PRAISE FOR BECKY SARAH'S
Grandmothering Real Life in Real Families

"Are you a new grandm___ ___ ___ ___ ___ ook is for you! Filled with honest truth ___ ___ ___ al advice, Becky Sarah has done a great servic___ ___ ___ ___ the families they love."
—Harvey Karp, MD, FAAP, Creator of the DVD/Book *The Happiest Baby On The Block: The New Way To Calm Crying And Help Your Newborn Baby Sleep Longer*

"At last! This is the book we've been looking for, one that we can recommend to the many women who come to us for help with the questions and challenges of grandmothering. Everyone who steps into a grandmothering role will find herself in these pages, whether this role is expected or not, traditional or not, joyful or not, new or not … We will be adding *Grandmothering* to the MIT Work-Life Library immediately … We also can't wait to give it to friends as they become grandmothers."
—Kathy Simons, MA, Director, and Rae Simpson, PhD, former Parenting Program Director, MIT's Work-Life Center

"What we have learned as mothers doesn't always translate directly to being a grandmother. Becky Sarah gives us a wise and comprehensive look at this deeply meaningful, joyful, and sometimes complicated new role. A rich and valuable resource, full of illuminating stories and creative ideas for being supportive and engaged, yet respectful of both our adult children's needs and our own."
—Myla Kabat-Zinn, co-author of *Everyday Blessings: The Inner Work of Mindful Parenting*

"Becky Sarah has written a warm and wise book about grandparenting in an age of non-traditional and recombinant families. The joys are more complex today, and Sarah's gem of a book helps grandparents to sagely navigate the challenges—and to help out their own children as new parents along the way."
—Robert Kuttner, author of *Family Re-Union*

of the most important questions and complexities facing multigenerational families today."
—Susan Linn, author of *Case for Make Believe: Saving Play in a Commercialized World* and Director, *Campaign for a Commercial-Free Childhood*

"...the kind of accessible and reassuring handbook that all grandmothers should read. It will help them contribute to the quality of life and development of their grandchildren as well as enrich their own understanding, skill and satisfaction of grandparenting in today's changing world."
—Diane Levin, PhD, Professor of Early Childhood Education, Wheelock College, author of Beyond Remote-Controlled Childhood: *Teaching Young Children in the Media Age*

"Becky Sarah seems to sit by the reader's side at the kitchen table while she offers practical advice ranging from what kind of baby carrier would suit an aging grandparent, to how to find one's way to grandchildren bewitched by electronic devices, to how to give advice to parents (mostly not to give advice)."
—Robbie Pfeufer Kahn, Associate Professor Emerita, University of Vermont, author of *Bearing Meaning: The Language of Birth*

"Think *What to Expect in Your First Grandparenting Year* crossed with *Chicken Soup for Grandma's Soul* and you have a hint of what *Grandmothering, Real Life in Real Families* is like. Becky Sarah's straightforward user's manual contains common sense, real life stories, and insight into age-old issues (delivering feedback to your children about their children) and dilemmas more newly prominent (children of same-sex unions)."
—David Valdes Greenwood, author of *Homo Domesticus: Notes From A Same-Sex Marriage*

Grandmothering

Real Life in Real Families

Becky Sarah

Whittier Street Press
14 Whittier Street
Cambridge, MA 02140

grandmothering.net

Book and cover design by Elaina DeBoard

Library of Congress Control Number: 2013948590
ISBN 978-0-9897918-0-9

First Edition, Printed in 2013

For Finn, Violet, and Emlin

Contents

Acknowledgements

Like most books and creative work of all kinds, this book could not have been finished without the help of many people.

I want to thank:

My husband, Frank Ackerman, brilliant writer and editor, wise mentor, patient listener, and loving grandfather. The ideas and content are mine, but the expression of them has improved greatly from his astute recommendations. I would never have finished without him.

Gail Shapiro, expert editor, ingenious source of all kinds of information, wise about the process of writing. Her many skills, so generously shared, made this a better book.

Toni Amato, who carefully and thoughtfully critiqued the entire manuscript, saving me from errors large and small, and deftly helping me say what I meant.

Elaina DeBoard, who designed the book, and Ellen Biewald, who designed the book's website, www.grandmothering.net, brought their considerable talents to this project. They were patient with endless revisions and a joy to work with at every stage.

Angela Bailey, Fanshen Cox, Trudy Cox, Linda Cox, Barbara Goldoftas, Myla Kabat-Zinn, Marion Kilson, Florence Ladd, Beverly Larsen, Judy Osborne, Rae Simpson, Maria Tramontozzi, and Linda Varone, all read drafts and made insightful comments, or took time to advise me from their knowledge and experience.

And above all, the dozens of people I interviewed, who shared their lives and their wisdom with me.

Introduction

When my first grandchild was on the way, I was delighted. I also had a lot of questions, and was quite curious about this new stage of life. I wished that I had a lot of other grandmothers to talk it over with, as I had talked with other mothers when my children were growing up. But none of my friends had grandchildren yet. Like many women, I had been hoping for grandchildren but I really had no idea what to expect.

I wondered whether this would be like mothering, or very different.

Could I make suggestions? In addition to raising two daughters, I had studied child development in college, and had been a preschool teacher. Would my grandchildren's parents welcome my knowledge of child development and child safety, or would suggestions be annoying and intrusive?

I wondered what it would feel like. Would I love a grandchild as much as I did my own children? Was there any way to get some tips on mistakes to avoid?

I went right to the library and to my local bookstore, but didn't find what I wanted.

As a mother, I had read many insightful, interesting books about raising children, but now I found that very little had been written about having a beloved child in the family, a descendent, when you are not the parent. What does it mean to be committed to, and responsible in some ways, for a child, to love her, yet also know that your adult child (and often a child-in-law you don't know very well) are the parents, and they will be making all the decisions? Where are the books about being a parent's parent?

So I decided to write the book I wanted to read.

I drew on many sources of information – starting with my own professional experience. In reflecting on my work with women, children, and families in several different jobs, I realized that grandmothers were often an important part of the picture, but one I had paid little attention to.

I was a home birth midwife and a childbirth educator for many years. As I started to plan this book, memories of births came back to me from a different point of view. I started thinking about the grandmothers.

So often I heard one end of a phone call: a woman who had just given birth, exultant and amazed, cuddling her newborn, and calling her own mother. Or, the mother of the laboring woman at the birth, suddenly distraught at painful memories of the abusive treatment she got in the hospitals of the 1940s, memories that came to her with jolting immediacy as she helped her own daughter with backrubs and hot compresses in the comfortable, nurturing environment of a home birth. I noticed that when there was an older sibling, often the grandmother was in the house to care for him and she was the only adult who could calmly focus on making peanut butter sandwiches or taking a toddler to the park, in the midst of the momentous drama of birth. Several times at the hardest parts of labor, I saw everyone encouraging the laboring woman, but only her own mother telling her, "I wish I could take the pain for you."

What had been minor details in my focus on midwifery care moved to the center of my thoughts.

While writing this book, I also worked as a parent educator. At the Massachusetts Department of Public Health I developed and taught a class called "Help Your Baby Stop Crying," for parents who were worn out by babies who cried for hours on end. Sometimes grandmothers came, too, and several said that they had swaddled their infants, wrapping them firmly in soft cotton cloth, just as I was teaching their adult children to do. Some of what I was teaching these young parents, they could learn from their own mothers.

In a different job, I created and taught workshops for parents called "Don't Wait Till They Ask," about talking to children and teenagers about sex and reproduction. There, I met with groups of parents crowded into living rooms, or clustered around a table in an elementary school. Many were struggling to protect their children from damaging stereotypes of both girls and boys, and from a callous, exploitative view of sex in the media. I remember a father who dashed in late, having left work early to get there, because he was sure he didn't want his children learning about sex and relationships from the Internet, but he didn't know how to talk to them about it himself. Many mothers and fathers remembered the more wholesome messages their own parents had given them, and wished that their children could hear more from their grandparents' worldview and a lot less from today's media.

Of course, writing this book led me to remember my own parents and grandparents with fresh understanding of what they had given me. Seeing how different parenting is today made me appreciate my childhood, in the Midwestern suburbs in the 1950s, and how smart and sensible my mother was. I started to think about how the social context affects parenting, creating pictures in everyone's mind of what's possible, what's normal, and what's safe. This subject came up often in my talks with grandparents.

But my own experience was just a beginning framework; I needed much more. I wanted to hear the collective wisdom of grandmothers with widely different situations and points of view. I wanted to hear from parents about their own parents, too, and from adults about their grandmothers.

I interviewed more than 80 people. I started by asking everyone I knew to help me find grandmothers interested in talking about their experiences, thoughts, and ideas. I met with women I knew and with strangers. We talked, at my house or theirs, sometimes for longer than either of us had planned. There were phone calls with women across the country. I was invited to a grandmother discussion group and got to know this group of women who had been meeting for years, sharing joys but also supporting each other through hard times. Co-workers and friends introduced me to their grandmothers. Sometimes I was able to talk with two generations, a mother and her mother. I talked with grandparent couples, too. Colleagues from the world of childbirth professionals – midwives, lactation consultants and childbirth teachers – told me what they had seen in families they cared for. Many of these women had grandchildren themselves by the time we talked, and wove together their own stories with their professional experience. I heard complex stories spanning decades, not all of them happy.

I heard from elementary school teachers, a novelist, a painter, therapists and social workers, a copywriter, a Girl Scout troop leader, an actor, a middle school principal and a UPS driver, from administrators and activists, the owner of a diaper service, a daycare center director, a college professor, a public health program manager, nurses, an engineer, a Tai Chi instructor, and from a young man who remembered his paternal grandmother rescuing his family after his father abandoned them and they had run out of money and food. The advocacy organization PFLAG (Parents and Friends of Gays and Lesbians) helped me reach grandparents whose grandchildren had gay and lesbian parents.

Everyone had a lot to say. I asked some questions, but mostly I listened to whatever was important to the person I was talking with. Two people said seriously, "My grandmother saved my life," and went on to tell me how.

I also looked for experts to advise me on topics I didn't know enough about. I found a young woman who vividly and thoughtfully described what it was like to grow up identifying as biracial, a science writer who has studied teenage development, a marriage and family therapist who specializes in stepfamilies. I read novels, blogs, and books by feminist social scientists and journalists.

I had less formal conversations, too. People told me what had happened to them, while we walked our dogs in the neighborhood park, or chatted at potlucks or parties.

Many ideas and circumstances came up again and again, and I saw they were important to include in the book.

It was hard to know when to stop listening and start writing.

For some, privacy was important. Their stories became part of my understanding and gave me ideas, but they do not appear in this book as anecdotes or quotes. For other people I interviewed, I changed names and identifying facts, and in some cases merged two or more interviews to create composite characters. I tried hard to preserve the speakers' words, voice, and meaning, and the emotional truth, even as I changed specific details to protect their privacy and that of their families.

I will always be grateful to these interesting, generous people for sharing their thoughts and their insights with me. Many told deep, fascinating stories. Being a grandmother is sometimes easy, easier than being a mother. For many women it is full of pure joy. But it can also include loss, mourning, and conflicts. I heard about heroic caretaking, difficult decisions, and a few real rescues, along with lots of wisdom, creativity and resourcefulness.

I learned much more about something I already knew. Grandmothers are not sweet, simple, static people, with quiet, sentimental lives. We do love our grandchildren deeply and happily, and a few of us are great cookie bakers. Some of us carry photos of our grandchildren, nowadays often on our phones. But overall the stereotype of grandmothers is silly and wrong. In reality, we are complex adults with strengths and weaknesses, problems and goals, accomplishments and regrets. In addition to beloved children, we have jobs, and intellectual, political, and creative passions, and romantic love in our lives. We continue to learn and grow, just as people do at all stages of life.

Part One, When Your Children Have Children, begins with a look back in history to see what remains the same and what is very different in grandmothering now than it was for previous generations. There is a chapter on hearing the news and making the transition to this new role. Women think differently about their own lives, and there are effects on careers, time, and responsibilities. Families change when a new person enters them, and I heard about the shifts among adult siblings when one of them becomes a parent, the need to timeshare somehow with the other grandparents, and most of all about how it feels when your children are suddenly parents. (It often feels sudden, no matter how long you – and they – have waited for this.) Other chapters are on creating a party or ceremony to celebrate becoming a grandmother, and on giving advice. Is it ever right to tell the parents what you think they should do? And why is it so hard not to give advice, even if you think you shouldn't?

I include here in this section some of the many wonderful ideas and anecdotes I heard about ways grandmothers have found to help and support their adult children in raising children. Grandparents listened patiently to exasperated sullen teens, took them on trips, and introduced them to the rewards of volunteering. One grandmother made curtains decorated with pictures of spaceships and rockets for a five-year-old, another did the laundry every week – for years – for her overwhelmed adult daughter. Grandmothers took children to swimming and ballet lessons, took them hiking and skiing. Grandmothers saved so they could help with college tuition, and paid for summer camps and new shoes.

Many parents told me their mothers and mothers-in-law were a big help. Many grandmothers were the opposite of critical; they steadily reassured their adult children that they were doing fine.

When things weren't fine, grandparents stepped in, caring for the household in an emergency. Some teamed up with the other grandparents. A gay teenager, who was thrown out of the house by his father, turned to his grandmother, and found a loving home with her.

I also heard a lot about the ways in which parenting has changed, and how mystifying some of those changes are to grandparents. I wanted to offer some answers to the grandmothers who say, about their grandchildren's parents, "But I don't understand why they...." There is plenty of individual variation in families, of course, and plenty of individual reasons why your children do many things differently than you did. But some of the change is due to a very different social context, with new economic realities, ever-changing technology, and altered employment norms for mothers.

Part Two, You and Your Grandchild, is about your time with the children. It is full of practical tips on activities, gifts, money, visiting from far away or living nearby. Here are many stories I heard from grandmothers about creative ways to serve healthy foods, ideas for fun projects, storytelling, choosing toys that are safe and help children grow, ways to avoid having on-screen entertainment dominate family life, ideas for sharing what you love with children, and tips for travel with children and adolescents.

Here, too, is a discussion of Grandmacare. This word was invented by a young mother I know. When her friends asked if her toddler was in daycare, she'd say, "No, but he's in Grandmacare two days a week." Her situation was not unusual; many grandmothers take care of their grand-children. I heard about evening babysitting, women who travel across the country to stay with children during school vacations, grandparents invited to move in with their adult children and care for grandchildren while the parents work, and parents with young children who moved in with the grandparents during a crisis, and stayed for years because it turned out so well. Grandmothers left their jobs to care for new babies when mothers had to go back to work. One grandmother had a house-ful of grandchildren every day after school. She told her adult children there could be only one child under two years old at a time, and let her children negotiate among themselves about which toddler would be dropped off at her house each day. Another grandmother took a four hour bus trip each way every weekend to help with premature twin babies.

This section includes a chapter on how to make Grandmacare work well for everyone, what to discuss in advance, what might be too hard to talk about, and updates on safety, media, ways to comfort a crying infant, and other practical matters.

Making Grandmacare work also involves saying no. It can be very rewarding to care for grandchildren and be a help to one's children, but grandmothers need to care for themselves too. There are times to set limits.

Part Three, All Kinds of Families highlights issues that may be new to some readers. Many of us are grandparenting in kinds of families we never parented in. Many of us have stepgrandchildren, adopted grandchildren, or grandchildren with gay or lesbian parents, and far more of us live in multiracial families today than a generation ago. But not all of us have experience in the kinds of families we now are part of, and even if we do, laws and cultural norms have both changed. These chapters pass on the wisdom from families I talked to on what to expect, and how to support your grandchildren and their parents. Each chapter has practical tips and suggestions: on how you can insightfully support an adopted grandchild as she makes sense of what being adopted means to her, on deflecting intrusive questions, updates on how the world has changed, how you can help protect a family that may be victims of prejudice, how you can connect with stepgrandchildren while respecting the growth of the stepfamily, and understanding the ways your teenage grandchild may think about racial identity very differently than you do.

Part Four, from Generation to Generation is the shortest section, just one chapter. It is about recording and sharing family history, passing on your culture, and teaching respect for other cultures. This can be lots of fun, and interesting for you as well as for children. It can include making scrapbooks of the children's lives, family recipes, storytelling, or learning about how your ancestors lived. This chapter addresses the difficult decisions, too, about family secrets, privacy, and how and whether to talk about the sad or embarrassing parts of your family history.

❧

The conversations, the listening, the writing, all took years, far longer than I ever imagined when I started. I had no idea how much effort is involved in writing a book, or how hard it would be to do it while working at a demanding job in public health. I certainly did not expect it to take so long that I would have three grandchildren by the time the book was done. But this book is not about them, or me. It is about women everywhere who are lucky enough to have this relationship in their lives.

I loved this project. It felt like another stage of midwifery, and a chance to look deeply, and talk in deep ways with other people, about some of the things that make our lives meaningful.

Part One:

When Your Children Have Children

1

The 21st Century Grandmother

Longer life spans, control of fertility,
nontraditional families, and new options for
women have changed grandmothering.

Some things will never change.

Some aspects of grandmothering never change. The deep emotions
you feel on seeing your child with his or her newborn baby make for
poignant moments no different now than for women in other generations. Grandparents have always tried to stay close to grandchildren
who live far away, just as they do now. Some moments and feelings are
universal, such as the way you feel when your adult child tells you a baby
is on the way, or the first time you hold your new grandchild, or your
happiness for your grown children as they discover the joys of parenting. Experiencing these times can draw you closer to your own mother
and grandmother.

Some difficulties are timeless, too. You probably worry about some of
the same things that plagued your own grandmother, and generations
of women before her. Women in all times and places have struggled
with how to connect with a daughter-in-law, or what to say to a teenage grandson who is withdrawing into risky behavior, or how to pass on

culture and family history. Chapter 4, Advice and Help, and Chapter 14, Family History, Childhood Memories, discuss these issues and how today's grandparents approach them.

21st-century grandmothering is different.

Your memories of your own grandmother might be a model for you of special times, of warmth and grace that you want to make part of your own experience of this stage of life. But in some ways it's going to be very different. Grandmothering is substantially different now than it has ever been in the past. Women's lives have new boundaries and expectations, family structures have changed, and technology has brought enormous innovations to communication, travel, and health.

Women have more rights and choices.

Although there certainly is much room for improvement, women now have more freedom and more legal rights than their mothers, grandmothers or great-grandmothers.

Women can vote, be elected to public office, earn advanced degrees, and sign legal contracts. Our great-grandmothers had none of these rights, and even our mothers didn't have all of them. You may have a job in a field that was closed to women a century ago. Your experience in the workplace is safer, and with less discrimination than your own grandmother faced.

Today's grandmother can leave a miserable marriage if she chooses, unlike many women in earlier times. Access to modern birth control and knowledge about her body has afforded her a far greater chance to control the number and timing of her pregnancies than ever before.

More control over money.

Women born at the beginning of the 20th century gave up their wages to their husbands, and couldn't own property or get credit in their own names. Women, including mothers, have always worked outside the home, but today's grandmothers have had more education and a new access to professional jobs and more equitable pay. Even if she lives modestly, or has financial worries, today's grandmother has unprecedented financial independence. That brings more control over her own life, and perhaps the ability to help grandchildren with college or other needs.

Of course, some grandparents have always helped grandchildren financially, and many married couples made financial decisions in respectful cooperation. Today, grandmothers have the legal power to make independent choices about money.

More choices.

The image of a grandmother as a quiet elderly woman, home all day, is no longer realistic, if it ever was. Today, most women become grandmothers in their fifties, although it can be earlier or later. The majority are working outside the home, some at the peak of their careers with the most responsibility and the highest earnings they will ever have. They may be married to their grandchildren's grandfather, or may be divorced, widowed, remarried, or single. They may have second careers, have done a stint in the Peace Corps, or gone back to school. They probably welcome grandchildren, and also relish their free time and are busy with work, travel, creative pursuits, new relationships, or political activism. They still bake delicious cookies. Now they can also advise their grandchildren about professions, or bring them on exciting trips.

Health and life expectancy.

We live longer and healthier lives than women of previous generations. Today's grandmother is more likely to live to see all of her grandchildren grow up, which for her own grandmother's generation was less common. She's probably healthy and vigorous longer, too. She has many more years when she can travel both to visit family and for her own enjoyment. She'll be able to lift a squirming toddler, or take a teenager hiking, until much later in her life.

Childbearing and infancy are far less full of grief. You may remember in your own lifetime your parents' fear of the polio epidemics 1952 and 1953, with schools and swimming pools closed.

Before the advent of antibiotics, vaccinations, clean water and safe food, most women buried a child, or a grandchild, or several. Genealogy enthusiasts see this in vivid ways. As they look at the records of births and deaths several generations earlier, they often find much bigger families, very often with a child or two whose birth and death dates are in the same year. These simple, factual records paint a picture of women's lives when birth control was not accessible to most women, many families had far more children, and the death of an infant was common. Now, these tragedies are rare. Parents today have many fears and challenges, but childhood death from disease is not usually something they worry about.

Families are different.

Nontraditional family structures your own grandmother couldn't have imagined are increasingly common and accepted today. Your grandchild may have two moms or two dads. You may have a grandchild who is internationally adopted. Multiracial families are much more common. Or, your grandchild may have parents who are happily not married. A grandchild may be the planned child of a single woman. In Part Three, All Kinds of Families, are detailed chapters on nontraditional families and how grandparents can support them.

Rapid social and technological change.

Because the world has changed so quickly in our lifetimes, grandmothers watch their own children parenting in far different ways than they did themselves. There are very different medical customs now for childbirth and infant feeding.

Your adult children are coping with the effects on your grandchildren of media, the Internet, and fifth graders text messaging in class. The context of parenting then, and now, is explored in detail in Chapter 6, Parenting … New and Improved?

Travel and staying in touch across distance.

Our children are also more likely to move far away from the homes and places in which we raised them. Grandmothers in the United States who were interviewed for this book have grandchildren living in Morocco, London, and New Zealand as well as all over the United

States. Some of these children had lived in several countries and traveled internationally.

That distance doesn't matter as much as it used to. Travel to visit faraway grandchildren is much easier, and safer. Today's grandmother can stay in touch over thousands of miles through email and webcams. Even as thoughtful parents and grandparents try to limit children's time on electronic devices, they also see ways technology can connect families. They find that a faraway grandparent can read to a child, or look at their projects and school papers, through a webcam, even have real conversations with grandchildren this way. Many parents post videos and frequent updates on a family website, so a distant grandmother can hear a toddler's new words, and see pictures of a child's first swimming lessons.

As we think about grandmothering now, there are ways it is different in this generation, and ways it is universal. You may feel a kinship with your own mother, grandmother, and great-grandmother as you enjoy your grandchildren, and you may also have to find ways to cope with problems and changes that earlier generations never imagined.

2

Becoming a Grandmother

Ready or not! First reactions to hearing
the news.

Watching your children become parents can be one of the great joys of being a mother. This stage of your mothering has its own complexities and challenges as well. It may be filled with worry, or with struggles to understand your children's choices. Some women feel pushed into a role they don't like or aren't ready for. For some it means new responsibilities. Yet even if there are difficulties, it's usually wonderful to have a grandchild. For many, the new status of grandmother is a special and delightful one.

> "At my sixtieth birthday party, my daughter told me, 'I'm pregnant.' I was so happy. For her and for myself."

Even before your grandchild arrives, your connections to other people change. Your relationship with your own child is irrevocably altered. You are now the parent of someone who has taken on the most adult responsibility there is: raising children. If this is your first grandchild, you are also beginning a new kind of relationship. There are unique pleasures, not like those found in raising your own children.

This new role may also have an effect on how you think about yourself and your own life. It's a symbol of aging, and also of continuity and renewal.

How it happens.

There are so many ways we can become grandmothers.

Your daughter, a freshman in college, calls sobbing from her dorm room. She's pregnant, she doesn't love the father, she needs both practical help and comfort and she is afraid you will reject or criticize her.

Or, your son, recently married, stands up at a Passover seder, pulling his young wife to her feet next to him, hugging her with one arm while he taps on a glass with a spoon to get everyone's attention, grinning and looking around with an impish, delighted look on his face that you know from the happiest times in his childhood. He's proud and elated to announce they have a baby on the way.

Or, your single thirty-nine year old daughter, with a good job and a comfortable, lively, interesting city life, sends an e-mail saying she has finished her home study and is adopting a daughter from China. You can sense her excitement and happiness, and you also see that she's wondering anxiously if you and her father will welcome and love this dark haired child who doesn't look like you.

Your son, over forty, resigned to a single life, falls in love. This time, the woman is just right for him, and you like her immediately, too. She has a three-year-old, and your son, who had given up on having a family, eagerly steps into a fatherly role.

Grandchildren can come too early in our children's lives, unplanned. Or, they may not come for years, while our children look for a life partner they can make a family with, or spend years, and all their money, on fertility testing and procedures that look less and less likely to bring a baby. Grandchildren can arrive right "on time" to parents who want them and are ready. Unwanted pregnancies may galvanize the new parents into becoming focused, purposeful adults. Or, being a grandmother can be tinged with sorrow when our adult children cannot manage parenting well, or even abandon their children.

Our children may share with us every step of their decisions, their efforts to conceive, or the adoption process. Or they may surprise us with the news, leaving us happy, surprised, and scrambling to catch up quickly.

Finding out.

No matter how it happens, getting the news that you will soon be a grandmother is a memorable, poignant turning point in life. Before is different from after.

Often it's expected, especially if adult children are a couple and have talked about wanting a family. Dorothy raised four children in a big, child centered extended family.

> "My daughter-in-law was my daughter's best friend all through high school, in our house all the time, she was already like part of the family. We all knew they were trying and when she got pregnant, well, it was a very easy transition for me, it just felt like OK, next step."

Ruth smiled as she described her son announcing in an e-mail from the other side of the world where he and his girlfriend were both in the Peace Corps in Thailand, that a baby was on the way, a first grandchild on both sides.

> "Thrilling, just thrilling."

Another grandmother said,

> "They had been trying for so long, they had just started seeing an infertility doctor, getting those tests. Every month was such a huge disappointment when it didn't work. They were so sad each time, and after a few months they started to worry about whether they would ever have a baby. My heart just ached for them. In November, I'll never forget this, my daughter called me at work at eight in the morning. They had just done the test and she was pregnant. I was so relieved, and so happy for them. Later, I got excited about being a grandmother myself."

8

"I just want to tell you, you're going to be the grandmother of twins," Glenda's daughter informed her, in a phone call from the other side of the country. Glenda happily congratulated her daughter. Inside, her feelings were more complicated.

"All I kept thinking about was payback. Now she will understand what it's like."

These moments are memorable, life-changing, and every grandmother I talked to could remember exactly how she heard, what was said, and how she felt.

Often, the news is followed by many months for everyone to adjust and prepare, which can be both festive and sweetly, deeply meaningful. If the new parents live close by, the grandmother-to-be may be involved, often by providing practical help. If the new parents live far away, a grandmother-to-be might still help prepare for the new child by buying clothes or equipment. Sometimes an expensive stroller or crib is a gift from the grandparents. Making things, like quilts or baby clothes, can be lots of fun, and a way to connect with the baby while waiting. If you have saved baby clothes and gear from raising your own children, unpacking them and sorting through them to see what might be useful for this new child can bring back memories. Seeing and touching the clothes your children wore, the Snugli or backpack you carried them in decades ago, adds even more meaning to this time.

Telling your own friends makes it seem more real. Some women will travel long distances to attend a baby shower. Then there is an excited phone call when the baby arrives, and plans to visit, to help manage the household or just to see the baby. Sometimes a grandmother, usually a maternal grandmother, is invited to the birth.

But sometimes it all happens fast, and there's little time to prepare, either in practical ways or emotionally. If a couple has endured a series of miscarriages, they may not tell anybody about a pregnancy until they are well into the second trimester. Or, if a pregnancy is unplanned, or one of the new parents is ambivalent about it, they may keep the news to themselves until they sort out their own feelings. They may wait for results of an amniocentesis. When you find out about your child's pregnancy halfway through it, or even later, the feelings, the excitement, the adjustment to being a grandmother, and the preparation are all compressed into a shorter time. There's no chance to slowly, over months, try on the new role of grandmother and think over your feelings about it. There might not be enough time to make a baby quilt, as a way to get used to the idea.

Marilyn told me she didn't expect to ever be a grandmother. Her only daughter was forty, never married.

> "I knew my daughter had been dating, going to those various speed dating things, and those agencies or whatever where they match you up. I was really hoping she would find somebody. It was a big shock to me when she asked me to have lunch with her, and as soon as we sat down, announced she was adopting a baby on her own. I was just shocked. I was speechless, which is a rarity for me! Then I got excited, I came around the table to hug her, and we talked all about it. She said it would probably take about a year, maybe more. The next day I went out and bought some bibs and baby clothes, and I started to wonder about names. Then! Four or five days later she calls back and a birth mother chose her, and the baby was due anytime. So I went in three weeks from no thoughts about this at all, to holding my grandchild."

In addition to joy and excitement, there are other feelings and thoughts. Timing and circumstances can make a big difference.

Not yet, I'm not ready.

When grandchildren come to a woman relatively early in her own life, while she is still raising her own children, it can feel as though there's not enough time or energy to fully enjoy the grandchildren. Many women whose grandchildren came "early" – before all their own children were grown and out of the house – regret that the picture they have of grandmothering, a time of relative leisure, a chance to "spoil" children and "not be the responsible one" is never realized.

Donna's eldest is twenty-six and has two children of her own. Donna had more children in her second marriage, in her forties. Of her grandchildren, she says,

"I feel those children deserve more, they deserve a real grandmother. I've still got two teenagers, so I can't give them what I would like to. I see my friends all excited about doing things with their grandchildren that they did with their kids. They have all their museum memberships and art supplies. They're hauling out "The Runaway Bunny" and all those classic kids' books that they saved. I spend time with my grandchildren of course, but all my thinking and my creativity is going into my own two younger ones. If the grandchildren had come along a little later ... "

I'm not old enough.

Grandmothers may feel they're not ready in another sense too. For many women, a first – often unspoken – reaction is, "I'm not old enough to be a grandmother." The child is welcome. The role, with its connotations of aging and decline, may not be.

Sharon was thrilled, and celebrated with her husband, at a special dinner with champagne toasts. Yet she makes sure her clients don't find out she's a grandmother. She is an accountant and financial planner with an office in her house. This home-based business worked out beautifully when she was raising her own children. Clients came to see her during school hours, and she just made sure that the clutter of children's toys and possessions stayed separate from her office. Now, though, with grandchildren, it feels different. She says,

"Before, I would talk about having kids, if it came up, especially since so much of financial planning has to do with children and families, it didn't hurt that clients knew I understood their situation. Now I don't do that. The image of a grandmother is not of a competent expert. People expect it must be time for you to retire. So I never mention having grandchildren."

Gloria says,

"I am not what you think of as a grandmother. It's basically gray hair, soft, round, older. That's not me."

Ellen happily described her granddaughter, who had made a wonderful recovery from being born quite prematurely. Ellen wore a locket with the child's picture, which she opened and showed me. As we were winding up our conversation, she lowered her voice and said quietly,

> "Now that she started to talk, she calls me Lala, and I'm just going to go by that, I don't want to be called Grandma, it sounds so old."

Right on time.

For others, the title and role of grandmother are eagerly embraced.

> "I told everybody. I was proud, I felt like I had accomplished something," said Florence.

Janice told me,

> "I was astounded at myself, I felt so empowered. Tall, proud, strong. It just came over me like that, the morning he was born."

Maria laughed when I asked her about feeling old.

> "Some of my friends are that way, they say they don't want to be old. I just say, this is what's happening, so do whatever you have to do to feel good about yourself, to enjoy this. Take care of yourself. This is part of life, the best part I think, so get with it."

Finally!

For other women, grandchildren come late, long after their own children are raised and long after they themselves begin to want grandchildren. Some have looked forward to grandchildren for years and for some expectation has turned to hope and then to resignation. When I talked to older grandmothers, in their seventies or beyond, being – or appearing – "old" isn't the issue.

Gloria felt she had waited quite long enough.

> "I thought, finally!! My sister had ten grandchildren by then, from four daughters."

Hannah told me,

> "I was almost eighty when my son called me so excited, 'Catherine's pregnant.' I had pretty much given up hope of being a grandmother. I married very late for my generation, and I was forty when I had my only child. And then my son, he was almost forty himself at the time, when the baby was on the way. I was extra happy because it wasn't something I counted on."

My kids aren't ready.

Sometimes the expectant parents don't seem prepared, or ready, or able to take care of a child.

> "I was quite anxious, I didn't see how they could manage to do it. Their apartment is the size of a teacup. As I visited them a few times I realized that's normal for New York City. I grew up in the suburbs myself, and when I was raising my kids, we lived in a suburban neighborhood of big old houses with big yards and big families. I have come to see that this is the world they are living in now, they are living in a city. And they can have a baby there. I had to get used to it."

But sometimes the grandmother's feeling that her children are not ready or not able to parent sadly turns out to be all too true. If the new parents are in disarray or disagreement, complex events can happen fast and chaotically. A woman just getting used to the idea of being a grandmother is suddenly caring alone for a new baby, or has the entire new family living with her. Perhaps she finds herself sleeping on the couch while a son, his girlfriend, and a newborn crowd into her only bedroom. Or, she may gain and lose a grandchild all at once if the child is born and the parents separate, or are never really a couple, and one of them, usually the mother, leaves with the baby. A paternal grandmother, especially, may lose a grandchild abruptly in this way.

Nancy told me her heartbreaking story.

> "My son showed up unexpectedly one evening with his girlfriend and said she was pregnant. They were both old enough to know better, but they were drinking too much, living chaotic lives, walking out on a job, not paying bills. To make a long story short, they stayed with me until the baby was born. I was with her for the birth, she was very strong for the birth. Afterwards everything just fell apart. My son was coming and going, mostly going. And she wasn't really up to taking care of that baby girl either. She would leave her with people, friends, or just in the car seat while they partied. Once she left the baby alone in the house. I had a lot of health problems, I work full time, I couldn't take on that baby all by myself which is what it was going to be. So I said to the girlfriend, 'You have got to find your parents, see if they can help.'
>
> "Eventually, she did go back to her parents, and they ended up raising the baby. When I call, they won't talk to me. They send back the packages and presents I send for her. So, I've lost her, my granddaughter."

Often, though, our children grow quickly into new, capable adults. Louise and I talked in her apartment, where pictures of her grandson adorned every wall, and scribbled drawings in the unmistakable style of a two-year-old covered the front of the refrigerator. She had been sure initially that her son was nowhere near ready to be a parent.

She told me cheerfully,

> "I never had a problem with my son being gay. And his partner, Raymond, is like another son to me. However, when they told me they were going to adopt a child, I

didn't think it was a good idea. For one thing, to be honest, at that point I couldn't really picture two men creating a good home for a child, without a mother. And I especially couldn't see them doing it.

"Everything in their house was either white or breakable. And they were young and acted younger. Because when I say Raymond is like a son to me, I mean a teenage son. They would decide on Friday afternoon to fly somewhere for a long weekend, and go. They never saved any money. They started things and didn't finish them, guitar lessons, planning to open a business, refinishing furniture. They were always out, restaurants, clubs, dancing, concerts.

"I didn't say it but I was thinking, 'At most, get a cat. At most.' So I wasn't very enthusiastic and I'm sure they could tell. I'm glad I didn't say it, because it turns out I was wrong.

"Everybody changes when they have kids, and they did too. Their whole lives are centered on that little boy now. They're up early, they have every book about parenting and babies ever published. Now it's all about the best pediatrician, and various kinds of strollers, and baby gym classes."

Louise can tell her story entertainingly, and laugh at her own certainty that a cat was the very most her son could take care of, because she was wrong. Her son and his partner were much more ready than they looked and now have an organized, child-centered family with a thriving toddler.

Mothering and grandmothering.

Becoming a grandmother is usually full of joy, even when that joy is mixed with other feelings. We learn new things about our children, as we watch and help them. Our children can surprise us, and we can surprise ourselves.

For some of us, watching our children with their children makes us see our own lives more clearly. Some stages of life are behind us. The delight of holding that tiny baby can be a vivid reminder of the first days of our own mothering, and some of those feelings and experiences will come back into our lives with grandchildren. But even as our children become parents, we are still mothers, as well as grandmothers. The challenge is to balance all three things: our love for the littlest family members, reflection on our own lives, and continued parenting of our grown children. They may need our practical help and support. Most importantly they need our confidence in them as they move into this new stage of life.

Resources

Nonfiction

Your Baby is Speaking To You: A Visual Guide to the Amazing Behaviors of Your Newborn and Growing Baby, by Dr. Kevin Nugent and Abelardo Morell

3

Your Children are Parents, and That Changes Everything

Grandmaternal feelings, attending to the older siblings, timesharing with the other grandparents, and your other children.

When someone enters or leaves a family, a lot changes. A new grandchild, especially the first one, or the first one to those parents, alters other familial relationships. It's a delightfully happy time but can also bring mixed feelings and some sadness about losses in your own life, even as you focus primarily on other people in your family.

Your relationship with this new little person is obviously a change. Your relationship with the child's parents is modified enormously too. And if the new child has siblings, then their world is different now and you may find yourself in a new place in it. Your relationship with the other grandparents, your other children, and even your friends may take on new forms.

Grandmaternal feelings.

I love the word "grandmaternal," which I believe was first used outside of a scientific context by the writer and sociologist Robbie Pfeufer Kahn, to describe families and feelings.

For some women, grandmaternal feelings develop slowly. Their first concern is for their own adult children, and their emotional involvement is with their own child's welfare. There is much to enjoy. One of the great pleasures of motherhood is to see your adult child having the profound, delightful moments of caring for a newborn. Watching this, you also know what's to come, often better than the new parents do. You can picture this infant as a one-year-old and a five-year-old, which first-time parents usually can't. You know how much fun it will be for your adult child when this new little one starts to talk, and you can imagine the poignant mix of loss and pride the day she starts kindergarten.

Betsy told her daughter, "I'm coming to take care of you, not the baby."

> "It was a pleasure to watch my daughter mother. She had all the right instincts. I cooked, I just really wanted to do everything to give to my daughter at this time, and it was a pleasure to me to watch her mother her baby. That's what meant something to me."

Some women find their attachment to infant grandchildren growing slowly over months.

> "It felt strange. I had to talk to myself, tell myself that this baby is connected to me. I don't know what I felt. There was no bond instantly."

Robbie Pfeufer Kahn writes about the first days of her first grandchild's life, and the gradual beginnings of her own grandmaternal feelings.

> "I became very relaxed, really for the first time with the baby. Up until that moment I found myself unexpectedly like Tolstoy when he first saw his newborn, the little tomato-colored baby with a scrunched up wizened looking face. Not that this baby looked like that. What I shared with Tolstoy was a feeling of strangeness, as if my grandson were alien, not kin, an unexpected emotion because normally I love babies. I realized that those alien feelings visited me because this wasn't my own baby.

"Later that first day I had discussed this odd turn of events with a friend and she understood entirely. I needed her understanding because everyone I had talked to before I left Vermont said, 'You'll see, it's better with a grandchild, it's so much better than with your own.' I think that hormones have a lot to do with a newborn's appeal, that they draw a mother and father to their baby. When the baby was a day old, my son said to me, 'Smell his hair, isn't it amazing?' I bent over to smell my grandson's dark hair and discovered that the damp, warm odor was nothing I recognized or was drawn to, although I said, 'Oh yes, it smells wonderful.' My own baby's hair when he was little intoxicated me and I couldn't smell it often enough."

Not every grandmother is interested in babies, and this too may keep focus on your own grown children. One woman said to me,

"I'm really looking forward to later on. Let's face it, at this point it's kind of like a carrot, doesn't really know you."

Others enjoy being with the baby but don't relish long sessions of infant care with its remembered exhaustion.

A father of two elementary school-age children described his mother's visits. Now that the children are five and eight years old, she is willing to get up with them at dawn, she is interested in everything they have to say, and happy to indulge them in many ways.

"When they were babies, she didn't want to take care of them herself, really. She would ooh and ahh over them, and take lots of pictures, and send presents. She told us right at the beginning that the diaper technology is not what she's used to, and she didn't want to learn how to do it at this point. Last summer, for the first time my wife and I got to go away for a weekend together and she stayed with them, and it was great. When they were little babies, no dice."

Melanie wanted to go slowly because her daughter was in the midst of a legal risk adoption. The six-week-old baby had been placed with them by the state social services agency, and the social workers and lawyers said they would most likely be able to adopt him, although his biological mother had not given up her rights.

Melanie called me to ask,

> "Am I a grandmother now? Or later, when he's legally theirs?"

She hadn't seen him yet, and he didn't feel like a grandchild to her, more like a potential grandchild.

We talked about this for a while. Of course she was frightened of getting attached to a child she might lose and even more fearful about her daughter having such a devastating loss. Melanie enjoyed picking out presents, and she called her daughter, who lives on the other side of the country, to hear about the baby. But she didn't put up pictures of him in her house. She knew she would feel very differently once the adoption was final.

For other grandmothers the attachment is instant.

Marilyn says,

> "That baby drew me like a magnet. I just wanted to hold him. I asked my daughter, can I just come over and hold him for a while? She said, sure, come any time. So I started going over most days, to just sit on the couch and hold him. It was peaceful for me. Short. A little while was enough. I just really wanted to do it. I was over there other times, to bring food, to take their laundry home and do it and bring it back. This was separate. I needed to see his face. He didn't seem like my own baby, like I've heard other women say. He seemed like my grandbaby from the first minute. I would sit on the couch and just feel him breathing for half an hour. Then go home."

Another grandmother was surprised to find the arrival of the fifth grandchild such an intense experience.

> "I have five grandchildren. With each of them I was excited and thrilled, from the first moment of seeing them,

holding them. Especially the first one, that was the biggest. All of them, really. It was something I had looked forward to for a long time. When my own youngest left home, I was very sad, and my husband wisely said to me that he thought I would really enjoy being a grandmother, which is true, I really have enjoyed it so much. The last grandchild, I thought I was getting used to it, I thought it wouldn't be quite as exciting, the fifth one. Actually, I found myself feeling that she was even more of a miracle. She's adopted and how she found her way into our family and her parents found her, was just a wonder. Even more of a miracle."

Erica decided to use the power an infant has to attract adults to help her make a relationship with a faraway grandson. She had spent lots of time with her first three grandchildren, who lived in her state. Her last grandchild was born thousands of miles away.

"It's going to be harder with him, to love him as much as the others. To get to know him and let him feel how I love him. So I went out as soon as I could. Luckily, when he was two months old, my daughter had to go to a professional conference, three full days. She had two presentations to give, and she had to be in the other sessions, working, talking to people, learning stuff. She had to stay in a hotel, three hours from home. So I went, and stayed there too and took care of him. Three full days in a hotel room, not comfortable, pretty boring, waiting so when she had a break she could rush out and nurse him. It was exhausting, really.

"I knew if I spent that time with him, holding him, touching him, I would get attached to him just on a biological level. And I hoped that he would feel that I was familiar to him when he saw me again. It worked, by the time I left he was my grandbaby, I just ached when I had to leave him which is how I wanted to feel."

After many grandchildren, and watching grandchildren grow up, it's different again. Edna is eighty-three, with eleven grandchildren, some of them adults now, with their own children. About the last few, she says "Oh, you get used to it," with a cheerful casualness that shocks women welcoming their first grandbaby. Edna has watched her adult children parent and run their own lives for years, and she's delighted not to feel responsible for other people any more. She's quite happy to see another grandbaby, but it doesn't change her own life.

Mixed feelings and regrets.

It's normal and common to have some mixed feelings and some very emotional memories, even as you focus on your adult children. Seeing your children's pregnancies and births and newborns can bring up powerful memories of your own, and powerful feelings about those memories.

I attended births at home and in the hospital for more than ten years as a doula and midwife. I had some poignant and intriguing times with grandmothers in families I took care of.

A new baby can rekindle grief over bad experiences and regrets in a grandmother's own births or mothering. When Lorna and I talked about being a grandmother, she needed to start with the story of own births. Her first, in the early 1980s, was breech. She had planned a home birth, and spent the last weeks of her pregnancy looking for a doctor skilled in breech deliveries and willing to do one. She found an older obstetrician, who had delivered many breech babies, but at thirty-eight weeks, when the baby put one little foot down to the cervix, her doctor kindly told her a vaginal birth wasn't the safe way to go. Her son was born by Caesarean section. For the next baby, she went to the only medical practice in her area that would let her attempt a vaginal birth after a Caesarean. After twelve hours of labor she ended up with a second Caesarean.

Twenty-five years later, she was thrilled when she was invited to the birth of her second grandchild. But during the labor she was overwhelmed again by her grief about her own births, so different from what she had wanted. She had to leave the room, and found herself sobbing – silently – in the tiny hospital bathroom with paper towels soaked in cold water pressed to her eyes. When Lorna and I talked about this, she was embarrassed to admit that her sadness had been revived by the birth, a time when she was expected to be happy and to be thinking about other people, not about herself. She said,

> "Eventually, it was really healing for me. I kind of accepted it more and moved on, more than I had ever been able to. I never talked about it, there was no one I could say that to, everyone expected me to just be happy, happy, happy."

A new grandmother is also often coping with reliving her own choices about birth, breast-feeding, infant care, and childcare. This intense time can revive any regrets she has, and almost everybody has some. Perhaps she wishes she had been more patient, or enjoyed those years more. For some women, there's a renewed sadness about marriages that didn't last, and parenting not shared with the children's father. You may be seeing your daughter starting a hard life mothering in a difficult situation, or even feeling envious she has it so much better than you did.

> "My son is a wonderful husband and father. I sometimes wonder if he's appreciated. He's devoted, he's waiting on her hand and foot with the new baby. No one did that for me."

Or, if you remember your own babies and mothering mainly with pleasure, this time can create a different kind of sadness or ambivalence. Yes, it can bring back wonderful memories in a very vivid way. But these happy memories can make you wish your adult child could have the delightful milestone experiences of birth you had. The culture has changed a great deal. You may find that the next generation of mothers does not want or value the same things you did. Especially for maternal grandmothers, if your birth experience was important to you, it can be surprising and sad if your daughter chooses to have a very different birth experience, or just doesn't care at all about how the birth goes or doesn't care to breastfeed.

One grandmother I interviewed was shocked at the decisions of a daughter-in-law she thought she knew well.

> "With the first baby, they had a beautiful natural birth, with

a midwife. My daughter-in-law's mother was there, and I was too, and we were all so joyful. It made us all closer. Now, ten years later, they're having their second baby. And she's going to the closest hospital, which is not family friendly, with an obstetrician, and an epidural, maybe even a planned Caesarean if it's even one day late. She told me on the phone, 'Been there, done that. I just don't have the energy this time.' I am just despairing, because I love her like a daughter, and the thought of my grandchild coming into the world that way... I called her back and tried to talk about the risks, the things she would end up having, I sent her two new books, All that did was alienate her. It's just awful."

Holding a newborn may bring feelings about your own fertility, and stage of life. You might not have actually been thinking about having another baby, but if those precious moments are in the past for you, a new grandbaby focuses your attention on the reality that you aren't going to, or couldn't even if you wanted to. This can be sad. Or it can be just fine, exactly what you want.

For the woman who does welcome the end of fertility, this stage can feel like the perfect next step. Some grandmothers are delighted not to return to the world of interrupted sleep and no time for themselves.

One grandmother said very cheerfully,

"To my mind, there's a reason why God gives the babies to the YOUNG women."

And of course, we may feel both at once—sadness and relief that childbearing is over, regret and delight in the happy memories of our own newborns.

This changes further as more grandchildren arrive. With the first one, a new grandmother may be vividly reliving her own pregnancies and first days of mothering, even as she wants to focus on the present, and her own adult children. Later grandchildren don't usually have as big an effect in that way; they don't represent a role change, or a new part of life. They can be enjoyed for themselves, just as later babies mean something different to parents than first babies do.

The siblings.

Another way that later grandchildren are different is that you have the older siblings to think about. Everyone knows that children, especially young children, are usually distressed and threatened by the arrival of a sibling. But nobody does anything about it. Grandparents usually act just like everyone else, as if the newborn is the most interesting and adorable person they have ever seen. Newborn babies certainly are uniquely attractive. However, they don't really need your attention. If the new grandchild is adopted as a toddler or older child, he or she may already be overwhelmed and probably needs time to adjust to and bond with his or her parents before starting a relationship with you. There are times when it's best to concentrate on the siblings.

Jackie is an African American mother of four sons, and grandmother of six. She is also a pediatrician, so she has plenty of experience with how children feel, and behave, when a new sibling arrives. And, she has a plan.

She tells the new parents what she's planning to do, and reminds them later on. They tend to forget, and the last thing she wants is for them to feel she's not interested in their baby.

She arrives at the soonest possible moment, dressed up as if for church, excited and bearing flamboyantly wrapped presents. The person she wants to see, though, is the sibling. They have her whole attention. If they want to tell her about the new baby, fine. Sometimes they lead her off to another part of the house to discuss something else entirely. She pulls out her gifts, saying, "This is a big day for your family, you're an older brother now, and I've brought you something to celebrate." If the older child wants her to, she takes a picture of him holding the new baby, which also turns into quite a satisfying picture for that child to take to school, since it features him primarily, with any cuteness the newborn may possess not really visible. Jackie doesn't even hold her newest grandchild for days. She manages to give the impression that her older grandchild is the most interesting person in the family, and that becoming a big brother or sister is quite an accomplishment. In the first few postpartum weeks, she spends as much time as she can with older siblings. She tries to be helpful to the new parents, too, and take the older children on outings at times convenient for their parents. But most of her focus is on what those older children would like.

One of her granddaughters was four years old when a baby brother was born. A couple of days into Jackie's visit to the family, Jackie was reading aloud *Peter's Chair,* a classic book about a new baby sibling, to the little girl. When the story was over, her granddaughter announced the news, "Grandma, *we* have a new baby. Would you like to see him?"

Jackie has her own way of contributing to the household too.

> "I have four lovely, capable daughters-in-law. I stay out of their kitchens. I am not much of a cook anyway, so I will get involved in cleanup of course, and I will bring a dish to a Thanksgiving. That's it. When there's a new baby, I offer to hire one of those postpartum doulas as my gift, and so far my daughters-in-law have said yes. That way there is someone in the kitchen, and it is someone my daughter-in-law has picked out and is answerable to her."

Betsy, a preschool teacher, had a similar idea. She focused on her four-year-old grandson, taking him to the park and to children's music concerts and patiently reading his favorite books over and over. She was careful not to act too interested in the baby, and she thought the little boy appreciated that.

> "My daughter didn't get it though, she was kind of hurt, she was saying, Look mom, Nickie is smiling, he wants to get your attention."

Your children-in-law.

Grandchildren create a new chance to get to know and appreciate your children-in-law.

Some grandmothers, in contrast to the popular stereotype, find their daughters-in-law easy to get along with.

> "My daughter and I are very close, but with the grandchildren in some ways it's easier with my son's children than with hers. If I say something to my daughter-in-law, she just takes it the way I mean it. I would say, 'Is this the coat he's wearing?' My daughter thinks I'm criticizing her, like

he should be wearing something different or something warmer. She's still back in her teenage years in some ways, where with my daughter-in-law we don't have that history. To her, I'm just asking about a coat."

The other grandparents.

Before, they were just your child's in-laws, a relationship created by choice and perhaps legal commitments. You might have liked them very much, or not at all. If you live far apart perhaps you rarely saw them, or you may even have never met them. At that point, it was a relationship that could be ended by decisions and choices, too. Yiddish has a wonderful word, the machatunim, meaning your adult child's in-laws. These people are your grandchild's family, so they will always be related to you.

Now, as one grandmother said,

> "We're sharing a human being. We're relatives, we're family. Permanently."

The midwives and postpartum doulas I talked to all said the same thing. when a baby comes, the parents of the new mother almost always visit first. "The wife's parents go first," Betty, the mother of three sons, told me ruefully. This seems to be an unwritten, unspoken rule that many people don't find out about until they are in the midst of it.

Claudia, a paternal grandmother, wishes now that she had done it that way. In her family, all four grandparents arrived immediately after the birth, and it was odd and not as satisfying as she had wanted it to be.

> "We were outside the bedroom, though. Her parents went in, we didn't. We were helping more in the house, the meals, which I was glad to do of course, but I kind of thought it was too much that we were never invited in, the baby was brought out to us sometimes. If it was me, I wouldn't have minded having my parents-in-law in my bedroom, I would have wanted all the help I could get."

In this short postpartum time, new mothers are in disarray, with leaking breasts, postpartum bleeding, and perhaps unwashed hair. They feel out of control of everything: their emotions, their bodies, their houses, and in this vulnerable state they often prefer their own mothers, or no one.

Even if a paternal grandmother is poised to be helpful and nonintrusive, a new mom may need to keep some boundaries.

Lois Freedman, a childbirth educator and author of *Birth As a Healing Experience*, says,

> "They don't want to feel better about their mother-in-law than they do about their mother, or need their mother-in-law more. There can be competition between the grandmothers, and a woman doesn't want to give her mother-in-law more involvement than her own mother."

Also, new parents are usually not aware of what this event means to the grandparents. They can't empathize very well because they have never been in your shoes, and they usually have no time or energy to think about what this means to you.

The postpartum period is over quickly, but competition between grandparents doesn't necessarily go away.

Over time it can get worse. Competition can become ferocious, although it's usually unspoken, or acknowledged only as a joke.

> "I was visiting, and me and the other grandmother were in the backseat with Carly in the car seat between us. She lives nearby. And it was like she couldn't let go of that even for a second. She was competing with me even as we rode in the car, to get Carly to look at her, not me. She had brought snacks, juice, books, toys, she was madly entertaining her over there, keeping her attention."

An experienced grandmother can find ways to reverse the tendency to competition. Erica has four grown children and two grown stepchildren, and six grandchildren.

> "I've seen everything, and I've made plenty of mistakes. I've learned some things, too. Now, I have one of my grand children living nearby and I take care of him after school.

I know the other grandmother loves him just as much as I do. She's a wonderful grandmother and I want him to have that. She visits, and I welcome her, which is easy because I really like her. Also I make a point to back off completely, I say to the parents, this week is for her, I'm available, but let her take him, let her have the time alone with him, whatever she wants. And I've invited her to stay with us, because their house is tiny with no guest room, and I don't want her to have the expense of a motel or something. So I hope that makes it easier for her to spend time with him."

Betsy has four adult children and many grandchildren. She advises:

"Don't preempt traditions, holidays, gifts, or names that might be important to the other grandparents also. One set of grandparents can't have every special holiday meal, or nickname like Nana or Pops, or give every gift that is special. Compromise, alternate, or do things together. Even if you always expected to be called Nana, maybe the other grandmother did too, and you can use your names, like in our family we are Nana Betsy and Nana Sharon. Holidays and birthdays aren't always going to be at your house; maybe both sides of the family can celebrate together, or you will have to alternate."

Kay and her husband found that the other grandparents were fine allies in times of serious troubles. Their eleven-year-old grandson was using the Internet to gamble online and watch pornography when he was alone in the house after school, and late at night.

"The other grandparents thought we would take it all lightly, not be concerned, because we're liberals. Not so, we were horrified. We thought they wouldn't want to help, would just blame and criticize. Not so, they dropped everything else, and did so much."

All four grandparents worked closely together to solve this problem.

"I was desperate. I was basically hysterical. I called Edith and Carl, Sean's other grandparents, just because they were the only other people who I knew really cared about him. We aren't close with Edith and Carl, they're very different from us. I was like a drowning person reaching out to anything that might save me.

"We ended up all sitting down together to talk, all four grandparents and my daughter and son-in-law. I can't say our talk was wonderful, but all us grandparents stayed pretty calm and all said basically the same thing, which was that this couldn't go on. I think my daughter really just couldn't believe that her eleven-year-old was looking at pornography. We had planned to offer help taking care of Sean and occupying him in a good way, so he wasn't alone in the house after school, or other times when they were both working. Anyway the upshot was, we had gotten to the point of talking about a lot of details about how my husband and I could take care of him after school a lot of the time.

"I'll never forget this, Carl had been pretty quiet, and then he just got to his feet and said, "I can take the hit on this." He went into Sean's room, and just turned everything off and unplugged it and started carrying it out to his car. Naturally, Sean put up quite a fuss. Before anybody really knew what was happening Carl had Sean's TV and his computer loaded into his car and the car locked. We were all kind of stunned. I'm not saying it was the right thing to do, it wasn't very respectful of his son. Somebody had to do something.

"Anyway somehow we got out of there that night with a plan that my husband and I would start picking Sean up after school. And then Edith and Carl pretty much decided that the money and time they've been planning to spend on travel would go towards travel to Boston. They come up for a month in the summer, and school vacations, and they make several other trips every year.

"I don't agree with everything that they do. For example, Carl offered Sean rewards of tickets to the Red Sox if he would improve his grades. I don't believe that is the way to encourage real learning. I'm not crazy about the values some of these athletes seem to promote either. But I have to admit it's a lot better for Sean to be going to these ballgames with his grandfather than what was happening before. And he is doing better in school.

"We've come to an agreement with Edith and Carl that some topics we just won't ever discuss. Religion, politics, abortion. We are in this together, and we need to get along."

Less dire situations can benefit from grandparents' cooperation too.

Two grandmothers who lived near each other became good friends and partners in giving to the children. Barbara and her grandchildren's other grandmother shopped for baby clothes together before their grandson was born. They found that they could do more for the children if they continued shopping together. These children have wonderful parents, but little money.

"We wouldn't give them money and they would never in a million years accept it, that would be like an insult. But we can give gifts. Even extravagant gifts. That's what grandparents do. So, the two of us grandmoms, we went in together on a big swing set and climbing toy for the backyard. And also swimming lessons. It's fun, and the two of us like to shop. Which neither of our husbands will do with us, so we go together, and look, and pick out the best thing for them. Music lessons, too, and beautiful dresses for the girls. And it doubles my purchasing power. Hers, too. We can do more together."

In talking with grandmothers, I heard some heartbreaking stories about one set of grandparents preventing the other grandparents from seeing the grandchildren. This sort of thing never ends well. If circumstances have given you the power to do so, and you are tempted to cut them out of your grandchild's life, think about how you are going to explain that to your grandchildren twenty years from now.

Your other children.

Your other children are aunts and uncles now. They may be delighted. This can bring grown siblings together.

Two adult siblings who are both parents suddenly get more connected now that they have such an important common preoccupation. They have lots to talk about.

A younger brother becomes the fun uncle, much appreciated for his rowdy playfulness. He's not ready to be a father, he may never want to be one, but he's great at piggyback rides and teaching kids to skateboard. Warm, fun times like this can make his siblings appreciate and enjoy him more. An aunt, whether she wants her own children later or not, may enjoy sharing things she loves with the children. The parents may name their own siblings as guardians of their children in their wills, or show in other ways that they rely on and respect what their siblings offer the children. In one family, the young mother hired her sister-in-law as the after school babysitter, talking about how she could really trust her children's aunt more than anyone. Her choice to do this, and the way she talked about it, nurtured a deeper friendship between the two women.

Or, if your children live far apart, and are in different stages of life, the young aunts and uncles may not pay much attention.

Most delicate for you is if one of your grown children wishes she had a family, too, or even just a romantic partner. She can feel sad and resentful of all the fuss, especially if she is older than the new parents. The arrival of a new generation means everyone gets new roles. Although you may still call them your kids, they are the adults now and the little ones are the kids. One new father, Carlos, whose story is in Chapter 4, felt deeply his new status when he became a father: he was suddenly more equal with his siblings. A childless adult can feel that she's not quite seen as a grownup in the family, because her brother or sister has gone ahead of her into a new life stage.

"My older daughter was pretty surly when my son and his girlfriend announced the pregnancy. I was sort of peeved at her until I thought more about it and remembered she has been dating and not finding anybody, for so long. Now her little brother has a family, and she's still single."

Change.

This stage is another step in separation, as well as a time of connection. For some women, this feels like a loss. For other women, it's a relief. Many women go from one reaction to another: first the sadness of the "empty nest" and later enjoying time for themselves and not feeling responsible.

"When she became a mother, it was clear she was all grown up. It's not up to me anymore. It's very relaxing. I can just enjoy them, and get on with my own life."

New roles can bring you closer, in a different way. Seeing your children have the poignant lovely experiences of parenthood can be a great joy. Shared love for the grandchildren and delight in their antics and achievements gives you and their parents something new in common. Although your lives are very different in some ways, each generation does share many experiences with the preceding one. Your adult children may gain a greater understanding of you, and you may think, "So this is what it was like for my mother."

Your children have children, and that affects all the relationships in the family. Connections change, and there are new experiences to enjoy together. It may take a while to notice and get used to it all.

Try this:

• Give yourself time to adjust and to explore the range of complex feelings this change brings for you.

• If the other grandparents live further away, or other circumstances mean they have less time with the grandchildren, be considerate.

• Don't take over all the holidays or special moments that may have just as much meaning for the other grandparents as for you.

• Watch for chances to enjoy and support your children-in-law in their new role.

• It's easy to get absorbed in grandchildren. Remember to pay attention to your other children too.

Resources

Nonfiction

Becoming a Grandmother: A Life Transition, by Sheila Kitzinger

The Scientist in the Crib: What Early Learning Tells Us about the Mind, by Alison Gopnik, et al

The Shelter of Each Other: Rebuilding Our Families, by Mary Pipher

Everyday Blessings: The Inner Work of Mindful Parenting, by Myla and Jon Kabat-Zinn

I Married My Mother-In-Law And Other Tales of In-Laws We Can't Live With and Can't Live Without, edited by Ilina Silverman

Family Re-Union: Reconnecting Parents and Children in Adulthood, Robert Kuttner and Sharland Trotter

I Only Say This Because I Love You: Talking to Your Parents, Partner, Sibs, and Kids When You're All Adults, by Deborah Tannen

Fiction

Daughters-in Law, by Joanna Trollop

4

Advice and Help

Why is it so hard to not give advice? And what kind of help really helps?

There is a lot going on when your adult child becomes a parent.

One of the biggest things is the touchy issue of advice and help. Advice and help are not identical. They overlap and they carry some of the same emotional meaning. Feelings about this can be very intense when a new child arrives, especially the first grandchild. New parents are learning. Actually, everyone is learning, and everyone's emotional.

> "Letting go of the mothering role is the challenge of being a grandmother. Not being in charge, not being the decider."

It can also go on for years. You probably have thoughts and feelings and opinions about a five-year-old who only eats macaroni and apples, or whether skateboarding is safe, or how to handle a child who wakes repeatedly in the night, or a teen who comes to the table with an iPod and earbuds, listening to music throughout the meal. Or about what school the children should go to, or whether it makes sense to leave an older adolescent alone overnight. Wondering when, or whether to say something, being tempted to advise or suggest or criticize, wanting to offer practical or financial help but not sure if it's appropriate ... these can be questions – or problems – for years. Your adult children's reactions can go on for years, too, especially if they aren't sure of themselves, or if you have come across as critical in the past, or have left them with the impression that you think they aren't good parents.

Why would parents not want advice and help from their own experienced parents?

Many people feel like adolescents again when they are around their own parents, at least sometimes. At best, it can be kind of nice to "go home" and be taken care of, fussed over. At worst, it can be confining and infantilizing. When a young adult is moving into an overwhelming new role as a mother or father, *both* these aspects can be heightened.

So, all parents need help sometimes ... yet getting it can make them feel worse. Your adult child may resent being dependent on you, and may feel like a teenager again, just when he or she wants so much to feel competent as a parent.

In many other countries, new parents want and expect help from their own parents, both practical hands-on assistance, which allows the new mother to rest, and guidance on how to care for a baby, and then ongoing care of their children while parents work. This works well in some families here in the U.S., too, of course, but the dominant cultural picture here and now focuses on independence, and portrays both help and information as intrusive.

The linguist Deborah Tannen has written in several of her books about how giving advice or information carries a message of criticism, as if you are telling your adult child that you think they need information, or that they don't know enough.

A grandmother of three said,

> "I realized with my second set of grandchildren that giving advice to a daughter, the message is, 'You need me. You can't make it on your own.'"

Offers of practical help can convey a similar unintended message. You may intend to offer a bit of ease, or a good solution to a challenging situation. What looks to you like a frantic, disorganized household where some things are neglected may not feel that way to your adult children. They may think they are doing just fine.

Offering help might be welcome. Or, it might not, because to your grandchildren's parents, it can carry the message, "your household is not OK," even if that's not what you meant to convey.

One new grandmother noted,

> "My daughter-in-law knew nothing, infants terrified her. With the baby she looked awkward, like she had three arms. She wanted and needed help but any offer of help was like a slap in the face to her feeling of competence."

Why is it so hard to not say anything?

Although there are certainly times and families and situations when an adult child welcomes a parent's suggestions, the most common pattern by far is that grandmothers know it's a bad idea to give advice. They readily talk about this, and yet they are profoundly tempted to do it anyway.

Almost every grandmother I have talked to said in one way or another that she knew she shouldn't tell the parents what to do. Actually, the very first thing many grandparents said to me was something like, "don't give advice." The words "bite my tongue" were used often. Even that phrase "bite my tongue" implies that one wants to speak and has to actually bite a part of one's own body to stop it. It's not an accepting or serene image, but one of conflict and pain.

If grandmothers know what they should do, and have confidence in their adult children, as most say they do, then why is it so hard?

I think there are many reasons, all powerful, and they add up.

It's natural to want to use your hard-won knowledge of child raising. You've taken care of children for decades. You've learned a lot. How tempting to just offer an idea: "Try holding him this way," or "I can show you how to give him a bath." It's also natural to hope your knowledge will be respected by people you care about. If you are a good cook, dog trainer, or tax preparer, if you're known in the family for editing skills, or experience in international travel, people probably often ask you for help or information, maybe more often than you'd like. Now, when the people dearest to you in the world – your children – seem to be struggling to get your beloved grandchild to sleep, or to behave reasonably, it can be odd or even hurtful that you can't offer suggestions about how you've successfully solved such problems.

> "We do stuff for our kids. I have been doing all their taxes for them for years. And both daughters call my husband and his sister, who are in business together as contractors, about their houses all the time, and they appreciate it a lot when little things get done for free on their houses. Bigger stuff, or stuff our business doesn't handle, they still want advice. Hours spent talking about my one daughter's roof. When it comes to the grandkids … they don't want to hear a thing, even though we raised the four of them."

Another reason is what I call the whiplash syndrome. You've been hit by an abrupt reversal of direction. For years, as a parent, you were responsible for making all the decisions, and implementing them too. You had to. It wasn't just an understandable impulse to say or do something to care for your child; it was your responsibility, every minute. Everything was up to you. Whether you were tired, distracted, needed a break, or caught up in a crisis of your own, it was still up to you to take care of your child. Now suddenly, there's a child you love dearly, and nothing is up to you. It can take a while to adjust to this very different role.

The cues all send you in the wrong direction too.

> "It isn't my kid. But it feels like my kid, he even looks like my kid because he looks just like his father, my son Allan, looked as a child. I've had to physically stop myself from scooping him up sometimes."

Sometimes, you think that your child is making big mistakes as a parent – the exact mistakes you made and now regret. How tempting to want to step in and fix that, for both your child and your grandchild's sake, to say, "No, no, no, I tried that. I was wrong!!"

I talked with several grandmothers who just couldn't seem to hold back, or didn't realize how their well-intentioned strategies were going to sound. One woman told me, "Whenever something comes up, I say what I think just once. Then they can do as they like." I cringed as I heard this, because I can imagine how it sounds to the parents. If you say what you think just once about everything, that's a lot of opinions. That "just once" may be sounding like a stream of criticism. Also, it's probably not really just once. We all repeat ourselves constantly in normal conversation. People close to us are pretty familiar with our views.

Books are another red flag. One woman happily told me that her daughter-in-law is pregnant, and added, "I have a big suitcase full of books I want to give her." Another woman says, "When I see a book about raising children that I think is important, I just order it and have it sent to them." Of course, a book can be a wonderful, thoughtful gift, and these might be eagerly welcomed and enjoyed. If you are tempted to send one – or a suitcase full – ask yourself, is it something the recipient said she wanted? Would she want to buy it herself, if she saw it? Or is this a way of trying to convince her of your point of view? Would you like it if she sent you the books that she thought you ought to read? Is this a shared interest, or a way of promoting your agenda?

A grandparent couple told me about the recent difficult visit from their daughter and her three little boys. The younger ones, fearless and energetic two-year-old twins, were exhausting but sweetly responsive and fun. The older boy, who was almost eleven, had everybody worried. He was angry, glum, and defiant in a way he never had been before. They didn't agree with how their daughter was handling this. While they tried to be supportive, there had been lots of discussion that had turned into debate at times. They were worried they hadn't helped at all, and remorseful that they had left her feeling judged. We talked this over for a while, and finally the grandfather said he had a book in mind to send their daughter.

"What book?" the grandmother asked nervously. She thought he had been too critical and interfering with their daughter.

"Oh, the only conversation we had that was at all relaxed was about backyard chickens. She's seriously planning to get some, so I picked up a new book I saw about it."

We all laughed in relief. Send her something she wants!

The kind of help that helping is all about.

Of course, help and advice don't always turn into difficulty.

Sometimes the parents do ask for help—and guidance. A woman whose first grandchild was on the way got a call that surprised her from her son and his wife, talking on separate phone extensions, asking her to come and help after their baby was born.

At first the older woman was very reluctant, saying, "I don't want to interfere."

The expectant couple was ready for her resistance, and prepared to talk her out of it. They both said cheerfully, "Interfere, interfere, please, we don't know what we're doing. Come show us."

Did it make a difference that they were both in their early forties? They had long since established lives as knowledgeable independent adults. His mother never commented on what they should do; in fact she asked them for advice about all kinds of things, from getting a new cell phone to how to buy airline tickets online, and whether it was bad for the environment if she put salt on her sidewalk in winter. There were no financial ties; they had supported themselves for many years, and she never gave them money. Asking for help didn't make them feel helpless.

In another family, things changed over time.

> "When the first grandbaby was born, I saw that they were wonderful parents, and also I was busy with my youngest, still at home, so I didn't get into giving advice like I saw a lot of my friends doing. And I could see my daughter and son-in-law didn't want anybody to weigh in, they had their own philosophy, and they knew what they wanted to do. Now, my daughter asks me stuff, she says, 'Mom, it's easier to ask you than look it up somewhere.' And if she doesn't like it, she just ignores it."

Gender can make a difference, although of course it doesn't necessarily. Fathers sometimes are more open to asking for information, and being shown how to do things at the beginning because they don't think they should automatically know. They expect a learning curve. Of course, they don't want to be ordered around or treated as inept. And nobody wants continual comments and suggestions once they've made a decision, or they feel they have learned how to do something. Fathers usually see taking care of an infant or a young child as something they need to learn, while mothers may have absorbed the idea that they should instinctively know. Some grandmothers notice that a son may find it easier to ask questions than a daughter, or to consider suggestions.

"It's real different. My son can take what I say if it's useful or he can just tune me out. If I suggest something he doesn't like, he just takes no notice of it. With my daughters, they are reactive, they respond, one way or another, and it can be a button-pusher."

Marina found that her son was more relaxed than her daughter.

"With young men, there is a certain skill acquisition process. They don't feel threatened by what they don't know."

If your son, or son-in-law, is open to suggestion, be sure your suggestions are respectful. Offering to show a new father how to swaddle his newborn is one thing, continuing to give advice on basic baby care when he's the confident, although tired, father of a three-month-old is probably not as welcome.

Rachel, the mother of four daughters, has a different challenge. The difficulty is finding time to do all she would like to for her grown children, and all they ask for. All of her daughters have children. When I asked, she said yes, sometimes her daughters had taken offense at unwanted recommendations from her. But that blows over. The big issue is when they ask her to come, and she can't be two places at once. She described a time when one daughter had surgery and another daughter had a bout of flu while a contractor's crew was renovating their kitchen.

"At the time all this was going on I was helping my parents move. And I have an elderly aunt who's alone, I had to help her.

"What has been the hardest part? Not having time to help out when I need to. I had to say no to my daughter in New York last weekend. We are having some carpentry done in the house and there are things I had to do to get ready for that. I only have the weekends. I wish I had more free time to help out."

Rachel has to be careful that her daughters feel that her attention and time are divided fairly among them … just as she did when they were children.

In another family, the two parents saw it differently. They had very different needs, and a grandmother's assistance got opposite reactions from her son and his partner, the two fathers of a newly adopted infant.

Gary remembers the first few weeks vividly. He can laugh now, but at the time it was awful.

> "My mom came over and basically started telling us what to do. I found it infuriating. Looking back, it's obvious we actually had no idea! We had expected to adopt a one-year-old, or a toddler, and we thought it would take months. But a birth mother chose us pretty quickly, and then he was born four weeks early. So we never had a chance to take the baby care class at the hospital, or even read much.

> "I can remember lying in bed, trying to take a nap after both of us being up in the night with him, and I could hear the doorbell, and apparently it's my mom because Carlos is going, 'Miriam, come in, wow, lasagna, let's put that right in the oven, can you take a look at these little white spots on his forehead. What is that?' And on and on like that. So I'm supposed to be getting the great luxury of a nap while Carlos has the kid, and I'm lying in there fuming while Carlos and my mom are just getting along great. She's showing him how to do everything, reorganizing the changing table, how to hold the baby, making Carlos sit down while she gets dinner on the table, the whole thing.

> "It was like being twelve years old, with my mother running things."

Listening to this story, funny but obviously painful too, I found myself trying to decide what Gary's mother might have done, and what other grandmothers might learn from her story. Should she have done less, said less? At the time, Gary certainly thought so. And yet now he acknowledges that he needed information from somewhere, because he really didn't know.

Carlos wanted attention and help. He had spent his adult life as the uncle, a distinctly minor role in his large child-centered family of origin. Schedules were arranged around grandchildren's naps and school vacations. Spare bedrooms went to married couples, and if anyone ended up on the couch, or the inflatable mattress in the living room, it was Carlos. Easter dinners were at the houses of his siblings who were married with children, and he was not involved in the planning. He sent checks when nephews graduated. But he wasn't invited to baby showers or expected to visit the hospital to see a newborn niece or nephew, the way his married brothers and brothers-in-law with children were.

Now, his baby was the youngest, to be talked about, inquired after. Now, the ordinary conversations of parents included him; he could join the discussions about various car seats, strollers, and preschools. Now, when he brought seven-week-old Gabriel to his mother's house, he was seated in the most comfortable chair, while his mother and sisters cooed over the baby. He was part of the cycle of passing on outgrown children's clothes, and could enjoy his sisters holding up onesies, and toddler shirts for his approval. Now, he wanted everybody to visit, to call, to send presents, to make him the center of attention as a new father. He listened to every piece of advice, from everybody. It made him feel supported and nourished as he did the hard work of caring for a baby. He and his mother-in-law had always gotten along. They made a closer, warmer connection because to him, her help felt like respect for him as a father. When she explained that those white spots were infant acne, and how to get rid of diaper rash, he felt that it was because she knew he was in charge of Gabriel.

For Gary, having his mother show up and tell him what to do made him feel inept, like someone who can't manage.

Over time, and especially through watching his sisters become parents, Gary realized that his mother's advice was useful to them, and probably had been for him too.

> "What I didn't realize, and Carlos did, was that we needed advice. We had no idea what we were doing, like most new parents, and we learned like everybody does. Things kind of settled down as our son got a little older. I didn't really get

over it until my sister had a baby. I thought she was ridiculous to be so touchy with my mom, instead of appreciating all the help, and Carlos said I was just like that. At this point, I consider my mom to be pretty much a saint, because she not only raised all three of us but then she stuck with us through having our own kids too."

Perhaps this family's story shows us there is no perfect way to be a grandmother, nor is it necessary to look for one, and that upset, and mixed feelings, are an inevitable part of growth and change.

So, what can you do?

What is the best way to enjoy your children as parents, and perhaps actually be helpful at times? How can you handle your own mixed feelings without annoying your grandchildren's parents or ending up with the proverbial "sore tongue"?

I talked to many grandmothers who also have relevant professional experience and they had good suggestions about this.

Midwife Nancy Wainer advises,

> "With a newborn, it's not a good time to emotionally connect with your daughter through talking. She is absorbed in her own self and the baby, as it should be. She has no energy for a relationship with mom or mother-in-law. So, don't criticize. Go prepared to work. Have an attitude of joyfulness and serenity. Nurture a mom and baby together, don't take over the baby. Don't become the authority on the baby."

A nanny who has worked for many families over decades counsels:

> "Mothers, especially with the first, don't want judgment from their own moms. They want pure love and acceptance. They want to be empowered by their mothers, validated. But the mothers have an uncanny way of always saying, 'I did this, I did that, try it, do it my way.'"

An experienced grandmother of six children, infants through teens, says,

> "The mistake grandmothers make is undermining their competence as parents. For the grandmother, for all of us really, I would say, the more you realize you don't have all the answers the better off you are."

Jackie, a grandmother, aunt and great aunt, and pediatrician says:

> "Would you say it to your sister, or your friend? If not, don't say it to your kids."

Joan, grandmother of five including three adolescents, advises,

> "If you are asked to do something, or they take you up on an offer to do something, just do it. Don't say, OK, but wouldn't you rather this or that other way … ? Don't take it as an invitation to improve a lot of other things. Don't rewire the house with your own two hands while they're out."

Everybody got promoted to something they aren't very good at.

If raising these kids and making the decisions about them isn't your business, what is?

As a grandmother, you do have a problem to focus on, or at least a new stage of life to learn about. You are the parent of an adult and no one automatically knows how to do that. We figure it out when we are in the situation, maybe getting some help from other people, just as we do with the other stages.

You may have been negotiating a new relationship with your kids as adults for a while now, and even felt pretty comfortable in it, but the arrival of grandchildren creates chances for more growth in this part of mothering for you.

I talked with a very frustrated grandfather who surprised himself and me by figuring this out in the middle of complaining about a beloved six-year-old grandson who ate little, liked very few foods, and made meals into contentious negotiating sessions … just as his own mother had done as a child! I talked with this grandfather, and his wife, after the latest visit from the child who refused what was cooked for him. His relentless bargaining about what he had to eat, and what he could have instead, had made many family meals argumentative and tense.

The grandfather said,

> "I know something about this. I raised a picky eater and I learned some things. I think I could really help. But she doesn't want to hear it, every time she visits she has a different strategy with him, she's read some other book about it or she's making him separate meals, whatever. I think I know what to do, but I'm not supposed to say anything."

His wife, the child's grandmother, said kindly,

> "Honey, that's not your job anymore, a picky eater. Your job is figuring out how to be the parent of a grown up."

He laughed, and said,

> "So, everybody got promoted to something they're not very good at."

I think he really got to the heart of the matter. We all do get promoted to something we're not very good at. His daughter, the young mother, wasn't very successful with her picky eater. It wasn't getting better, and everyone was exasperated, including her. Her own parents, these experienced grandparents, probably do have some good ideas about this problem, but she didn't want their guidance. She wanted to figure it out herself, her way. The grandfather was certainly stuck as he tried to move into his new role as a respectful and supportive parent of an adult. He was trying but he wasn't very good at that, yet, either.

Sometimes, you can find a model and advisor in your own family. You can even call her and talk it over. Jackie found an unexpected blessing when she did this. She reconnected with an elderly great-aunt.

> "My aunt and I are really not alike in a lot of ways, politics, religion, but when I ask her about grandmothering, we can

completely connect. She's given me good tips. She's been through a lot and it's great talking with her."

You might actively seek out other grandparents to talk with.

"My closest friends, there are a group of four of us, we all have grandchildren. We share a lot of interests, we've taken cooking classes together. And we all remind each other, 'It's not your child,' we say to each other, when we're tempted to interfere or get bossy with the parents. That's our refrain, or sometimes, we say, 'It doesn't matter what you think!' It's a lot easier to see when it's somebody else. We can laugh about it, together, and help each other keep our mouths shut when we should."

You may also see ways that you can actually help your grandchildren's parents. Many families have told me about ways a thoughtful grandparent stepped in to solve a problem, or do a task that really eased the family's life. There's no formula for what works; each one is unique. It's usually easier for the parents to ask you for something if you generally show you have confidence in them and aren't critical.

Grandparents can really help.

I heard many wonderful stories of families where grandparents had found ways to really be of help. It's rarely telling the parents what you think they should do. What most families today need more of is time, not advice, and grandparents may have it to give.

Being available to care for your grandchildren when needed can be a great help to the parents. You may find ways to help with household chores or errands or other tasks, too, but look for something your adult children actually want.

The parents might love it if you show up with new outfits for the grandchildren. A mother with a very modest income told me happily about how her mother-in-law would take the children out for the afternoon and bring them back wearing new shoes.

This was a help to the parents financially, and it was an errand taken care of, too.

Such a thing can also feel like criticism. The parents might think those too small, stained, fraying T-shirts from vacation spots they've visited still look great on your grandson, and carry wonderful memories, and don't need to be replaced.

> "I just ask if I'm thinking of doing something for them. I stay with both sets of grandchildren in the evening so their parents can go out. In one house, I do the dishes and they love it. In the other, now I just bring my knitting or a book for after the kids are in bed."

When you look around and see something that you think needs doing, consider whether your standards have changed. Wasn't your house messier and your laundry a little more haphazard when you were a busy young mother than it is now?

Every family has its own culture and for some, grandparents can give a child something that helps out the whole family economically. As long as it's framed as a gift to a child, the parents' independence is preserved. Giving a swing set or music lessons is not like writing your adult children checks to subsidize their basic living expenses.

Sometimes grandparents can do something that saves time for the parents.

> "I went to small claims court for my son. And I've stayed occasionally to wait for a repairman, because I'm retired from my full-time job, and working part-time free-lance now, so I can do it."

Betty had the time, and because of her longer life experience, she also had a good idea of what her grandson needed. She solved a problem that nobody else knew what to do about.

> "My littlest grandson, we called him the Tornado Baby, and the Curtain Climber. He is constantly in motion, fearless, everything is fun to him, falling down doesn't bother him. When he was a toddler he was always climbing up on top of anything he could. If you looked away for a minute, he

would be standing on the back of the couch. He would go right up a ladder, and he would just head off down the street if the gate was open. When he started kindergarten, his teacher right away told his parents he had ADHD and he had to be medicated. The parents didn't want that at all, but they didn't know what to do, and he is a handful at home, too. They could also see that his teacher was starting to not like him, and he was frustrated at being expected to sit still so much. Then a child psychologist told them he doesn't have executive function. My husband laughed at that, he said, 'Hey, that's why five-year-old boys aren't executives.' But something had to change.

"When I was a child nobody ever heard of ADHD, so we could all be as rowdy as we wanted, and run around and make noise and have all kinds of projects and all that happened was your parents told you to go outside. Boys were expected to be rambunctious and loud. My three brothers climbed trees, went where they weren't supposed to, and got up on top of the garage, and threw balls in the house unless somebody stopped them, and no one thought anything of it. My dad would yell at them, but it was just, 'Get down from there' or, 'Stop that' or, 'Listen to your mother.' He loved them, he was proud of them. They were outside in all weather, they came home every night at dinnertime sweaty and dirty. So, I tried something. I was taking my grandson to school, so the parents could get to work. I would walk him over. And I started to get him about half an hour or even an hour earlier and we would go to the park, and I would just run with him, and play, and then by the time he got to school he was a little worn out. And I put up a basketball hoop in the driveway, which the older kids had been wanting, and we got the older ones to play with him after school. It was funny to see because he is so little. They taught him to shoot baskets, and they chased each other around. I've taken him bird watching with me too which nobody thought he would like, but he does, he comes home with his pockets full of rocks, and bugs in a jar.

"This helps. The teacher is still pressuring them but she admits he's a lot better. We're looking into swimming lessons for him, and I'll take him, because the parents are just so overloaded."

Linda is a labor and delivery nurse. We worked together for several years and she told me a wonderful and unique story.

She has three sisters, and they all got in the habit years ago of turning sex education of their own children over to her, because she's a nurse. It started when one sister turned up on her doorstep with her eleven-year-old son. "He's got some questions," she said, pushing him in the door. Others called her whenever anything came up they didn't want to explain, or when their daughters were approaching the time they would begin to menstruate. As Linda's nieces and nephews grew up and became parents, they brought their own kids over to Linda, and eventually her grandchildren were included too. By the time I knew Linda, she was a grandmother and great aunt, and this was a family tradition.

Eventually, there were a lot of kids and Linda got tired of calls from her daughters and her sisters, expecting her to drop everything at short notice to deal with a question they were too embarrassed to handle themselves.

So she set up a regular schedule. She made an appointment with every child in the family around age ten, and went over the basics with them. Around the Christmas holidays, when more relatives were in town, and children didn't have school, she also had an additional session with all the girls, and a separate one with all the boys. This was a combination of everything she wanted them to know, and any questions they wanted to ask. She established right away that any question was legitimate and there was to be no teasing, no swearing, and no disrespectful language.

In this family, none of the parents have figured out how to talk about sex or reproduction or birth control, because they can count on Linda to do that. The family has established a culture that lets kids know these topics are interesting and important and serious, and that responsible behavior is their responsibility.

I had a chance to talk with one of Linda's granddaughters, when she was about twenty-five years old.

"I always knew everything," she said, rolling her eyes and laughing. "I had to educate a lot of my friends. And boy was I ever careful about birth control. I just could never have faced my Grammy with an unplanned pregnancy, after she went to so much trouble to make sure I knew all about birth control."

Grandmothers, or both grandparents, pitch in to help in other ways, too. In another family, an exhausted frazzled mother in the middle of a divorce was glad when her own parents offered to take her daughter to visit colleges.

It's an emergency.

Some families have a time when a grandmother's intervention is crucial. A young man told me this story when he heard I was working on this book.

"After my dad left, when I was ten, my mom was working but we were running out of food and we had no heat. My dad just took off and things got worse and worse. Finally I went down to a pay phone and called my grandmother, my dad's mom. She was there the next day with a big truck, with her sons and sons-in-law. By the time my mom got home from work, all her stuff was in the truck. My grandmother said, 'Get in. I don't have room for the houseplants.' She took us back to her place, and there was a trailer on her land for us. We lived there and she made sure we didn't lack, she would come down with a turkey, or a bag of groceries. In the fall, she took us shopping for winter coats, and shoes for school."

When is it your job to interfere?

There are times, mercifully rare, when you do have to say something, and you may have to interfere.

Is the child suffering or in danger? If you answer no to this question, if this is just a difference of opinion, then it's time for working on your

51

job of being the parent of a grownup, and helping and advising when asked, whether that's often or never.

If the answer is yes, then you must intervene. This is a very different matter. If a child is suffering or in danger, then your dilemma is what to do, not whether to do something. Grandparents can err in saying too much, but it's also easy to shrink from the awful task of admitting to yourself and others that your own adult child is not able to care for your grandchild.

One mother watched her son, who had been raised with great tenderness and gentleness, become a really harsh punitive parent to his three-year-old daughter. He yelled. He yelled angry threats and insults. Sometimes, he hit. It was tempting for the grandmother to see her daughter-in-law, who was just as severe and harsh to their child, as the source of this behavior. But blaming others did not really change anything. Her son was not the kind of parent she expected him to be, the kind she valued, the kind she thought she had been.

She spoke in a calm and carefully planned way to her son and daughter-in-law. She urged them to think of how the child felt, she reminded them of what a three-year-old could understand and what she couldn't. They listened to her in a somewhat abashed silence, more receptive than she had expected. Later that afternoon, she and her son were at a playground together, with the child. The little girl had gotten worn out, and the grandmother was carrying her home. She said to her son "She's so little, I remember carrying you like this, and now you're so much taller than me." He stared as if struck by this final evidence that his child was small and deserved tender care, and after that day the grandmother saw a calmer and less punishing family life. Yet, her son and his wife were still colder and less nurturing than she had expected, or thought possible. It was very painful for her to know her son was capable of such behavior toward his own child. It shook her confidence in herself, and in how she had raised him. She knows she may have to intervene again.

Other grandmothers see worse. A grandparent couple was devastated to find out that their teenage granddaughter had attacked her four-year-old brother, injuring him badly. The bruises were alarming enough, but the little boy also had a broken arm. The grandparents realized over the next few days that their son and his wife, the children's parents, were in denial about this, and had no real plans to keep it from happening again.

"It's hard to see someone you raised who can't give that nurturing."

Troubled about both children, they offered to take the little boy to live with them. The overwhelmed parents agreed. Then both grandparents sat down with the teenage granddaughter and tried to talk to her about what had happened. She was sullen and silent, but eventually did agree to go to church with them.

> "We got her into the youth group at our church, and that's a start. We're still worried, we can't figure out what's next, but everybody's safe for now."

In another family, the grandmother's ability to step in made a huge difference when her son couldn't parent his own son. Her seventeen-year-old grandson decided that he didn't want to act ashamed of being gay anymore and it was time to come out to his parents. He didn't expect it to go well.

One evening after dinner, he packed his most important possessions into his backpack, sought out his father, and said simply, "Dad, I'm gay."

"I've got three things to tell you, then," his father replied, stiff and red-faced. "The first is you are not my son anymore and you will never spend another night under this roof. The second is you will not see your brother again."

The boy picked up his backpack. "Well, if I'm not your son, I don't have to listen to the third thing," he replied and walked out of the house.

He went down to the corner and called his grandmother, his father's mother. His courage was used up. He found himself alone on the dark street, and he was a rattled frightened child again as his story spilled out to her on the phone. She immediately drove over and picked him up. He lived with her until he finished high school and went off to college. Knowing what can happen to homeless teenagers, I think she may have saved his life.

What to say, what to do.

Grandparents are like a family National Guard in some ways. You might not be doing anything to help out, or you might be needed, and respond, at times. In an emergency, you might have to quickly drop everything else.

You might be enjoying your grandchildren, while mostly paying attention to your own life. Or you might be picking up grandchildren after school every day, and making sure they get their vaccinations and new eyeglasses. If a crisis or emergency comes up you might suddenly be managing the household, or temporarily taking up the responsibilities of a parent. In some families there are true emergencies, when a grandparent has to step in, perhaps unasked, and do more for the children than you ever thought you'd have to.

You'll get better at this complex job over time, and it offers new windows on understanding your own adult children, and on yourself as a parent and grandparent.

Try this:

- How can you help? Frame your questions like this. It may work better than thinking about how you can get your grandchild's parents to do things your way. It doesn't have much to do with whether you're right about what's best. Maybe you are. Probably you are completely, absolutely, 100% right about everything you are thinking. But that's not so important.

- Give yourself a break. Give yourself a little time to get used to being a grandparent, and the parent of an adult. Acknowledge, at least to yourself, the frustration of not being called upon for your wisdom and knowledge. It's OK to *wish* they would ask your opinion.

- When you are tempted to give advice to your adult child, ask yourself if you would say it to your own sister or brother or to a friend or a colleague.

- Reframe. You did a good job, you raised a competent adult, and that is something to enjoy and be proud of.

• Is too much of your energy focused on your grandchild's family? Is enough of it focused on your own projects and interests, your friends, spouse, and other people who matter to you? Your health, your work?

• If your children do ask for help, just do it and stop there. Don't respond with, "Wouldn't it be better ... " and fill in your ideas about how to handle everything else, too.

• Be prepared to take decisive action in an emergency.

Resources

Nonfiction

You're Wearing That? Understanding Mothers and Daughters in Conversation, by Deborah Tannen

Family Re-Union, by Robert Kuttner and Sharland Trotter.

Addressing ADD Naturally, by Dr. Kathi Kemper

5

Celebrations

Rejoicing in this new stage of life, and making space for mourning and healing and forgiveness, too.

Why celebrate becoming a grandmother?

All over the world, human communities acknowledge and celebrate many of the milestones and achievements throughout life. There are a wide variety of events acknowledging the maturity of young people, from Mexico's quinceañera, and the Jewish bar mitzvah and bat mitzvah, to America's debutante balls. Achievements like high school or college graduation and retirement are often marked with ritual and honor. Housewarming parties, engagement parties, weddings and wedding showers, and anniversaries, are all happy celebrations of important life events. Becoming a mother involves baby showers, and all kinds of other exultant, fun events that are also chances for new mothers to connect with each other.

We can begin a tradition of celebrating becoming a grandmother, too, in some of the same ways. Becoming a grandmother is an important, joyous, and complex life transition. It's a new role, a transformation in family relationships, and best of all as we welcome a new beloved child into our lives, often a source of deep happiness.

In this chapter we'll look at many ways to celebrate, and also rituals to mourn and heal the pain and losses that can be part of becoming a grandmother.

It can be casual and fun, or solemn. Some of us are lucky enough to have good friends who are also becoming grandmothers, and can share this experience.

Surprise a grandmother-to-be with a gathering of mutual friends, or a special time for just the two of you. Plan a celebration for yourself, perhaps using some of the ideas below.

Fitting it in.

A new grandmother may find it hard to focus on celebrating for herself, even if she likes the idea. One of the pleasures of grandmothering is helping the new parents, and participating in events like baby showers. These are lovely experiences and not to be missed. But you may lose track of your own feelings in the midst of the attention you want to give to other people. Taking some time to celebrate and acknowledge this transition can be enjoyable, and deepen the importance of what is happening for *you*.

Your celebration can be fun and meaningful for other people too. Moments like these can nourish connections between friends and family members.

You can create a celebration for yourself, or for a friend or relative. Just as women often arrange parties and give practical gifts to each other as they become mothers, we can create traditions of enjoying and acknowledging grandmotherhood together.

When a grandchild is not the biological child of the grandmother's biological child, a celebration may be especially appreciated and useful because people often question the validity of her relationship and her commitment to her grandchild, and she may have trouble feeling quite like a "real grandmother" herself. These are wonderful occasions for the new grandmother's friends to create a celebration for her. The grandmother of the adopted grandchild, and the stepgrandchild, may especially enjoy a heartfelt acknowledgment of her new role and relationship. So, too, can the mother of a lesbian daughter whose wife or partner gives birth to their baby.

What is there to celebrate about becoming a grandmother?

Becoming a grandmother is similar to, and linked to, becoming a mother. It is also very different, rich with meaning and emotion unique to grandmotherhood.

Grandmotherhood is about continuity and renewal, nurturing new life rather than creating it, nurturing the whole family, not just children, and giving without controlling. It may have other specific meanings to you that you want to recognize and express.

Honoring grandmotherhood is a positive acknowledgment of aging. Becoming a grandmother can be a creative, generative, and lively part of middle age and old age.

This is the time to honor stepping into a new role and giving up an old role. The time for having babies is ending or is long over. Your relationship with your own child is changing irrevocably.

> "On the one hand, my daughter needed me more than she had in many years. On the other hand it really hit home that she wasn't my little girl anymore, she's somebody's mommy now, she's a grown up."

If this is not your first, then you have already made the transition to grandmotherhood. Even so, there is still much to celebrate in becoming a grandmother to this particular child.

When to do it.

Right after a child's arrival, grandmothers living nearby are often quite busy helping, and don't have the time or attention for anything else. Grandmothers may be bringing dinner to new parents, shopping for baby clothes or equipment, finding and paying for diaper service or a postpartum doula or a housecleaner, and taking photos. Some women live far away and are poised to dash to the airport the moment that crucial phone call comes saying a daughter is in labor or baby has been born.

In these situations, they are not focused on reflecting about their own lives.

For some, celebrating well before the child's arrival can work best.

It might be as soon as you find out about the pregnancy or adoption.

> "My two best friends and I go out to dinner, just us, each
> time there's a grandkid on the way."

If the grandchild's family lives far away from you, and you won't be traveling immediately to visit, then soon after the child's arrival can be a good time. A grandmother can feel quite an anticlimax soon afterwards if she gets a call, or even an e-mail, that a baby's been born. This grandmother can feel that she is "all dressed up with no place to go." It can feel odd to simply go to work, or go about normal activities when something so wonderful and life-changing has just happened.

A similar situation arises with some adoptions. Parents who adopt older babies or children are often advised not to have any visitors at all for the first month or more. Social workers experienced in adoption suggest that they create a quiet intensive time for their new child to adapt and to learn that they are her parents, before introducing other new people and relationships. Even if the child is much older, this time is much like the first days with a newborn, when the baby and her parents get to know each other and become attached. Although the grandmother of this child may understand and support this plan, she might feel at loose ends herself. Or, perhaps the advice makes no sense to her and she feels shut out and impatient. In these circumstances, those first weeks after the child's arrival are a great time for her to celebrate for herself, or for her friends to make a special occasion for her.

> "My friend who is also a grandmother, we get together
> around the time of the birth to celebrate for ourselves. And
> we've done it with each new grandchild, just the two of us."

Or, the best moment could be a year later. When Flora talked with me about her first grandchild, she said,

> "I wanted to celebrate with my friends. For the first months
> everybody was too busy and my grandson's parents were too
> exhausted. I finally had a party and invited my friends to
> meet my grandson just before he was a year old and that
> was perfect. His parents had more energy and he was old

enough to relate to people a little bit. I have a great photo of him sitting on the couch with one of my oldest friends, looking at books."

Celebration could also be much later. Perhaps you didn't think of this, or have time for it, until you had grandchildren already in school, even older.

"My fourth grandchild was born on my sixty-fourth birthday. The others are older, six, and eleven, and fourteen. And about three months later, there was a week when they were all going to be in town at the same time. And I wanted to have them all together, and just enjoy it. I cleared it with my kids, the parents, and I invited just a few other people, my closer friends. With all the family, it was enough people to fill the house. I got my picture taken with all the grandkids, and I made a little speech at dinner about how happy I was to be their grandma, and I thanked their parents for making me a grandma, and I can tell you there wasn't a dry eye in the house. We have several musicians in our family, and they played later on and people were dancing and it was really a great time."

Choose any time that feels right to you and is not crowded with baby showers, or other events.

If you are thinking of honoring a friend who is Jewish, don't surprise her. Ask her how she feels about the Jewish tradition of waiting until after the birth to give gifts to a new baby. If this tradition is important to her, or to the baby's parents, then she might feel more comfortable celebrating after the baby's arrival.

What to do.

Your celebration can be as simple as a meal with friends, or a brief time you set aside for yourself alone to reflect.

Or, you may enjoy doing more. Many meaningful transitions in life are celebrated with ritual that is special about this occasion. They often involve commitments or hopes for the future. They can be solemn and well planned, or just a casual gathering in someone's kitchen, with food and merriment, and a few congratulations. Holidays, graduations, birthdays, weddings, retirement, housewarming, funerals, baby showers, can all be models and inspirations. Below are some ideas you might enjoy using.

You can do this with your friends and family, or you can create a special occasion for yourself alone if you prefer or if that is your situation. Don't miss the opportunity even if circumstances don't allow you to have an elaborate party with others. Even if you are alone, or if things have not gone well and there is sadness or uncertainty, or outright grief, it may help to take some time to honor your new role and focus on happiness.

Simple celebrations.

A very simple small party can be wonderful. When I complimented Elizabeth on a beautiful silver and turquoise necklace she was wearing, her face lit up.

> "My friends gave me this when my granddaughter was born," she told me.

Three friends, a Sunday brunch, and this necklace were all it took to make a joyous day and something she remembered with great pleasure. Barbara said,

> "Us two grandmothers went shopping for baby clothes together. Then, we were going crazy waiting – he was nine days late – and just before the baby was born, we went out together to a very fancy lunch and had champagne."

A social worker described for me an impromptu celebration at a professional conference where one of the attendees told others that her first grandchild had been born the day before. Most of these social workers didn't know each other, and those that did were colleagues, not close friends. Although they wouldn't necessarily stay in touch after this conference, they wanted to do something special together to mark the day. Several women at the conference got together in the morning and quickly made a plan, and by lunchtime, amazingly, they had created a party for her.

> "We just got a cake from the bakery down the street and balloons, and when we had lunch together we told her it was a party for her. I think it really meant a lot to her."

A little food, congratulations, and hugs and attention created a very special moment for the new grandmother, and also for everyone else there.

Sharon says,

> "My husband and I went out to dinner and toasted each other, as Saba and Savta, Hebrew words for grandfather and grandmother."

You might also enjoy a more formal and ritualized celebration. You can borrow from other rituals, the ways holidays, birthdays, and other special events are acknowledged. There are also unique elements of grandmotherhood that call for special specific ritual.

Elements you may include in your celebration.

Joy.

It's wonderful if you can invite other grandmothers, and ask each to share stories of the joys of being a grandmother. Ask each person to bring a picture of her grandchildren, and pass these around so everyone can enjoy them.

Or you may be celebrating with friends who are not grandmothers. Often some friends have grandchildren and some don't. Ask those who do not have grandchildren to bring a poem, a memory of their own grandmother, or to talk about how they see you in this next age of your life.

You could talk about what you are looking forward to, and anything you know about your grandchild. If you have a picture, bring it.

If your grandchild is internationally adopted, you might share what you have learned about the child's country and culture of origin, or serve food from that country as the beginning of making this culture part of your family life.

Food, and nourishing yourself.

Whether you are feeding others or celebrating by yourself, create a meal that has connotations of your ability to nourish yourself and through that to nourish your grandchild. What is the meal that makes you feel strong, and satisfied, including foods that are healthy and pleasurable for you?

Is there anything that your mother or grandmother used to cook that you would like to include, or anything you plan to teach your grandchild to cook?

If you are putting on a celebration for a friend, bring food to symbolize your support in this new part of her life.

One woman always brings her signature lasagna when she wants to help anybody out. Her lasagna pan has been to all her friends' and relatives' houses after births, deaths, divorces, in the midst of kitchen renovations, and when someone got back from a long vacation and had no food in the house. So lasagna is her contribution to grandmother celebrations because it's a reminder that she is a supportive friend who will nourish her friend in this new role.

Gifts.

Bring the new grandmother a scrapbook or a photo album. Or, if she will be caring for the child regularly, perhaps ask her if she would like a cloth baby carrier. A stroller to keep at her own house so the new parents won't have to move one back and forth with the baby might be very convenient.

Typical baby presents like a hand knit sweater or hat, or a toy, can be joyous and fun.

One grandmother bought herself a necklace with her grandsons' birthstones, which she wears every day, "so the boys are always near me."

Take up your responsibilities.

There are many responsibilities to being a grandmother. You might use this occasion to clearly and formally make three commitments: to the child, to the grandchild's parents, and to yourself. You can strengthen those commitments by sharing them with people who are important to you. Ask your community for their support, encouragement, and guidance in your new role. Or just think about it yourself, as a serious and thoughtful addition to the happy parties, showers, and baby sweaters.

Responsibilities to your grandchild.

Are there specific things you want to do or be for this child? As I listened to grandmothers, I heard wonderful, varied commitments,

> "I will love her 100% no matter what for the rest of my life."

> "I will teach him what it means to be Christian."

> "We will have fun."

> "I will teach him to make good bread."

> "I will put money aside every year for her college education."

Responsibilities to your grandchild's parents.

You may wish to plan on being a support to the whole family, and to helping the child's parents. This is a challenging task, one that can benefit everyone.

A grandmother of six told me,

> "I am there to support the whole family, not just the child."

If you've had a distant or difficult relationship with your child's partner or spouse, or with the grandchild's other parent, now is a good time to focus on appreciating that person. You don't have to like everything about them, but talking out loud about what you like and respect about your grandchild's mother or father can help you focus on those good qualities.

If this family is multiracial, or headed by gay or lesbian parents, they may face prejudice, discrimination, or even just isolation. You may also want to work actively for equal rights and good treatment for them in your community, as well as being a loving grandmother to them as individuals. Contribute to advocacy organizations, get on mailing lists that will alert you when it's time to contact legislators ... you can find many ways to work for inclusion and tolerance.

Responsibilities to yourself.

This is a good time to get serious about taking care of your health. You will have a lot more fun if you are in the best possible health in the coming years.

Make some serious promises about regular vigorous exercise, both aerobic exercise, which increases your heart rate, and strengthening exercise. One good source is Miriam Nelson's book, *Strong Women Stay Young*. A copy of this book would make a wonderful gift.

Eating well will make a big difference. How can you best nourish yourself? Write down everything you eat for three days. Make an appointment with a nutritionist, or consult one of the many excellent books available. You don't have time to waste thinking about what you should have done in the past, or feeling hopeless about changing long-standing eating habits, so don't bother with that. Instead, pick something you can realistically do, like eating more fruits and vegetables and resolve to make that part of your life. If you smoke, stop now. You can't smoke around your grandchild anyway.

> "I've seen this in other families, where a grandparent smokes, and the parents don't want her holding the baby, don't want to come to her house. She's out on the porch in the cold and the rain, smoking at their place. And I knew my daughter-in-law would be that way, and why shouldn't she? I didn't want that. I've quit before, for years once, and I know I could do it. I've got an appointment to get the nicotine patch."

Are there other things you need to do to take care of yourself? Martha says,

65

"Menopause and being a grandmother came at the same time. I know now I'm not going to live forever, so I'm going to do the things I really want to do."

If you have a goal or dream that is important to you, now's the time. Martha graduated from law school at age sixty-one, and practiced domestic law, specializing in adoptions, until her death at seventy-eight. She loved this work. Being a creative, satisfied person is setting a wonderful example for your grandchildren.

Some grandmothers find or make a symbol of these commitments to keep in their homes as a reminder. This can be anything that connects you with your deepest intentions. For some, a spiritual or religious symbol will feel best. Barbara, grandmother of two, has a beautiful hand-crocheted shawl made by her own grandmother. She hung it in her meditation room, and it links her with a family tradition of strong and nourishing older women. For Maria, working in her vegetable garden evokes happy memories of her childhood, especially time spent gardening and cooking with her grandparents, and reminds her of what she wants to give her grandchild.

Mourning, healing, making amends, and forgiveness.

Distress, as well as happiness and hope, can come along with a new grandchild. Arrival of a grandchild can force you to revisit sad and painful events in your own life, and sometimes brings up unfinished business of your own. There are very few families who haven't suffered from losses, bad decisions, struggles with alcohol or drugs, or terrible behavior. You may have made mistakes that affected your children, or not have been as good a mother as you wish. You may need to protect your grandchild from a violent or sexually abusive person. Abuse or abandonment may have hurt your family.

Some of these things you can do something about and some of them you can't. This can be a time for committing yourself to do what you can towards healing and protection of yourself and your family, forgive where appropriate, and then put pain and grief behind you.

The root of the word crisis means a turning point, an unstable situation. Having a grandchild can be a crisis, and can be most useful and healthy. It can force you to reevaluate, to grow, to take the next steps in your own life. Some women find becoming a grandmother pushes them into changes that they need.

Marina said,

> "The day my son's baby came, I said to myself, 'Who wants a drunken grandmother?' I poured the liquor I had down the sink, and I went to AA that night. I never had another drink."

Linda found she had to revisit the worst thing in her life.

> "My older brother was a grown man when I was ten, and he molested me. Later I told my mother. She didn't really believe me so I never talked about it again. I made sure my children were never alone with him. With the grand-child on the way I knew I had to do more, to protect my grandbaby and other kids. I picked up the phone and called every single person in our family, plus a couple of longtime friends who know him, and told them everything that had happened. Then I called my brother, told him I remember everything and everyone knows all about it now. There's a lot of uproar going on. I really don't care. My grandchild is safe from him – my son will make sure of that, now that there's no secrets."

Some women find they can be better grandmothers than they were mothers. Some women regret mistakes they'd made, or wish their lives had been easier when they were raising children, so they could have given their children more. They now may have more time, more energy, be happier or have found ways to heal from old wounds. It can be comforting to give grandchildren that time, energy, and warmth, or to be a practical help to one's adult children.

Another new grandmother knew it was time to forgive her ex-husband.

> "My daughter is adopting from Haiti and she'll be a single mother. She's going to need all the help she can get. It has really made me think about her father, my ex-husband. We had an awful divorce; he did things that really hurt me. He

threw away all our money on crazy business schemes, and gambling, and eventually left me for a younger woman. I was furious for years. Now I do see that he tried through it all to be a good father … maybe not very effectively, but he tried. He's a sweet guy in some ways. And now, I have a really good life, all that stuff with him is in the past. I don't want my life to be about that, or have bad feelings in the family when the baby comes.

"So when my daughter left for Haiti to get her daughter, I created a kind of healing ritual for myself. I did it alone, I was kind of embarrassed that I was still mad at him and I didn't want to tell anybody. I wrote down every bad thing he had done to me, and then I took it out into a forest. I hiked in a ways, and I burned each piece of paper, each bad thing. And let the wind blow away those ashes. I had a little bit of a cry there too. Some of the things I wasn't actually mad about anymore, others were still painful. But when I walked out of that forest I felt lighter. I actually went home and called him, just planning to say something brief about how nice it was about the baby. We ended up talking about what we could do. My daughter has asked me to come and stay with her for a week after she gets back from Haiti. My ex asked could he get them stocked up on groceries, pick them up at the airport, and make a nice dinner for them the first night. I agreed with him, even though I was a little disappointed not to be the first one to see her. The most important thing, though, is it seems like our daughter will have two parents helping her now, not just me. And that's worth a lot to me."

Mourning and celebration, loss and joy, growth and healing, may be woven together in the experience of becoming a grandmother as they are woven together in the rest of our lives. Giving our full attention to all of these matters can help us move on and can make the happiness of becoming a grandmother more rich and complete.

What is meaningful for you and your family?

This chapter is full of ideas and anecdotes. No one will do all or even most of them. They are intended to give you a sense of possibilities and ideas to choose from, or to spark an invention of your own way to mark becoming a grandmother. Choose what works for you.

Resources

Nonfiction

Strong Women Stay Young, by Miriam Nelson

6

Parenting... New and Improved?

What is different today in childbirth, infant and child care, and teen behavior? You may be surprised, even disturbed, by your children's parenting.

Much has changed in the ideas and theories of child rearing since you were raising children. The practical realities have changed too. Your kids are parenting in a very different context. The choices your grown children make as parents are not just individual choices. Their world is different. They couldn't do everything the way you did even if they wanted to.

Getting pregnant.

Now, as always, not every pregnancy is intentional.

But for women or couples who do decide to have a baby, even getting pregnant doesn't always just happen – or not happen – anymore. The general public knows a lot more about conception now. Books and blogs and conversations include pinpointing the fertile days of a woman's cycle, and details of sperm motility. Couples with no reason to think they'll have trouble conceiving often start with temperature charts and ovulation predictor tests, instead of just throwing away their birth control and making love. Getting pregnant can appear more difficult, requiring extra planning and arrangements, not just a natural result of sexual intercourse. Because of the vast publicity given to the successes of fertility technology, achieving pregnancy can also appear more controllable, something a person can make happen at his or her convenience. Of course, that doesn't always work.

A woman of sixty says,

> "I work with a lot of younger women. In their thirties, I mean, younger than me. And they all are waiting to have a baby, waiting till they have more money, or finish this or that, have a house. And I tell them I think you can miss your fertile years that way. It just doesn't sink in. I got pregnant sort of by accident my senior year in college, I was engaged, I graduated pregnant and I'm glad, because we had the kids we wanted, real easily, it actually worked out fine for us. Even though we were too young by today's standards."

Pregnancy is different now.

Of course, in some ways pregnancy is universal and will never change. But the context means that most women experience it quite differently now than in our generation. Normal pregnancy is far more monitored and medicalized than when you had your babies, with many ultrasound pictures and more testing at every stage.

For many of our age group, childbirth education classes were an important part of pregnancy. For seven or eight weeks, we spent an evening every week in a church meeting room, or a day care center, or the teacher's living room. We learned about the biology of birth, and about practical techniques, the Lamaze method, the Bradley method, or another approach that would make us knowledgeable consumers and help us cope with the pain of labor. Fathers learned how to help in significant ways, or a close friend or another family member was invited into that role.

I taught childbirth preparation classes for many years and I saw the effects of this way of preparing for birth. Classes starting in the middle of pregnancy and lasting for two months gave people a chance to think about what they'd learned and come back with questions and concerns. Pregnant women and their partners saw these classes as a way to learn how to get what they wanted in their births, and make informed choices. They had opportunities to talk about the issues with each other after class, or at the break. Expectant fathers could meet each other. Many women in my classes would call me after they had their baby, telling me the story of their birth and asking about the other people in the class by name. I saw real friendships develop among the new parents. Sometimes I would see these women years later, in the grocery store, or on the street, and I would hear that they were still friends with someone they had met in the childbirth class.

Now, such classes still exist but are no longer the norm. There are shorter classes, often based in hospitals, and they are much more about simply transmitting information on what to expect. Online childbirth education or a few hours on a single Saturday morning are common.

Birth.

Childbirth customs have changed dramatically too. Now, epidural anesthesia is very common, almost universal. Some grandmothers are surprised to find not just the father at the birth but lots of friends, including someone with a video camera, or two, and those videos shown in very public places.

Many of today's grandmothers wanted the least possible medical intervention when they had their babies. In addition to taking classes in natural childbirth, they tried hard to get through labor without pain medication. Some switched hospitals or sought out a doctor who would be receptive to changing hospital routines to keep the new family together throughout their stay, and to reducing medical intervention, including routine episiotomy and electronic fetal monitoring. Some women found a midwife and gave birth at home; others hired their childbirth teacher to come to the hospital and advocate for them, and coach them through the contractions without medication. Women who didn't care about avoiding medication still wanted the father, or other family with them, and wanted to hold their baby right away. Hospitals changed a great deal in those years, in response to consumer activism. That's when they started allowing fathers to stay with laboring mothers, and to hold their babies, rather than waiting somewhere else, alone and anxious, while women gave birth in the company of strangers. Keeping baby and mother together, instead of sequestering the newborn in a nursery, away from the parents, became the norm.

Many grandmothers are shocked when they first hear that most women in the current generation, while they want the father of the baby with them, don't see avoiding medicalization of their births as a goal at all. Most grandmothers, and their friends and peers, wanted to avoid a Caesarean section if possible; they may hear a daughter or daughter-in-law planning one in advance for convenience. A great-grandmother told me,

> "My own grandmother would never have had a baby in the hospital. She thought they were dirty. And actually, they were at that time, there were lots more infections in hospitals back then because no one knew about bacteria, or how they were spread. When I had my first baby, my doctor had a maternity home, a house by his office, where patients came to give birth. He was an older guy, he said to me, 'It's just a matter of me catching this baby. Women know what they're doing.' And that's how it was. Then, twenty and thirty years later, I watched my daughters spend eight months preparing for the births, all these classes and talking, talking, talking. And they did have natural births like they wanted but somehow it got a lot harder. Then my granddaughters and granddaughters-in-law...now they don't care about that, they want the anesthesia, the epidural. They watch television during their labors, it's like getting a baby from UPS. So I've learned it's always going in another direction."

Baby care.

These days, far more mothers of young children are working, and need to work. They often have only a few weeks of maternity leave, sometimes no paid leave at all. Partly because they will need to accustom their infants to taking a bottle when they work, many young mothers use bottles to feed their own breast milk to their babies.

"Mother's milk used to be the easy way, because it was

always right there, and you didn't need to bring anything, or get it ready. Now, my daughters-in-law think breastfeeding is expensive because they have to buy or rent an electric pump, for hundreds of dollars."

Grandmothers also notice there is a lot more equipment.

"When they come over, they need a suitcase. There's all these various things to put the baby in, and special nursing pillows, and all."

We know more about safety, and the recommendations have changed. Babies are supposed to sleep on their backs now, and car seats have saved many lives.

How to raise children.

New parents are bombarded with advice. They always have been, in every time and place and culture, and that's usually a good thing because human beings do not know instinctively how to care for our young. We need to learn.

Through most of human history, this advice – and practical assistance – came from face-to-face encounters with familiar people. In our generation, it was from family and friends, or neighbors, or our own doctors who knew us and our children, and from books. As a mother, you may have read some of the popular manuals by pediatricians and other experts and talked over the challenges with your friends who had kids. You may have consulted your own parents and siblings, and observed what they did—whether you followed their example, or made sure to do just the opposite.

Your adult children can do those things, too, but they also have instant access to far more information on the Internet, and also to plenty of misinformation. Calling a pediatrician is only one way for them to find out about child health, and not the easiest.

The sources of advice to new parents have changed. So much of the information, ideas, and ways to consult experts and peers is now online, not face-to-face. Much of it is from corporations selling something, institutions including hospitals, and anonymous Internet sources.

Connecting with other parents.

Our generation of mothers, and the ones before us, met other mothers in the park, schools, or at kids' classes and activities. Often, we just shared casual, enjoyable camaraderie and conversation on long afternoons at the playground, or while waiting for children at music or dance lessons. Sometimes we got to know other parents better, through our children. Daycare parent meetings led to carpools, children playing together, and sleepovers. Sleepovers and carpools led to making friends. We could help each other with emergency pickups, and pass on outgrown skis, and ice skates, and barely used winter jackets. Sometimes, these mothers became close friends, and our whole families would invite each other to barbecues, and trips to the beach or the amusement park. Some of these friendships outlasted the raising of our children; they are the women we are close to today.

Your adult children may meet other parents that way too, but they also find them in other ways now. Instead of talking to people they already know who have children, or in addition to doing that, they can read blogs by parents they don't know and will never meet. They can join an email list or a meet-up of local moms.

Children's lives are different.

> "It's hard to even visit because they're so scheduled, so busy.
> And why does a seven-year-old have a cell phone?"

Children today spend much more time indoors, with far more time in organized activities supervised by adults, and are far more influenced by media.

> "My grandchildren never just play by themselves or with friends in the neighborhood."

Telling children to go outside and play is a thing of the past for most. The world feels more dangerous to parents now, whether it really is or not. Neighborhoods are not usually full of playmates, either. Children don't necessarily go to neighborhood schools, so the other children they know may not live nearby. With both parents working, many children are in afterschool programs. Even weekends are much more structured with sports leagues run by adults, academic tutoring, and lessons.

Grandchildren today don't know as many of the traditional games that groups of children used to play together, like Dodgeball or Mother May I. They are used to adults helping them play, and to having their time with friends arranged by their parents.

Most of us found friends and played with them on our own.

A grandfather remembers this:

> "There were two other boys my age in walking distance. Their parents weren't friends of my parents, but that didn't matter. No playdates, I just walked over there."

Media.

> "When I was little, car trips meant reading, reading, reading. And games, license plate bingo. My sister and I each had a pile of books for the trip. I can still remember some great books I read in the car. My own kids were the same way, and once they learned to read, I could take them anywhere. Now my grandchildren watch videos in the car. When are they going to read all those wonderful books?"

Another important cause of change is the electronic entertainment media that saturates children's environments, starting with videos marketed for babies, and then computer games, and more videos, and television shows full of ads for toys. Some of the newest toys and video games are marketed together, so the toys encourage children to ask for the video, and the videos advertise the toy. In addition, many of these toys are hard to use for creative play. They're meant to be used just to imitate the story in the game or TV show. So the imaginative play that is so important for children's development is curtailed. There's more on this topic and how parents and grandparents can cope with it in Chapter 9, Being With Your Grandchildren, and in the Resources for that chapter.

Watching screens impedes the learning of social skills and the growth of relationships. Social skills develop in young children as they play together, talk, listen to each other, decide or compromise on what to do together, teach each other games, or invent them together, have conflicts and learn to resolve them. But those opportunities are lost if they are watching on-screen entertainment, even if they do it side by side. Time spent staring at a screen is time lost to building friendships. It's time that could be better spent in developing language skills, and playing with concrete real objects, which is how small children do learn to understand the world.

In addition to the ways on-screen entertainment harms children directly, it also creates a vicious circle for parents. Busy parents are tempted to use TV or videos to keep children occupied.

> "My daughter-in-law says she has to let the kids watch TV, it's the only way she can make dinner."

When parents do this, children don't learn to enjoy playing by themselves. They can't occupy themselves, and so are harder to live with. Then the temptation for a parent to use electronic entertainment is much greater. And of course the more they do so, the worse it gets.

In contrast, when on-screen entertainment was a much smaller part of child's day, as it was when we were children, and even when we were raising our own children, life was easier for parents. A child who is used to playing by herself, and also has local playmates, (or even brothers and sisters) available for board games, fantasy play, building things, and impromptu backyard ball games, is easier for a parent to shoo away to amuse herself. "Go outside," or "You can play until dinner's ready," sounds good to such a child. She probably dashes out the door for a little more free time.

> "My kids had building toys, and made forts out of the couch cushions. My youngest was a kind of prop in his older brothers' games from the time he was three. I had to make them come to the table for dinner. I didn't worry about entertaining them."

In addition to undermining children's ability to play creatively, what children see in the ubiquitous entertainment media is another problem for parents.

Since 1984, when the federal regulations to protect children from advertising were removed, the content of media shown to children now includes extreme violence, explicit impersonal sex, and advertising directed to children.

> "My granddaughter visited and wanted to watch MTV. She says her babysitter watches it with her. I told her we don't watch that because we don't think women should dress like that."

You, and the parents, can make a big difference by limiting exposure to media, making the worst of it off limits, and teaching children critical thinking. As they get older, it helps to teach them to be skeptical about advertising.

A grandmother says,

> "They see shows that I wish they didn't. What I can do is talk about it with them. I try to get them to think about the violence. I ask them to think about how it would really feel if those things in the shows happened to a real person."

But this doesn't completely solve the problem. Children are not naturally critical analysts. They are curious, and they are literal thinkers. Their environment and their social world are still full of these influences. The children's friends will still talk about products with movie characters, or video games. Kids are affected by the play and the preoccupations of other children and other families.

> "My grandson's parents don't watch TV, and they keep videos and computer games to a minimum, and he is outside, playing, and making things a lot, which is wonderful. But when his friend came over, the friend just wanted to play this online game. It wasn't violent, it wasn't too bad, but it bothered me that they did that all afternoon. It was the only thing the friend wanted to do. We want him to have friends. We don't want to isolate him, make him different from the other kids."

Children are exposed to images that frighten and upset them in places parents can't control.

"I was on an airplane with my grandchildren, three and seven years old. And the movie they were showing was horrible, really violent. I had no control over the kids' seeing it."

Most of us didn't have to cope with nearly as much of this when we were raising children.

Challenges in schools.

Parents in every generation try to make sure their children get the best education possible. But parents now face different challenges than you did. Even the most advantaged schools struggle now with testing requirements that shape the whole day, loss of school time for the arts and physical education, and shorter recess. Your adult children may be advised, even intensely pressured, to medicate your grandkids at the first sign of what used to be considered normal rambunctiousness. The energetic shenanigans of an inquisitive toddler, or the anguish and hostile gloom of a thoughtful, reflective adolescent are now often seen as illness, rather than developmental stages and life challenges.

Advertising is everywhere, even in schools. Some schools show ads in the classrooms in exchange for funding for the school budget. Some use advertising materials as curriculum.

Raising teenagers has never been easy.

Parents of teens today face a more dangerous and toxic culture.

Alcohol and tobacco are marketed to teens, undermining parents' efforts to protect their adolescent children and teach them to make good decisions.

It is hard or impossible to monitor adolescents' activities on the Internet, which is full of truly dangerous sites, like pro-anorexia sites which explain in detail how to become anorexic, and violent misogynistic pornography, and online gambling. Other parents may not be dependable allies in protecting teens from this, or in talking with them about how to cope with it and what to reject.

Many teens feel they need to be available for phone calls or text messages all the time, including during the night and while studying, or they will be isolated with no friends.

"Our granddaughter, seventeen years old, visited for a long weekend, and we had a great time. But she was texting, her friends I guess, during meals, and while we did some sewing together."

We don't really know how many teens send nude photos of themselves via cellphone, called "sexting," or keep their phones on all night. But the fact that these activities are even possible is a challenge to your adult children as parents, one that most women who are grandmothers today didn't have to face as mothers.

It's the economy.

Economic realities determine some of the choices for today's families.

"My grandfather supported a family without even graduating from high school, as a house painter. My father could support a family with a college degree. My children have Master's degrees and they need both parents to work."

Now, financial independence comes later in life. The time a young person is dependent on parents after puberty has gotten much longer. For many of today's grandparents, college graduation was commonly the beginning of independent adult life. For some people, independence came even earlier, often at high school graduation. There were jobs. In the past few years, persistently high unemployment, and larger education debt, has meant that even young adults finished with college, or even with Master's degrees, have returned to living with their parents at a much greater rate, further delaying financial and emotional independence. It was much more unusual for young adults in our generation to do this. It's a shifting set of decisions and challenges for parents and young adults.

How to respond to change.

Some grandmothers just accept all this and try to get used to it. Others attempt to give grandchildren the best of what they remember.

"I taught my grandchildren to play Mother May I. The little one needed some coaching. We had it working, and we had fun, and they asked for it next time. But it never crosses their minds to play it themselves, without me, like my friends and I did. With the card game Go Fish, I taught it to my granddaughter and we play it, and then she taught her sister and now they play without me. I think it's fun, and good to have these ways to entertain yourself among kids, without a grownup doing it for them."

Claudia and her husband decided that they would get the grandchildren out of the house.

"My husband and I are both retired, and we try to get the kids outside as much as we can. We take them skiing and hiking."

Chapter 4, Advice and Help, has ideas and anecdotes about ways grandmothers have found to help their adult children in parenting. Mary Pipher's groundbreaking book, *The Shelter of Each Other: Rebuilding Our Families*, describes vividly the problems families face today and also many wonderful solutions, including practical realistic ways grandparents can help.

Some changes are improvements.

As grandparents, we do need to understand the challenges our adult children face in their parenting, including many difficult situations that we did not face. It's also important to be open to change and to see things that are not like what we are used to. Some things aren't worse, just different.

We need to notice and appreciate all the ways things are better, too. In some ways the world today is fairer, more diverse, and has less rigid gender roles, far more freedom for women, and less discrimination against people of color and other minorities. Your grandchildren have opportunities that you, and your children, didn't have.

We continue to make progress against prejudice of all kinds, racism and sexism and homophobia. Dating violence, bullying, and violence in the home are still huge problems. But they used to be secret problems that no one would talk about, or that were considered normal life. Now they are addressed.

The Internet can save time and connect people.

The Internet – certainly a source of terrible ideas and mindless distraction from healthy activities for children – has also put information at our fingertips, saved time for busy parents, and connected people.

> "I noticed that my daughter doesn't have to drive around after school with the kids doing errands, like I did. Lots of things she'll just shop online, and she'll have free time in the afternoon to take them to the park. When they get started on the playground, she'll use her phone to order stuff, and make quick calls, like scheduling appointments, and then when they're ready to go home she's taken care of all that. She's really organized and she knows how to use the technology to make more free time."

Online communities can be good sources of information and commiseration. They can make it much easier for your adult children to quickly consult a big group of their peers about anything from local schools, or where to find a good piano teacher, to deeper issues like a nine-year-old with frighteningly intense temper tantrums. These mothers usually never meet face-to-face, although they do sometimes decide to get together. A family moves to a new town, or is the first in their crowd to have children, and can find other parents to talk to quickly and easily. A single mother by choice can find a community of others in the same situation. If your grandson is more interested in chess than soccer, his parents can quickly discover the closest chess club, or people who will play with him by email.

In one town, an online community of young mothers organized practical in-person help for each other. When one of them had a baby, the other mothers would set up a schedule and drop off cooked meals, or be available for an errand. These young women had never met each other in person before, but they showed up with salads and chili and enchiladas.

Try this:

• Accepting change is one challenge for grandparents. So is holding on to your own values and common sense.

• Understanding the realities of your adult children's lives will make their parenting more comprehensible to you.

•Ask your children what they are reading about parenting, and read those books yourself. You'll understand the current culture better, and you may learn some things.

• Consider giving gifts of time and experiences rather than electronics. Give young children toys that encourage open-ended play rather than toys tied to products. Give lessons, books, trips, or take them to big cities, or to the wilderness. Support and encourage teenagers in healthy adventures.

Resources

Nonfiction

Remote-Controlled Children: Teaching Young Children in the Media Age, and *So Sexy so Soon, The New Sexualized Childhood and What Parents Can Do to Protect Their Kids* by Diane E. Levin

Consuming Kids: The Hostile Takeover of Childhood, by Susan Linn

Taking Back Childhood: Helping Your Kids Thrive in a Fast-Paced, Media-Saturated, Violence-Filled World, by Nancy Carlsson-Paige

Last Child in the Woods, Saving Our Children from Nature Deficit Disorder, by Richard Louv

Websites

The American Academy of Pediatrics website www.aap.org, has extensive up-to-date information about child health and safety.

Part Two:

You and Your Grandchild

7

Grandmacare

Taking care of your grandchildren while their
parents work, finish school, or go on vacation.

As I talked with grandmothers, what I now call "Grandmacare" came up
again and again, although at first I didn't have the word for it. Grandmacare is not raising children in a parental or custodial role. It's also much
more than visiting. It is taking regular responsibility for grandchildren
for a significant amount of time, so that parents can do something else.
Sometimes Grandmacare takes the place of daycare, sometimes it's filling in during just one section of the day that is hard or impossible for
the parents. It can be caring for children regularly so parents can finish
college, or work. It can be taking care of the grandchildren occasionally
so parents can go out dancing, or go to Mexico for a week. I talked to
grandmothers, and a few grandparent couples, who had moved in to
take primary responsibility for raising the grandchildren and running
the household that both parents could work. In other families, grandchildren and their parents – often in crisis or disarray – moved in with a
grandmother when they needed temporary or even long-term housing
and help caring for the children.

It's a unique relationship. It's not a professional paid caregiver, but rather a permanent, loving relationship to the child. The woman doing Grandmacare is not the parent, not the final decision maker. Ultimately, she is not in charge. She's also not a just a guest who tries to fit carefully into household routines and play with children, either. While they're in her care, she does make the decisions. For some women it means a lot of responsibility, long days, and the challenge of balancing work and children.

I believe Grandmacare is probably becoming more common and more needed. Because the current generation of grandmothers enjoys longer, healthier lives than any previous generation, more children have two living, active grandmothers than ever before. At the same time, nuclear families face increasing difficulties. Many experts, including academics, journalists and others, have commented on how busy, worried, and overwhelmed parents are. Mary Pipher has written about the ways our culture harms families with violent media, consumerism, and isolation from neighbors and community. Nancy Carlsson-Paige documents the damage done when children's play is being replaced by time spent in front of electronic entertainment. Susan Linn and Juliet Schor have described intensive marketing to children in recent years. Families are more vulnerable to these and other problems when they lack time – time to supervise children, time to take them to the park, read to them, set up art projects, play catch, have a friend over. As families with young children face increasing shortages of time, lack of high-quality child care, and economic pressures requiring both parents to work, more and more families may turn to Grandmacare.

There has been little study of Grandmacare. We do know parents throughout human history have turned to their own parents, especially maternal grandmothers, when they needed help with their children, but there are no comprehensive national statistics.

Grandmacare can start out as a way to help the parents, or as a way to be with the grandchild. It can turn from one to the other. It can be a delight, and it can be difficult. It inevitably complicates relations with the grandchildren's parents.

As I listened to stories about Grandmacare, there seemed to be four types: occasional Grandmacare, day care Grandmacare, extra parent Grandmacare and homemaking Grandmacare.

Occasional Grandmacare.

"We left the baby with grandma and went out dancing."

It could be a planned vacation for the parents, while grandmother stays with the children. Or it could be a difficult situation, or an emergency. Premature twins are born, and the new parents are overwhelmed, needing all kinds of help. A grandmother pitches in however she can, sometimes without much discussion. When one parent, or both parents, can't cope, is in jail, or in the hospital, grandmothers are often the first responders.

The situation doesn't have to be a problem; it can be a wonderful event, perhaps the arrival of a new child. For Marina, helping her son and his partner when their newly-adopted baby arrived was a wonderful time.

> "Kurt and Allen were both very clear they needed help, they wanted me to come, we had it all planned in advance. I arrived within two hours of when Olivia was given to them, twelve days old. The three of us parented together for the first three weeks. I lived there with them, I was up in the night with them. The first bath was all three of us."

Another grandmother described a trip that allowed her son to go on a long-planned rock climbing expedition with old friends, even though his wife had important last-minute business travel.

> "I go for visits, just for fun. I also go sometimes when they need me. Like last year my daughter-in-law was out of town on business and my son has this trip every year, rock climbing with old friends, planned way ahead, that week. So I went for a four-day weekend. The older two, they are both teenagers so they mainly need someone in the house, supervision, meals. The younger one is just eight, so with him it's everything, lots of driving for school and his violin lessons. It was a little tiring, really, also lots of fun. I know

the kids better because of times like that, and I know it helped them out."

Daycare Grandmacare.

"Is he in day care at all?"

"No, but he's in Grandmacare two days a week."

Some people, both parents and grandparents, believe that children should be with family members, if possible, rather than in a daycare center. Or perhaps there's no good daycare available, or grandma is more convenient, or more flexible. Others feel fine about daycare, but think a devoted grandmother is even better.

> "My mom is a pretty good deal," says one young mother, laughing. "She picks him up and delivers him back home, she serves him all organic food, she's a fanatic about safety, and she goes with our schedule. And she totally loves him, he has a great time with her. On the down side, she's taught him to like Johnny Cash, and the Grateful Dead, which I can't stand, and they go out for sushi all the time, which I also can't stand, so now he thinks that's a treat. But all the big things are really great, so I'm stuck!"

Sometimes parents ask, sometimes grandmothers, or both grandparents, volunteer. Talking with parents, and with grandmothers, I heard about many arrangements. In one family, the two grandmothers had become friends, and they offered to work out the details between them. They often went on outings with the three children together, or switched days with each other at the last minute. They always made sure one of them was available during the workday.

A first-time grandmother at sixty-two told me,

> "So my daughter, who is a physical therapist, needed to go back to work and she just couldn't bear leaving him with anybody but me. So I said OK, I'll do it, and I took early retirement."

Another woman described the special foods, and the vigilance, necessary to feed her granddaughter, who has celiac disease. The child can't tolerate any gluten, so that means no wheat, rye, barley or oats. In addition to the obvious – cookies, bread, pretzels – this means no salad dressings, ketchup, meatloaf or hot dogs, because they all contain wheat. She asked rhetorically,

"If the kid wasn't yours, would you have the patience?"

For grandparents Cathleen and her husband Charley, it wasn't any one particular thing, just a general distrust of daycare, which to them meant relying on the care of strangers, and a family failing to take care of its own. Cathleen, an administrator for the state highway department, was nearing retirement. She had another seven months to go before being fully vested in the pension system, and she was thinking about what she could commit to. Her husband didn't even have to think about it. He told everybody,

"They're not going to day care even if I have to work at night to take care of them myself."

Charley and Cathleen figured out a way to get through the last months of Cathleen's job, using vacation time and sick time, and complicated irregular schedules for both of them, as well as some help from the other grandmother. Then Cathleen retired, and the next morning happily started caring full-time for three young children.

Some parents with two demanding careers and little free time have invited one of the grandmothers, or a grandparent couple, to live with them.

"I am basically raising the children. Luckily my daughter and I agree on things. I get two weeks' vacation a year – we settled that very specifically before we started – and for that time I get a group of my women friends together and we go to Cape Cod."

Yolanda volunteered to care for her six-month-old granddaughter, when the baby's mother absolutely had to go back to work, and there was no good infant daycare available. Then her other three adult children started asking her to take their kids too, and now some days there are five or six children at her house after school.

> "I just told my kids, they have to work it out amongst themselves. I can only have one that's under two years old at a time, and I can't drive the kids, they have to pick up and drop off, make a little carpool amongst themselves if they have to. And they do, they get together and talk and make sure it's not too much for me. I love having a house full of kids again."

Some grandmothers travel long distances, or modify their own work schedules to accommodate their children's jobs or school. Terry commutes from her home in Boston to New York City every week to help her daughter with a premature baby and a toddler. She has rearranged her work schedule, and stopped teaching her popular class in Scandinavian baking to do it. She's tired, and always feels she should be somewhere else, but never doubts this is what she wants to do – which is just the way she felt raising her own children.

Money is a factor. Grandmacare can make the finances of working parents manageable, if grandmother can do it for free. Or parents may pay the grandmother, usually somewhat less than they would pay a daycare center or family daycare. She may not be able to leave another job to be available for grandchildren unless that income is replaced.

Extra parent Grandmacare.

> "Can you take Austin to soccer, so I can stay home with the baby while she naps?"

This kind of Grandmacare means being home for children after school, or available if they are sick when parents need to work. It means filling in, perhaps that difficult early-morning time when both parents, or the only parent, is off to work before day care or school opens. This grandmother cares for children often, but not necessarily at regular times each week. Or she may help out regularly but not all day. Some women doing this said they were "an extra parent," or "an extra pair of hands," or "I'm the fallback."

Danielle and her husband own and live in a small apartment building in a Chicago suburb, with four three-bedroom units. They sold one of the apartments to their daughter and her husband, so the grandchildren are right upstairs. The young parents are both doctors, and they leave early for work. So Danielle is up early too, as her three-year-old grandson, barely awake, arrives at her door in pajamas between 5:30 and 5:45 in the morning. Danielle treasures a leisurely beginning of the day with the child, breakfast and getting dressed for day care, with no rush or deadline. She drops him at day care, and some days she picks him up too.

Pauline told me about caring for her grandson after school every day. She's a third grade teacher herself, and there's only one elementary school in their small town. She doesn't worry about exact timing or dashing across town. She just brings young Joshua home with her every day when school is out. They snack, and relax, and then get started on homework until one of his parents gets there. It's easy, and Pauline knows it's a huge help to the parents. She told me about her sister Grace, also a grandmother. What Grace does is quite different. Grace's daughter got pregnant as a college freshman, and dropped out to have the baby. The young mother lived with her parents and Grace was very involved, happily so, with her grandson. Eventually her daughter married and had another son. Pauline sadly described the situation now,

> "Let's just say, that little boy, he needs his grandma. The new husband, well, I guess it's natural that he favors his own son. So Grace makes sure that little boy gets to be on the soccer team, and takes him shopping for school clothes every fall, and lots of other little things. She knows she's needed."

Latrisha did that kind of extra parenting too, though for a different reason. She saw that while her daughter's children had plenty of lessons and special trips and outings, her son's family was short on money and time.

> "So I signed those two girls up for ballet lessons, and I take them every week. At Christmas, I'll take them to the Nutcracker. I make sure they have those extras, too, like their

cousins do. It's fun for me, to take them, to see them have these things."

Homemaking Grandmacare.

"After his wife left, my son and the kids moved in with me."

I was surprised to hear about so many families with all three generations living in the grandmother's home. This arrangement is more common in some other cultures than in the United States. One grandmother told me that her son-in-law, who grew up in another culture, fit gracefully into her household on arrival in America. He immediately devoted himself to doing small repairs around the house, yard work, lifting and carrying for her. He was comfortable deferring to her about anything to do with the house, and comfortable in a multigenerational household. For most families where everyone has grown up in the United States, moving in with the grandmother usually feels much less natural and can be quite a struggle.

Laura, a widow of eighty-six, lives in her big suburban house with her daughter and son-in-law and their four children. She and her husband designed the house and had it built when their children were teenagers. It's beautiful and immaculate, full of light, gorgeous rugs, fabric in warm colors, and Laura's paintings. It didn't look like a house where children live, and after I heard the whole story I understood why.

"When they came back after living for years in Mexico with the children, we looked for a place for them to live but everything is so expensive now there was nothing in a good school district they could afford. We decided to try them living here, we tried it in my house for several months. We decided if we could do it, we would build on for them, a separate space so we could get out of each other's hair. At the end of the three months, I knew what it would take for it to work.

"We put on a new addition to the house for them, and I knew I absolutely had to have a separate kitchen. I couldn't stand the mess, they are eating at all hours, four children.

The town gave us a lot of trouble about that, they didn't want us to put a stove in. It's not zoned for two-family housing, and a separate stove is how they define that. I was determined I had to have it. So we just built it without that, and then put it in later after we had gotten approval and they were all gone. The building inspector knew I was going to do that. This way, the mess is confined to their space.

"What you have to do to live like this is know when to shut up. I didn't know and I learned the hard way. I have never been a critical person. If I ever said anything the slightest bit critical it would make a big resounding noise, much more than if we were not living here together.

"We have to have a smoothness. In order for us all to be together. I think they watch too much TV and video. I can't say that, ever. For one thing, they know I think that and if I say it, it's like I'm observing and criticizing them, it would be fatal. I can't say anything that could imply criticism. Once you become aware of it, it becomes automatic.

"It goes the other way too. They don't drink. I like to have a glass of wine, a couple of glasses of wine, in the evening. Then my daughter started saying to me as I would pour the second one, that's enough, or I think you've had enough. I got quite angry. We had to get through that, too."

For Betsy, living together wasn't planned but it has worked out beautifully. Betsy's son divorced and his wife immediately left the state, leaving him with two preschoolers, a new truck that was paid for, and a growing business installing new windows in old houses. The business made a lot of sense for the father of a young family; he enjoyed it, and it paid well, and he had a good future. "All these old houses are going to need new windows sometime," he told me, "especially with the cost of energy going up." But it didn't make any sense at all for a single parent with young children. Sometimes installations took more time than expected, so the hours were long and irregular. Within a couple of weeks, he called his parents and asked if he and the kids could move in for a while. All three of them knew what he really needed was care for his children. Betsy had recently retired and she told me,

"I was the mom. It was wonderful. I loved doing this."

For Sharon, the transition to living together was harder and scarier. Her daughter Heather married a man who quickly turned violent. Heather was afraid to stay and afraid to leave. Like many batterers, he threatened to come after her if she ever left him and kill her and their daughter. Finally, when the child was in kindergarten, Heather decided she had to get out. She planned her escape for weeks, calling Sharon, and her sister and brother-in-law, every day. Finally, one harrowing night when her husband was out of town, Heather's sister and brother-in-law came and helped her move out. They took her straight to the airport, and by dawn Heather and her five-year-old daughter were at Sharon's house. Heather's husband could find them. So far he hasn't. With housing taken care of, Heather can earn enough, and Sharon picks up her granddaughter after school every day. She treasures those relaxed after school hours with her granddaughter, and she can invite the little girl's friends over, too, to play. Their household is comfortable and stable.

Joys and satisfactions.

Every grandmother I talked with about Grandmacare said it was a joy and a pleasure, even if the conversation later revealed exhaustion, losses, and conflict. Grandmothers talked about the delight of a closer relationship with beloved grandchildren, and seeing them often, and about the fulfillment of helping their own children in such an important way.

For bicultural or new immigrant grandparents, there was also the satisfaction of passing on their culture, beliefs, and language. Tarja, who came to the United States from Finland with her family, says of her four-year-old grandson,

"He does understand Finnish. He only wants to speak English, because that is what is all about him, but he understands

Finnish. The other graparents speak it to him also."

All the adults, parents and grandparents, want the little boy to grow up bilingual. They all know it's only the grandparents who will actually speak Finnish to him consistently.

Many grandmothers love Grandmacare without reservation.

> "So far, Mikey is such a pleasure. My husband is seventy, and we want to travel. But it will be a long time before we go, it's so hard to part from Mikey even for a day or two. Each day is precious."

For Betsy, taking care of her two grandchildren every day was a welcome chance to do more mothering.

> "I loved doing this. I only had one child, which wasn't my choice; we tried for years to have another. I think if they had all the technology back then that there is now I would've had a big family. So, suddenly having the little girls was just fine, just fine."

For some grandmothers, taking care of grandchildren is more joyful, fun, and relaxed than raising their own children was. Retired or semi-retired, they have more time now.

> "As a grandmother, you have more time to spend. House chores are easy. I have more time to take pleasure as a grandmother."

Cathleen, seventy-one, takes care of all three of her grandchildren, a baby, a toddler and a four-year-old, during the workday. She says the difference between Grandmacare and being a parent for her is that she is:

> " … more relaxed and not so nervous. This is easier, I have more knowledge. My friends are surprised I can do this at my age, but it's fun."

June says,

> "I go one day a week to babysit. My daughter is a nurse, and her wife Penny is a UPS delivery driver. They both work part time. They make enough that way, and they're not so rushed. It's just the one day that they both are at work, Mondays. And I am so happy to do that day. It's best thing that ever happened to me. I have never been happier in my entire life. I was a crazy and controlling mother and I didn't enjoy it. I was afraid most of the time, homework, getting sick, everything. I became a very anxious mother. I missed a lot with my kids. I was so busy keeping them on track, it was more a responsibility than a pleasure. Now, with the boys, it's the best time in my life."

Closeness to the grandchildren is a joy. Erica gave up her volunteer work on her small town's crisis hotline, and reorganized her work schedule to one that is less convenient for her but allows her to take care of her new granddaughter three days week.

> "It's a little harder. It's tiring because now the days I do work, the days are much longer. But, I enjoy it, and I want to help out my daughter, and really I want to have that relationship with my granddaughter, which I know will be deeper and more attached if we spend this time together when she's so young. That's the biggest reason I do this, the kind of relationship I want to have with my granddaughter. And I do have it. When she holds up her little arms to me, it's just lovely. And we have all sorts of special things we do together, things she remembers and asks for."

Stresses, challenges, and sacrifices.

Even when grandmothers love the time they spend with their grandchildren, and feel lucky to have this in their lives, they often talk of some losses and challenges. Some grandmothers know exactly what they're getting into, and what they're giving up. Some realize as they go along, or only in retrospect. Grandmacare can be tiring, and hard on friendships, hobbies and creative interests, and careers.

Grandmacare can be strenuous.

"How was it?" I asked a woman who retired to care for her infant grandson while the parents worked.

> "Exhausting!" she said promptly. "I did it for two years, two days a week. I didn't remember from my own kids, what it's like."

The physical demands of caring for young children can be overwhelming, especially for anyone who has health problems or physical limitations. Lifting and carrying infants and toddlers wasn't the hard part of mothering for most of us, and for many grandmothers still in their fifties it isn't a real problem. As we get older it gets harder, and older grandmothers often mentioned it as the only negative part of Grandmacare.

Dorothy is grateful that she can see her baby grandson often since he and his parents live in the same town. Several times a week, she goes to her daughter's house to take care of the baby for a few hours. Dorothy is sixty-nine, and has emphysema. She gets tired easily.

> "It's worth it, but lots of times I come home and go straight to bed."

June says,

> "I have the kids once a week. I love it, it's the best part of the week, but it's tiring."

I asked June if she had any suggestions for a new grandmother who would be taking care of grandchildren regularly. She did.

> "Make sure she's got grandmother friends. Some other Unitarian Universalist grandmothers and I got together.

We have grandmother morning at the church. For three years we've got together one morning a week. We talk about our aching backs, and why the young people have the children. 'I love doing this, but it's almost too much.' We can say that there. And you feel like you're not a bad person for feeling that way."

Yolanda has another solution.

"I started lifting weights. I'm up to ten pounds. My friends think I'm crazy, but I can carry a toddler up two flights of stairs, no problem."

Work and career.

Grandmothers who make a specific time commitment to care for their grandchildren sometimes leave jobs or drastically cut back or re-arrange their hours. Sometimes they use up all their time off caring for the children while the parents are on vacation, or in a crisis of some kind. There is a "Mommy Track" for women with young children who choose flexible schedules and less demanding work, and accept less advancement in their careers in return. Some grandmothers find themselves back on that track. This can be welcome, if it comes at the right time in the grandmother's life. Or, it can be a real sacrifice meaning loss of income, retiring later, or accepting a less respected and less rewarding job.

The famous dilemma of balancing work and children has been transferred, in some families, from parents to grandmothers. More than half of all women between fifty-five and sixty-four are employed, according the Census Bureau's 2006 Current Population Survey. They face the same challenges as working mothers.

Some are grateful that an employer allows them to work part time or shift their hours to mesh with their grandchildren's needs. Others regret loss of jobs or opportunities they valued, and worry about retirement finances.

In addition, every working parent knows that missing work, or leaving early to pick up a sick child can be seen as not being reliable or serious about the job. Explaining these events is usually even harder for a grandmother. She is often met with incredulity, or the suggestion that she must be ready to retire.

A grandmother who takes a few years out of the workforce to help raise grandchildren will find it even harder than mothers do to explain that gap in job interviews. Many women have found solutions to this: workplaces that are genuinely family-friendly, part-time jobs, or job with schedules that mesh nicely with childcare needs. I remember a neighbor whose grandchildren went to school across the street from me. She is a nurse, and has worked a 6:30 am to 2:30 pm shift for many years, so she could be available after school, first for her own children, then for her grandchildren. She had no problem being outside the elementary school, with a snack, when the kids got out.

Some women struggle to keep jobs, and keep the respect of their supervisors and colleagues, just as they did when they were mothers. Some grandmothers make sure not to say why they're leaving early, or changing their hours for grandchildren—they find another reason to talk about. A grandmother who is the "extra parent" says,

> "Luckily, I hardly ever get sick. I use my sick days for when the kids are sick. Basically, I lie. What else can I do?"

Friendships.

There can be other losses that women don't anticipate. Friendships – both casual and important – can be lost or marginalized. In this way, caring for grandchildren is not like raising our own children. A mother can often make friends with other mothers. In fact, the community of parents in daycare centers, schools, and neighborhoods can be a wonderful source of adult friendships for both mothers and fathers. Whole families can enjoy visiting, passing on toys and clothes, doing things together. A grandmother caring for a toddler, or two, is more unusual. She will probably meet the parents of her grandchildren's friends, not other grandparents. Usually she finds that women her own age are in a completely different stage of life.

> "No one wants to go for coffee with me anymore, now that there's a baby in a high chair at the table."

It's hard to make plans with friends who either are still working or are retired with no children around, if you have to be home for nap time, and can only go places that are safe and fun for little children. Sometimes friendships fade away, because the other women do not want to limit activities to those that can include a baby or three-year-old.

Friendships can also be strained by radically different interests and preoccupations too. Many of us remember that when we first had babies, it could be hard to stay friends with people who didn't. We found new – often close – friends among other new mothers. Stephanie calls these "mom friends," and that includes her two oldest, closest friends. She met one at the parent co-op day care center, and the other waiting in the hall every week for their four-year-olds to come charging out of dance class. Their children grew up together, and the women's friendships were rooted in their intense shared experience of being mothers. Stephanie and Bonnie scheduled their turns to clean the daycare center together. Stephanie and Donna both started dinner right around five o'clock, and they often talked on the phone as they cooked. They had everything in common: struggles about how much time and energy to devote to work without shortchanging the children, money problems, the schools, and all daily pleasures of watching children grow. They had fun, too. They put on a Halloween party for their kids, with bobbing for apples, and they made a celebration of sharing the first watermelon from Stephanie's garden. Their children grew up together and are still close friends.

These three friends thought they would be moving into the next stage of life together too, but now Stephanie's days are very different than her friends'. She takes care of her two little grandsons four days a week. She says,

> "Bonnie is Director now, and is totally busy during the week. Donna is teaching full-time. We're still close, but now it's just because of what we've had in the past and because we make a conscious effort. We have preserved our friendship because we all made that effort. I'm back in mommy-mode, and they are professionals, and they are both making good money now, and I had to start Social Security at sixty-two. And when I look around the park, or the gymnastics classes I take the boys to, all the moms are the age of my daughter. There's nobody I can make friends with."

Time, and child-centered activities, aren't a problem for Danielle. Now that she's not working, the time she spends with her grandson leaves plenty of other, free time to do things with friends. She's very aware that the most fascinating thing in her life isn't necessarily interesting to her friends. She makes a conscious effort not to bore them. She doesn't talk much about either adorable things the child has done or her concerns or worries about him. She is careful not to show photos to people who want grandchildren but don't have them, or to talk to them about the child's doings. Sometimes she feels a little distant from her old friends.

Many friendships don't survive. Some women, especially those doing "daycare" Grandmacare, find themselves out of touch with colleagues, and less connected to friends.

Leisure can be a casualty too. Plans or interests are postponed or given up.

Flora says,

> "I love this, don't get me wrong, I wouldn't trade this time for anything. But it does mean that pottery, and travel, are out for now. And I was going to teach a scrapbooking class. By the time they're old enough not to need me anymore, I don't think I'll be up to going to Machu Picchu like I wanted to."

When they don't come over anymore.

A more painful and poignant loss comes to some grandmothers when the parents move or reorganize their childcare arrangements. Many grandmothers told me that they had a deeper bond with the children they cared for frequently. Yet, these relationships are dependent on the grandmother's relationship with the child's parents, and also on events and circumstances outside the grandmother's control.

A strained relationship with the child's mother makes such changes both more likely and more difficult to handle. Judith says,

> "When Mia was six, my daughter took over again, after I had her every day, since she was a baby. It got to the point where if there was a problem at school the teacher talked

to me first, and my daughter noticed that and resented it. Now I just see Mia every other weekend, and I miss her so."

Even when parents and grandparents are getting along beautifully, events intervene and a child is gone. A parent marries, or gets a good job in another city. There's an opening in the daycare right on the way to work, or a school-age child who has been coming to Grandma's after school every day for years starts sports or music lessons. A move to another city can mean that the child who was a regular, perhaps daily, part of the grandmother's life is suddenly two thousand miles away and seen only a few times a year on visits. Often, there's nothing that can be done about this. Sometimes grandmothers feel helpless, knowing that parents are doing what's best, or that even if they are not, the grandmother doesn't have a voice in the decision. In a divorce, family arrangements usually feel out of everyone's control.

Some grandmothers can negotiate. Betsy's son and grandchildren lived with her for four years, and it was an awful blow when her son remarried and moved with the children and his new wife to a town an hour away. "I want them every other weekend," Betsy told her son, "and for two weeks in the summer." He agreed, and the children do spend these times at Betsy's. But this is a rare happy ending.

Emotional issues and challenges with the child's parents.

For some women, the arrival of a grandchild improves their relationship with their own adult children and children-in-law. There is a common topic of conversation and fascination. Some young parents develop a greater appreciation of their own parents. The new grandmother has another chance to make up for mistakes she may have made in criticizing or giving too much unwanted advice to her adult child, and instead can express approval and support. The grandmother's helpfulness and appreciation for the good job her son or daughter is doing as a parent can bring them closer together.

Grandmacare can be the solution; it can make it feasible for parents to work or go to school. It can make the family's life easier, give parents a chance to have fun together, go on a vacation. But it doesn't always work this way, and taking care of grandchildren can make things worse, instead of better. Grandmacare can bring its own challenges, and it can inflate tiny, easily managed problems into daily tensions. Grandmacare can also create more friction between parents and grandparents.

Although mothers may need, welcome, and be grateful for the grandmother's care of their children, they can also be uncomfortable and sad about what they are missing or about feeling that they are being replaced in their children's lives. Some mothers wish they could afford to stay home themselves. They work because they need the income. At worst, the parents can sometimes resent the grandmother for what the parent misses during the day. When her newly single son moved in with her with his three children, Betsy could say, "I was the mom," because the children's mother had left and there was no competition for that position. Betsy's son needed a mom for his kids, and he trusted his own mother. In any other situation, grandmothers learn to be sensitive to the mother's feelings and not usurp her role. Many grandmothers I talked with are careful to absent themselves from decision-making, and make it clear all around that their daughter or daughter-in-law is in charge.

Cathleen says,

> "I think my daughter sometimes feels like she's missing time with them, not doing everything with them that I do. Last week she said to me, 'I am the mother, you know. I have to know where you're going with them.' So I have to be careful of her feelings. When Caitlin took her first step at my house, I just didn't say anything. Later, she called to tell me that Caitlin started walking. And I don't talk to teachers, if they bring up anything I just say I'll take a message to my daughter."

Grandmacare can also exacerbate tension with the parents if there is disagreement about child raising practices. A grandmother who can do everything her daughter or son's way when she's a visitor finds it much harder to do so when she takes care of a child for many hours each week. She is certainly not going to criticize the food her daughter-in-law serves. Does she have to feed the same things to the children in her own home? Dottie and her daughter have agreed that when the children eat at Dottie's house, they follow her ideas on manners, but when Dottie visits the family in their own home she doesn't comment, criticize, or suggest. They've made a clear agreement that works for them. It's not always so easy. A grandmother may not be sure how to discuss the issue openly, or may worry that her family won't find a compromise that works. She can be caught between silent seething, and doing things her own way when the parents aren't there and wondering if they would be upset if they knew.

> "I feel lucky it's just little things. I can't stand the way there's food all over the house at their place. That's one reason I like to bring him to my house. Since he was little, he totally accepts that at Grandma's house food stays on the kitchen table, nowhere else. Of course I never say anything about how they do things, and that seems to be working OK."

Another source of tension is that the parents can sometimes resent being dependent on the grandparents. Our culture promotes individualism in everything. Unlike most human communities all over the world, we expect nuclear families, and even single parents, to successfully handle all their own needs by themselves. Young parents may appreciate a grandmother's help, yet think less of themselves for needing it. It can make them feel like teenagers again.

Some grandmothers told me they felt taken for granted and unappreciated. They are on call when needed, but not appreciated or honored for their importance to the child and the family. One grandmother said,

> "I certainly don't want them to feel like they owe me or anything like that, because that can get uncomfortable. But I do just like to be thanked."

If you are asked to do more than you can, or want to.

A baby who cried for hours every day, no matter what anyone did to comfort him, was just too hard for his grandmother to take care of. She said sadly,

> "I had to tell my daughter, I just can't be the one to watch my grandson, I just can't stand the crying."

I asked Donna for her advice to other women about Grandmacare.

> "Don't overdo it like I'm doing. Two or three days a week is fine. You need time for yourself too."

Some women face pressure to give up jobs they love in order to be more available for grandchildren. Bonnie is Development Director for a major law school.

> "I have a thirty year career. I'm good at it. I would've worked even if I didn't have to, I've always enjoyed working. Now my daughter and son-in-law would really like me to be available more and on short notice. They really seem to think I should leave my job.

> "They wish they didn't need help, especially my son-in-law. They do need help, with three little boys under five years old, two of them twins. So they'll ask me to do things, but in this bantering way. They wish I would just always be available and volunteering so they wouldn't have to ask. There's a kind of tension to it. So it's not just me taking care of my grandsons, there's another layer to everything."

Some women just can't do as much as their adult children need or want them to. Health problems don't stop them from visiting, or happily spending time with the children. But they can't be responsible for kids for long days anymore. They can't lift a toddler, or keep going for nine or ten hours with an infant. Often, grandmothers find that they love spending time with the children, but it's difficult and stressful to take several young children out together. Or, they're happy to bring an older child to his sports or activities, but can't bring a heavy, mutinous toddler along, who has to be carried and may dash off in any direction if put down for a minute.

Adult children may not realize how their mothers have aged. They may find it hard to understand, or even too upsetting to think about, when she tells them her knees can't manage all the stairs in their house, or she needs a real rest in the afternoon. It's a reminder of aging and mortality.

Darlene's son asked her to plan her yearly visit during school vacation time so she could take care of his three sons, who are two, six, and seven years old. The daycare center was closed for this week, too, and it would have been expensive and difficult to find other care. Darlene has asthma, and arthritis in her knees. She takes medicine for her blood pressure. She was hurt and angered by the request because she felt her son was oblivious to her physical limits.

> "I'm not a grandmother machine," she said bitterly. "I've told them before I can't take care of the children by myself, especially the little one. They are just using me to save money."

Betsy and her husband Diego live in Seattle. They plan to retire next year and want to move to the small house in the beautiful coastal town of Port Townsend, which has been their vacation retreat. Their daughter, who lives in nearby in Seattle, is pregnant. Betsy says,

> "I love the Port Townsend house so much, it just makes me sane there. We've struggled with this, should we stay in Seattle to help? What we want to do is to sell our house in the city, and move into the house in Port Townsend and then rent a really small place, a studio, near them. It's a two or two and half hour drive away, half an hour by ferry, so we can be up here a lot whenever she needs us, we can help, but we wouldn't be able to take care of the baby every day when she's teaching the way she would like us to. I feel I'll be able to do more in a sense because I'll be in such a good mental state. I'm torn, about whether we should move, or stay close to them."

Grandmothers may be annoyed at the expectation that they always be available, or they may be delighted. Or both at once. Sometimes it's difficult to decide how much time to spend on Grandmacare and on what terms. The dilemmas are reminiscent of mothering – the pull between beloved children and the rest of life.

Some grandmothers decide not to do it.

Saying no to Grandmacare.

Some grandmothers just say no. For most women, there's a guilty ambivalent inner struggle surrounding the decision to say no. It goes against everything we have learned about being women who should take good care of our families. It certainly contradicts the image of a grandmother: loving, sentimental, caretaking, and available. There is not much precedent or support for a grandmother who says no, no thanks, sorry, no, can't do it, I'm running for alderman, going to New Orleans to rebuild houses, going to graduate school, going camping, joining a jazz band, getting married and moving to London, on call for Search and Rescue, getting promoted to Assistant Commissioner, making sculpture, finally opening my restaurant. Most of the grandmothers I talked with who said no to Grandmacare did so because they had something else they passionately wanted to do, but some just wanted their time to be their own. Most struggled with their decision, and found it hard to tell other people. Few had any support from anyone for saying no.

Mary was a grandmother who seemed like a natural for taking care of her grandchildren. Her daughter Pam was divorcing, with a preteen, a four-year-old, and a baby on the way. She and Mary had a good relationship, with shared beliefs and values about childraising. Pam lived in Newton, just outside of Boston. It's a place where Mary could have made a good life. It has public transportation, good city services of all kinds, lots of cultural and educational life, and a community art center, where Pam suggested her mother could take the art classes she was interested in.

Housing was no problem; Pam's house included a small studio apartment that could be rented, but it could also be Mary's home. Pam was exhausted, and overwhelmed. She was happy to have this third child on the way, but was terrified about the first few months, no, the first few years. She knew from experience how hard it is to take care of a small child, even with another parent on site. Now she would be doing it alone. She needed lots of help, and she knew it.

Mary promised to help. However, she didn't really like babies. And she had done as much housework as she could stand while raising her own five children, with a husband who was usually at work, and no household help, in a time before takeout food, microwave ovens, or clothes that didn't need ironing.

The day the new baby arrived, Mary was there to hold her daughter in labor, rub her back and encourage her.

But in the following weeks, Mary found herself deeply reluctant. She just couldn't bear to enter another grueling round of cooking and cleaning up. Even with her own babies, a newborn had felt like drudgery. "At that age, they're basically like vegetables."

Mary's time looked empty and available to other people, but she was taking a drawing course and a painting course at the Museum School at Boston's Museum of Fine Arts.

> "I was sixty-six years old that year, and I knew I had time for one more big thing in my life. I could paint, if I didn't put it off much longer."

Pam remembers,

> "My mom would come to my house, but she would just step over whatever was on the floor, just shove the laundry over to the end of the couch to make a place to sit down. She would play the piano, and after a little while the kids would come over and she'd switch to something they could sing, and they'd have a lovely time. In the meantime, I was exhausted, trying to clean up a bit and make dinner for all of us. I'd have liked her to send me off for a nap and take care of everything for a few hours."

That June, Mary's lease was up and it was time to decide where she would live. She and Pam talked it over. In a way it was appealing to Mary, as an older single woman, to move in downstairs from Pam and be secure in a family situation. She could have holidays with Pam and the girls, and, she said, "I'm sure I could be a help to you."

Pam said no.

> "I'd made my peace with how my mom was, and she wasn't at a point in her life to help me the way I wanted. I knew if she was living upstairs I would resent not getting help."

Mary bought a condo in a lively, integrated neighborhood in

Providence, Rhode Island, an hour away by car. She started classes at Rhode Island School of Design in mid-September.

She can laugh now looking back,

> "I'd already been accepted at art school, but I didn't tell anybody because I felt like I SHOULD move in downstairs from my daughter and babysit. I had these two parallel tracks going in my mind of what I was going to do."

For some women, though, it's simple, clear cut, and easy. They are sure. They do not want to spend a lot of time taking care of grandchildren. Georgianna told me,

> "I'm getting older and my daughter kind of suggested in a roundabout way that I might like to retire and move to Asheville, where they are, and help out more with the kids. I'm not going to. I want to be a summer vacation grandmother, and a Christmas grandmother, but I don't want to live near them and be expected to take care of them all the time."

Charlotte just wasn't ready.

> "I feel like it is too soon. I want to help my kids and I want to really be there for my grandkids and do things with them. The thing is, I just started playing in a bluegrass band, and that's led to going out at night a lot more, to hear music. I never did this when I was young. I played violin in high school but in college music just wasn't what I was doing, and then I had little kids and no money. Now, I'm loving it. Plus, I've got plans to go to Vancouver next summer. These are things I never got to do. And if the grandkids could have come along a little later, when I was more ready to slow down …"

Saying no – or saying yes – to spending a lot of time caring for grandchildren is part of a bigger decision. It's a choice about time, about what to do with the years left. Grandmacare can be a great joy, a chance to correct mistakes made raising one's own children, it can be fun, it can be all sorts of wonderful things. Saying no can be wonderful too. Saying no can also mean choosing one's own life, one's own ambitions, over other people's needs and expectations. For some women, it's a real turning point.

When I talked with Alice, I heard a story of growth and confidence, and also an account of how hard it can be to change when everyone else would rather things stay the same.

Alice is sixty-one, with three grown children, a son and two daughters. Her grandchildren are her son's twin eight-year-old girls.

We talked about the past two years of her life, a time of enormous upheaval for her. A divorce, a new love, and going back to college had sparked a transformation that affected everyone in her family.

The year Alice turned fifty-nine she was finally divorced, finished with years of bitter legal negotiations and free of the man she'd been married to since she was twenty-one. He appeared to be the perfect husband to outsiders but exploded in rage when he didn't get his way, knocked her against the wall, twice broke her arm. She welcomed the peace following her divorce, loved her tiny studio apartment, and was settling in to an interesting, active late middle age when she met Roger. They fell in love, and with his encouragement Alice went back to the college she had dropped out of thirty years before.

Alice and I talked in her little kitchen, on a hot Saturday afternoon in late August, right before classes started. It was the beginning of her senior year, and her kitchen table was piled with textbooks and papers: her class schedule, her reading lists, notebooks, photocopied articles, all the papers that attend a new semester. On top was a big three-ring binder labeled "Senior Project." She was excited, full of energy, ready to dive into the work of her final semester.

We talked about the advanced classes she had been waiting to take, and the environmental justice organization she works with. She lives in a small working class town, and an asphalt plant had been allowed to build right on the edge of a residential district, within three blocks of apartment buildings. Her small grass-roots organization is trying to get the city, or the state Environmental Protection Agency, to require filters to reduce the fumes emitted into the air.

"Now, I can't be as involved with helping my kids. I was a

doting mother, because of the situation with the domestic abuse I probably was an extremely doting mother. And I kept that up, even when my kids were into their thirties. They weren't growing up, and neither was I. It was hard for me to say no to anything, I hadn't the whole time I was married.

"We all needed to do a lot of changing, my son more so, he was having a rough time with mommy having her own life. My daughters, both said, yeah, mom, go for it. My son was more needy, he would call at five o'clock, we want to go out, can you babysit? I would say no, I have plans. I was not so available for every runny nose. He wanted me to be always ready to pick them up at school, stay with them in the evening so he and Ashley could see a movie or whatever. He basically thought that the kids were the main thing in my life, or should be. Of course, I love the girls. I like to have fun with them, take them out for something special, like the Christmas tree lighting in the Square, or the neighborhood block party. I don't want to be on call.

"Sometimes I would cancel my plans, with my friends or Roger. But, I said to myself, no, this is not good for you, Alice. It took a lot of therapy. Therapy really helped. I had to learn in small ways to say no. I was always available for everything, and I was angry at myself.

"Then, Roger signed us up for salsa lessons, it was on Saturday night. I was afraid to do it, afraid my son would be angry that I was going out, instead of babysitting so he could go out. Fear seemed to rule my life. Fear that my son is not going to talk to me, which did happen for a couple of months. I had to live through that. He's come a long way. Now, he resents it, but he accepts it.

"It's even more important for me now, because I'm going to go into social work, I want to work with women like me, with domestic violence and all the things that can happen to a woman. To do that, I have to know how to take care of myself."

Saying no to Grandmacare doesn't mean not caring, or not giving.

One of Alice's internship placements has already offered her a job after she graduates, and another agency is interested in her, too. Social work is not highly paid, but to Alice it looks like plenty. She's never had any kind of professional job before, just a series of entry-level part-time jobs, patched together in the midst of raising her children and getting out of a violent marriage. In a year, she'll have a full-time salary with benefits, and her living expenses are lower than ever before in her life. She supports only herself, and Roger convinced her to move into his house, which is paid for. Even though they share the expenses of the house, she'll have extra money. She has already opened tax-exempt college savings accounts for her granddaughters. They are small accounts; she puts in just $25 a month for each girl. She's learned all about tax-free compounding, and she glowed with pride when she talked about being able to give the girls a head start on college expenses. She never earned a significant amount of money before, never supported herself. She certainly wasn't the person anyone else could depend on for financial help.

Her children don't know about this. She's planning a big graduation party for herself and she'll announce it then.

I saw something else she's doing for her grandchildren and her children, too. Finishing college at sixty-two, passionate and effective involvement in social justice issues, and salsa dancing on Saturday nights … what a wonderful, lively picture of aging Alice gives her family! When her kids, and her grandkids, are in their fifties and sixties, perhaps they'll be more confident and having more fun because Alice has shown them what that looks like. And when the grandchildren become uncertain questioning adolescents, deciding who to be, and wondering what to spend their lives on, Alice will be a wonderful person to talk to.

Try this:

- Enjoy this time. Take pictures.

- If you are frequently in the parents' house, or live with

them, you see their lives up close and could even violate their privacy completely by accident. You may know more about their purchases, parties, diet, and housekeeping than either of you would have chosen. It's probably best not to comment on these things unnecessarily.

• Not everything has to be said. If you are worried about something, think before you speak. If it's actually going to be useful information to the parents, of course bring it up. Be truthful. But don't defuse your worries by talking about them repeatedly to the child's parents. Don't be a source of anxiety in their lives.

Resources

Nonfiction

The Happiest Baby on the Block, and *The Happiest Baby Guide to Great Sleep*, by Dr. Harvey Karp

The World According to Toddlers, by Shannon Payette Seip and Adrienne Hedger.

Dr. Spock's Baby and Child Care, 9th Edition, updated and Revised by Dr. Robert Needlman

Addressing ADD Naturally, by Dr. Kathi Kemper

Websites

Kids-In-Mind.com gives very specific information about a movie's content, so parents and grandparents can decide what is appropriate for children.

8

Grandmacare, The User's Manual

Practical plans for taking care of your grandchildren.

Preparation and planning can help Grandmacare work well.

Attention to safety, and some practical discussions with the parents, are important whether you are flying in from across the country for a few days, or bringing the children to your house all day while parents work.

Safety.

There is much you can do to reduce risk of accidental injury. Don't rely only on what you remember from raising your own children. We have new knowledge, and new ideas on how best to keep children safe. Consult one of the current, comprehensive childcare books; there are several in the Resources section at the end of this chapter. The web site of the American Academy of Pediatrics has good safety information in the section for parents. The injury prevention section of the website of the Children's Hospital of Boston is also an excellent source.

Also, make sure you know the safety rules and safety equipment (like cabinet locks, helmets and other sports safety gear, rules for crossing the street) that your grandchildren's parents use. Have the parents show you exactly how to use the car seats or booster seats, especially if you will ever need to take the seats out and put them back into a vehicle. Revisit this topic as the children get bigger, because correct use of car seats and booster seats changes as children grow, as do other safety equipment and rules. In most towns, you can have the car seat or booster seat inspected by a certified technician to make sure it is installed properly, is appropriate for the child's size, and is being correctly used. Check with the local police department, or the pediatrician to find an inspection site.

Preschool children can't be relied on to use common sense, or remember instructions, no matter how smart or well behaved they are. Nor can you watch them every second, because that's not humanly possible. Your vigilance and attention are very important but it's also essential to make the environment as safe as possible, and look ahead to make it safe for the next developmental stage, not just the one they're in now. Plan ahead for a baby rolling over or scooting forward so she can reach something she couldn't get yesterday, or a toddler realizing he can head off down the stairs to the basement, or leave the yard to explore the neighborhood. Having a safe environment will make you much more relaxed, too.

As children are older, of course, they can take more responsibility for themselves. There are still some things to keep an eye on, such as making sure they aren't exposed to pesticides or other poisons, monitoring their use of sports safety gear such as helmets, and teaching them to cross streets safely. The books and websites you consulted for babies and toddlers will help you as kids grow.

Planning with your grandchildren's parents.

Try to sit down with both parents and clarify exactly what you all expect. Such planning can eliminate surprise and hurt feelings and make Grandmacare a pleasure for everybody. Even in a crisis, starting with five minutes to get essential information about health insurance, emergency phone numbers, and children's school and activity schedules, can make things go more smoothly and calmly. If you're going to be doing regular childcare, knowing what media the parents approve of and what they don't, and how they feel about sugar, fast foods, and snacks before dinner, can remove sources of tension between you and your adult child or child-in-law. If you have an agreement from the beginning about who pays for outings and special classes, then it doesn't have to be awkward when you want to take the kids to the Aquarium or a concert, or sign them up for swimming lessons.

Emergencies. Make sure you have up to date contact information, the office location of the children's doctor, the preferred hospital Emergency Room, and all the health insurance information.

Schedules. Is it OK if the parents are sometimes late picking up the child? Are there times you know you won't be available? Do the parents want to be told in advance where you take the children? Can you meet the child's teachers, parents of friends they play with, or babysitters, so that in an emergency or unusual situation they know who you are? Will you be taking children to their lessons and activities? Some families use an on line calendar so everything is written in one place, and everyone can see it from their computer or phone.

Rules. What do the parents expect about naps, manners, how siblings treat each other, cleanup chores, and other family standards that they want you to follow? Generally it's best for the parents to make the rules. But there may be a few things that are important to you to do your way when the children are with you.

Discipline. What are the consequences for unacceptable behavior? No matter what, don't ever hit or humiliate or scare children. It doesn't improve behavior in the long run, and it teaches them to be afraid of you.

Money. Who pays for diapers, special outings, classes, car seats for your car, or admissions to museums or performances?

Food. If the children come to your house, do their parents send a lunch? Are there foods the parents want them to have, or don't want them to have?

Your time. If you will be the primary caretaker of your grandchildren, negotiate time off for your vacation, social events, classes or recreation, and medical appointments before you start. It might even make sense to have these important agreements written down, because even people of good will, who trust and care about each other, can remember a conversation differently.

Why didn't we settle that?

The above is an ambitious list, and it may not be feasible to talk about it all in some situations. As I heard grandmothers' stories of Grandma-care, I noticed how much wasn't talked about in advance, and how many reasons there are for this.

Sometimes the parents themselves don't know, can't decide, or can't agree. Sometimes things happen fast, and everyone's upset. The grandmother needs to know a few basics, but beyond that she may have to just pitch in and figure things out as she goes along. In the worst times in a divorce or when someone is having emergency surgery, the parents aren't going to be able to sit down with you and talk about rules and schedules and what to pack in a child's lunchbox. In a crisis where you arrive to take over short-term, you may have to just find out what you can and manage from there. You may be introducing yourself to surprised teachers and daycare directors, or even the pediatrician.

Or, if there's a divorce, separation, or strained relationship with a daughter-in-law or son-in-law, detailed conversations with that parent might be unwelcome or very awkward. Even then, your calm focus on the children's needs could open communication with your grandchild's other parent.

Happy situations can pose their own problems for the orderly transfer of information.

"My son asked me to stay with the kids when he and his second wife went on their honeymoon, and I was delighted.

The divorce from the kids' mother was hell. It's just hell to watch your son suffer like that. Then when he met Kimberly, it was wonderful, I just love seeing him so happy and she is a lovely, very sweet person, including to his kids. And she asked me to be in the wedding. Her mother and I were her bridesmaids, and that was so … well, it was just a very emotional day … and with everything to do for the wedding, all the arrangements and everything, it's a miracle he even remembered to give me the house key and a list of emergency phone numbers , and all the instructions about Justin's asthma. So the two of them, the newly marrieds, left straight from the wedding reception, and I'm standing there with the kids, waving, happy tears running down my face. When we finally got out of there and got home, it hit me. I didn't know what to do on Monday. What time did they have to be at school? Did I pack a lunch for them?"

For calmer, more long-term situations, like daycare Grandmacare, or extra parent Grandmacare, it might be good to have a regular time to revisit these issues.

A monthly or seasonal check in can also remind the parent to keep you informed of new friends, new school policies, new health insurance, and other changes.

New ideas.

You probably know a lot about caring for children. But grandparents often tell me they have forgotten some of what they knew, and need a refresher. Whether you remember everything about raising your own children or not, there is new information, and new ideas that can be very useful. This chapter started with getting up-to-date on safety, and that's the first thing to do.

If you are caring for an infant, you may want to learn about the "calming reflex," described by pediatrician Dr. Harvey Karp in his book *The Happiest Baby on The Block*. Many parents and grandparents have found this amazingly effective in soothing a crying baby. The technique can work wonders, even if the baby's been diagnosed with colic, and it can also help babies sleep longer.

Take a look at the new cloth baby carriers, too. Look for one with sturdy, padded shoulder straps that adjust to fit you. The most comfortable carriers will fasten with buckles, not ties, and will fit you symmetrically, with the weight evenly distributed on both your shoulders, and will have a waist strap.

This makes carrying your infant or even toddler grandchild easy on your back, and keeps your hands free.

You will also face challenges you didn't have when raising your children. The media, including entertainment marketed to children, the Internet, television, and advertising are much pervasive and more problematic than they used to be. Take some time to become well informed and think about these issues.

Media.

There are many reasons to be cautious about exposing children to media, even if it's marketed for children. The content is often much more violent, sexual and antisocial than the children's shows you remember, as well as containing far more advertising. Screen time crowds out physical exercise, time outdoors in the natural world, time for friends and family, and creative play. Repeatedly viewing violence, whether in a video game or a TV program or a movie, desensitizes children and teaches them that violence is fun, and the way to settle conflicts. Watching it is frightening for children, too. They don't know it's fiction. They aren't able to understand that the scary people and creatures they see on a screen won't appear in their own lives.

The American Academy of Pediatrics recommends no screen time at all for children two years old or younger. The Center on Media and Child Health at Children's Hospital has good access to research information and strategies for families on choosing the best media and teaching children to think critically about it.

If you take care of children for long stretches of time, you will certainly need a break sometimes, and it's tempting to use a video, or the Internet, to keep them occupied. Consider instead investing some time and effort now in teaching children to play together, play on their own, read for pleasure, play musical instruments, or help you with cooking and other creative pursuits. This will benefit both you and the children because kids will be harder to take care of later if they learn to rely on media, and they'll be pleasanter and happier if they learn to rely on themselves and other people instead. Grandparents grew up and raised their own children in an era of much less media, and they often have skills and ideas for ways kids can have fun without staring at a screen.

A routine including quiet time every day, when children read or play by themselves, or an especially fascinating toy that is available only while you take a break each afternoon, are popular strategies. If you work on it gradually, you can teach them to help you get a meal on the table. You will have a three-year-old or four-year-old setting the table, and older ones who can take their turn cooking, rather than bored children who can't seem to occupy themselves without electronics, while you do all the work.

You don't have to worry about your grandchildren learning to use computers. They have constant exposure to them. A computer scientist father said,

> "It's supereasy. It's like learning to use toothpaste. At Google and all these places, we make technology as brain-dead easy to use as possible. There's no reason why kids can't figure it out when they get older." (New York Times, October 22, 2011, "A Silicon Valley School That Doesn't Compute.")

Doing things differently than the parents do.

In a crisis or problem situation when kids are scared or worried, familiarity helps. Children will probably be calmer and feel more secure if you serve the foods they are used to, and follow their normal routine very closely.

Happy, planned vacations might be very different – just the time for looser schedules, eating outdoors, and playing card games past bedtime. If you are taking care of children while the parents go on a trip together, the parents may feel very relaxed, and have an "anything goes" attitude. Or they may still want to keep to rules and routines that are important to them. If your daughter-in-law really wants to minimize sugar in her children's diets, don't set your heart on daily visits to the ice cream store you loved as a child. There are other ways to have fun, and other ways to make the visit special.

Or, if you think their parents let your grandchildren eat way too much fried and sugary food, you can offer healthier foods, but you'll have to make some concessions to the food they are used to.

Taking care of children every week, either during parents' working hours, or as a frequently involved "extra parent," is another situation. Children can readily adjust to variation in rules and routines at Grandma's house if there's no conflict between parents and grandmother, and there's consistency and predictability in both places. Stephanie takes care of her son's two children at her own house. She says,

> "My daughter-in-law was great, she made it really easy. I know she thinks I'm paranoid about safety. But she tells the kids, 'Grandma's house, Grandma's rules.' The kids accept it because all the grown-ups are a united front."

Chloe was almost three years old, young enough to still be talking about herself by name as some little children do. Her parents told me about her efforts to reconcile the differing expectations of various grown-ups. One afternoon, she described to them all how the adults in her life respond to her wish to sit in the driver's seat of a car and pretend to drive. The family was standing on the sidewalk next to the car, chatting. Chloe pulled on their hands to get their attention, pointed to the driver's seat, and cheerfully explained to everyone, "Mommy let Chloe sit right up there. Chloe drive. Daddy, too. Grandma, no."

Another time, Chloe argued for a better deal. Her grandmother lets her push the button on the Cuisinart. Her mom does not. Chloe first tried telling her mother, "Grandma lets me do it."

"Yes," said her mom, "and at Grandma's house you can do it."

Frustrated, Chloe pleaded, "Can you just pretend to be Grandma right now?"

These incidents made funny stories because the adults were all comfortable with the discrepancies. Most differences are like this. Parents can probably accept that grandparents might need to set up their own routines, or their own rules about cleanup. Grandparents are usually careful to not do things that the parents really don't want them to. But if there is a serious difference it's probably best to negotiate and discuss, rather than having it come up unexpectedly.

The children feel more secure if all the adults in their lives are on good terms and nothing is hidden.

Even though your intentions are good, it doesn't actually make children feel good if you let them get away with something they know their parents don't want them to do. If you've given them something or let them do something they know their parents don't approve of, it can make them feel awkward and guilty if they feel they have to be dishonest with their parents.

Take care of yourself.

Nurturing yourself and respecting your own limits is crucial for the success of Grandmacare.

If possible, try to get together with other grandparents. Just as for parenting, it's great to have a place to discuss experiences, complain, share ideas, and admit it's physically exhausting.

Set the limits you need to. You be may responding to a crisis such as a hospitalization, or a divorce, or planning to take care of your grandchildren during the day while parents work, or being asked well ahead of time to come and stay with grandchildren while their parents take a vacation. No matter what, give some thought to what your own limits are. In a true crisis, you'll probably show up and do what you can first, then talk about it afterwards. Even in a crisis, if you really can't lift a toddler, or don't drive, that has to be part of the plan.

Consider your health, your own financial needs, your job, your time and energy, the other people in your life, and the other interests that are important to you, before you make a commitment to Grandmacare.

Try this:

> • Always support the parents' primary role. Avoid becoming the person that teachers or health-care providers talk to; take a message or refer them to the parents. Don't become the authority on the baby's development, or the children's feelings or food preferences. If a toddler docilely takes a nap every afternoon at your house, but puts up a struggle with parents, don't rub it in.

> • Ask your children what books on parenting they like and read them. If they've enjoyed a course or workshop,

you might want to take it too, to understand how they are thinking and what's important to them. You might not agree with everything, but you can look for parts you do agree with.

• If you've got something good to say about how well the children are doing, say it. Some people in your life will be bored by talk about cute things the children did, or their accomplishments, but their parents won't.

• Talking to the parents about changes you want to make in schedules, rules, or how an issue is handled could sometimes tactfully be done as a question. "What you think about...?" "Is it OK if we...?"

• If you have helped out during a crisis, then after the crisis is over, give back the parental role. This is one of the most difficult situations. The family may need you to take complete charge of everything at one point. Then you will need to know when to back off.

• In an emergency, it might not be possible to calmly talk over the details with the parents. They aren't at their best anyway. And even when the emergency is over, they may be too overwhelmed to be grateful for what you've done.

Resources

Nonfiction

Dr. Spock's Baby and Child Care, 9th Edition, Updated and Revised by Dr. Robert Needlman

Caring for Your Baby and Young Child Birth to Age 5, Dr. Steven P. Shelov Editor-In-Chief

Your Baby and Child, Penelope Leach

Websites

The website of the American Academy of Pediatrics has lots of child-care information, including comprehensive safety guidance.

The injury prevention section of the website of the Children's Hospital of Boston is another good safety resource.

Kids-In-Mind.com has movie reviews that give very specific information on content so you can decide what's appropriate.

The website of The Center on Media and Child Health at Children's Hospital, Harvard Medical School, and Harvard School of Public Health has lots of good ideas and strategies for parents and grandparents.

9

Being with Your Grandchildren

Baking cookies, Halloween costumes,
traveling together, and teens with tattoos.

In some ways, grandmothering can be easier and more fun than mothering, a reprise of the best times with children. Special outings, museums and amusement parks, crafts, games, classic children's books, cooking together and traveling together, all can be delightful. Since you aren't responsible for everything about the children, you can spend your time on the things you enjoy the most, or are best at. It may be especially pleasurable to repeat favorite activities you did with your own children.

> "I make all their Halloween costumes, and special dresses
> for the girls. It's really fun."

Time.

Your time and attention are what deepens relationships with your grandchildren, and what makes cherished memories. Talking is great. So is attending their games, or dance or gymnastics performances, or going to see their art on display in a school corridor. So is sitting quietly together reading, or taking them on a hike in the woods in silence, or listening to whatever they have to say. Some children enjoy craft projects or fixing things. You might have more time now to play in the sandbox or pay attention to the rambling remarks of a young child. You may have time and energy for goofy, fun things like putting on a birthday party for a beloved pet.

Things to do together.

Many grandparents find it useful to have a variety of short projects ready for visits. There are lots of books on activities to do with children, and you may want to consult them. Below are a few ideas for children from toddlers through adolescence.

Children today are often unfamiliar with old-fashioned games like Parcheesi, clapping games, or dominoes, and with paper and pencil games like tic-tac-toe, or Hangman. To refresh your memory or learn new paper and pencil games, check Wikipedia online for "paper and pencil games." Or, create a crossword puzzle together. These games are great for travel, or any time there's some waiting to do, or when a child is sick. To occupy them on the way back from an outing, you could make a crossword puzzle, using words about the day (museum, beach, tortilla, swim).

Try teaching children to play chess or checkers. One approach is to begin by giving them a big advantage: take a lot of your pieces off the board before you start. Set it up so they can win, especially at first. After they have learned the rules and developed some skill, stop letting them win every time. If you don't take a pawn – or a queen – when you can, they never learn the game.

Teach them to tell jokes. Starting at about four, some children find it very appealing to be able to tell a simple joke, like a knock knock joke, or a "Why did the chicken cross the road?" joke. At this age, you'll have to coach them, and practice with them; it may be surprising how confused they get.

> "This was so cute. I taught her to tell the simplest "Why did the chicken cross the road?" joke. We practiced it over

and over. Then, when I brought her back to her parents' house at the end of the afternoon, she wanted to tell it, but she got so excited she got confused and wanted to whisper it in their ears, and started saying it was a secret. She got a secret and a joke mixed up. A few weeks later, she was telling jokes just fine, and we were all laughing."

Drawing and painting are great, but there's more you can do with paper, scissors and pencil. Make paper dolls or snowflakes. A Mobius strip can be made in a few minutes with paper, tape and scissors. Show them how to draw a pencil line down the middle, starting anywhere, without lifting the pencil. If they keep going, they end up with a line on both sides of the paper. Then show them how to cut the strip lengthwise, as if cutting two thinner strips. It seems as if it will make two circles, but it ends up as one big one.

Kitchen table science.

- There are very simple, fun things you can do, and there are books with lots of slightly more elaborate ones if it interests you.

- Mix vinegar and baking soda and see the bubbles of gas.

- Sprout seeds and look at them closely every day to see what happens.

- Get a magnifying glass and look at all kinds of things … hair, a leaf, the couch.

- Put oil and water in a jar and try to mix them.

Taking things apart, and putting things together.

For a toddler, putting new batteries in a flashlight can be a fascinating activity. Let her try the switch…it doesn't go on! Help her do each step, from opening the flashlight, replacing the batteries and closing it, and then try the switch again. Light! Toddlers like to go in a dim but not scarily dark room and shine a flashlight around, too.

With a child five years or older, try taking apart a broken phone or appliance to see what's inside. If you can explain how it worked, all the better. Even if you don't know, it's interesting to see what's in there.

Some grandchildren would just love to help you with anything you've bought that requires assembly, from a picnic table to a tricycle for a toddler. This will probably go better with one child at a time, rather than a crew. A six-year-old can use a screwdriver, and a seven-year-old can read directions. A school-aged child may be able to do most of the work, if you are patient, go slowly, and let them take the lead with some coaching. Try putting up a pergola, or a shelf, or a coat hook together. Would they like to make play dough from scratch, as well as play with it once it's done?

Older children might enjoy helping you set up your new computer or music system.

They can teach you some things, too.

> "I wanted an iPod. I wasn't sure which one to get or how they work. My twelve-year-old granddaughter was my advisor. She explained everything; she was really sweet about it. She helped me decide which one to get. She set up the library on my computer, showed me everything."

Cooking.

It's enjoyable to bake with children, but there are lots of other ways to cook together too. We know more about nutrition now, and you can have just as much fun if you substitute some healthier ingredients for the ones in the traditional baking recipes saturated with fat and sugar. Grandchildren will benefit all their lives if you help create good habits and happy memories of healthy meals.

Joan, grandmother of five, found ways to serve healthier food.

> "I love to bake, and we do that together. But I have found that I can cut the sugar way back, to less than a third, and cookies still taste very sweet. In fact they taste better because

the other flavors come through also. And I make a smaller batch, I serve them on plates so everybody gets two, with a glass of milk, and then if they're still hungry, they're eating fruit. You can enjoy cookies without gorging on them."

Another grandmother, a professional caterer, suggests,

"I just put the salad and cut vegetables sticks and hummus, and whatever interesting that I have, like my orange and black bean salsa, or polenta rounds, grilled shrimps, all that out on the table first, when they first come in. They eat it, they're hungry."

Try making fruit salad or soup or lasagna with them sometimes instead of baking.

Help them learn how to cook things they like from scratch, like scrambled eggs, or a cheese quesadilla, or oatmeal. They might get a little more adventurous with these familiar foods, adding a few more ingredients of their choice.

If you make bread, your grandchild may enjoy parts of the long process, especially watching the yeast proof, and kneading and shaping loaves. An older child might want to learn how to make bread all by himself.

"My grandsons aren't interested in cooking generally. They like to just eat macaroni and cheese, and apples with peanut butter. But they do love to help me shape bread dough for the final rise. They make the long rolls and braid them together and they're so proud of the loaves. It's the only whole wheat they eat."

Fruit juice popsicles are a classic, fun for young children to make as well as to eat. Try adding nonfat yogurt, chunks of ripe fruit, or layers of juice in an array of colors.

"My grandson doesn't like a lot of foods, but this year he likes sushi. And he made it at summer camp. I was sur prised he wanted to do that, but I got a sushi cookbook and we did it together. It was surprisingly good, I didn't expect to like it, but I did."

Cooking can link with other fun activities. Farms or orchards where you can pick your own fruits and vegetables are a great outing for all ages. Shopping at a farmer's market, or having an apple tasting party in the fall, with slices of many kinds of apples to compare, may surprise your grandchildren with how interesting fruits and vegetables can be, and help them slow down and really pay attention to the taste.

Janice and Pete, whose story of taking their grandsons to Europe is later in this chapter, are both very serious cooks. They take classes, and they grow their own herbs and vegetables. When they were raising their own children, Janice made appetizing meals every evening, and Pete's way of relaxing on the weekend was cooking Italian or Mexican dishes for friends. Once their kids grew up and left home, both expanded their repertoires. Now, Janice says,

> "Food that comes in a box is just not happening at our house. We've taken our grandkids to cheese specialty stores, and the Armenian grocery, and the Indian grocery, and let them choose something to try. One made a soufflé with me – that's tricky with a ten-year-old! Pete made a mole sauce with our oldest grandkid, and chiles rellenos. We've drafted them to really help us when we're making a multi course meal. We always have on hand some things they're used to at home, but we try to broaden their horizons, too."

As you are cleaning up, if you have cut the top off a carrot or the bottom off a bunch of celery, show children how to put those in a shallow dish of water so they will sprout leaves.

Be prepared for children to change as they grow. They can lose interest in what was a favorite activity between visits. Or, the opposite can happen. As kids get older, they often like spicier food and become more interested in trying new dishes and cuisines. A teenager can suddenly decide she's a "foodie" and want to learn how to cook everything, the more flavorful, exotic, and complicated the better.

Cooking together can serve other purposes too.

> "My daughter looks so tired. When she visited last time, I told my grandsons to run out to the kitchen as soon as they are up, without making any noise, and we will make muffins for breakfast. I'm up early anyway so I'm ready for them, we bake whole-wheat muffins with apples and raisins and cinnamon. By the time we do all that, make them, and eat them, and clean up, my daughter has had a chance to really sleep in."

Family history, family newsletters.

Consider making a family newsletter, or learning your family history and the contributions of your ethnic or racial group, or making a scrapbook of the child's life. There are detailed ideas of many ways to do this in Chapter 14.

Gardening and outdoor play.

Most kids won't want to order seeds with you, or choose new varieties or plan which annuals will go where, a favorite February activity of serious gardeners. Nor is weeding likely to be popular.

But if you keep it to short sessions, many young children are eager to participate in certain parts of gardening. They will love planting seeds, and be fascinated to see the tiny seedlings appear. You just have to accept a clump of seedlings all in one place instead of a neat row. Most children also like watering with a child-sized watering can. You might want to get one that lets the water out of small holes, rather than a single open spout. That way they can't dump too much water on tiny plants, and you don't have to issue as many instructions, or try to hold back an enthusiastic three-year-old. Even better is the hose. Set it to a very fine spray, so they can't knock things over with a hard stream, and let them loose.

Growing something they can harvest and take home appeals to almost everybody.

Composting has an attractive "ick" factor. Show them all about it, and tell them how it works.

Using tools is appealing. A child with no interest in growing flowers might still love to be able to handle a giant long-handled pruning shears.

> "My grandson is six. It's hard to get him to clean up or help out in the house, like most kids. But this spring he really wanted to garden. Last time I headed out there, he was running ahead of me, yelling, 'Grandma, I want to work with you,' grabbing the biggest rake. He cut the big rose bush back all by himself."

In hot weather, it's fun to get wet. If you have a lawn, or a big enough outdoor space of some kind, turn on the sprinkler and let them run in and out of the spray.

Getting soaking wet *in their clothes* is extra fun for little kids. On a really miserably hot day, take them outside with small non-breakable containers of water, and let them pour water over themselves, in their clothes. This can make an oppressive day into an adventure. The wet clothes and hair will keep them cooler, too.

For preschoolers and younger, fill a bucket or dishpan with water, sometimes with soap bubbles. Add a few containers, a toy that can be a boat, maybe some corks. Don't ever leave them alone with a container of water, though; young children can drown very quickly, in just a few inches of water.

Share what you love with them.

Are there skills you want to share with them, or special places, or experiences?

> "Children's lives are indoors now. My husband and I talked, and our unique contribution will be to take them outside, walks in the woods, camping."

Another grandmother finds ways to share her art with grandchildren.

> "I'm a fabric artist, and I want to show them all how to

make things. I'm always getting that stuff out. Sometimes they take to it. One liked embroidering when she was just four. They love using the sewing machine. This year the twelve-year-old wants to knit."

A grandmother in a big family says,

"I tried to always take them up to camp ... a big old house we have on the lake ... when their cousins were there. I wanted them to grow up together. I think it worked, the cousins are close. I love to hear them laughing and staying around the table after dinner, talking. Now they all have their licenses, and the drive is too much for me, so they drive me up."

Almost anything you enjoy doing has possibilities as long as you think about the child's age and abilities, and don't take offense if they don't like it. Skiing, ice skating, bicycling, hiking, bird watching, chess, crafts, dogs, drawing and painting, boats, scrapbooking, card or board games, or playing music, are all worth trying to share with children. You can enlarge their world by showing them what you love and enjoy.

Giving.

"You want purple hightops? Sure, let's go."

Toys and presents.

Choosing and giving presents to your grandchildren can be great fun. One of the joys of grandparenting is the chance to be more generous and indulgent than you were able to be as a parent. You'll probably want to bring gaudily wrapped presents to birthdays and gift giving holidays.

But everybody will be happier if you can figure out how to indulge without spoiling, and to give special treats and wonderful presents without annoying or undermining the parents. In some families, generous birthday and holiday gifts are welcome and a highly enjoyable part of the family culture.

Plan a little and consult the parents before you start shopping. For many grandparents it's easy and tempting to buy lots of presents, but when I talk to parents they often say their kids have too much stuff already, and get way too much more on holidays and birthdays, with the grandparents being major culprits. Sometimes lavish presents can be just right, but more is not always better. Children won't be three times as happy if they get three presents.

Toys raise other issues too.

You probably remember when toys were just toys—blocks, model cars and trucks of all sizes and complexity, train sets, crayons, dolls and doll houses, chemistry sets, many kinds of building toys, plastic models of horses, potholder weaving looms, all sorts of sports equipment, board games and puzzles.

If you look in a toy store now, you'll see some very different things. Many toys are linked to movies and television. Others are electronic and do just one thing when the child pushes a button, but don't really allow for creative or self-directed play. Some of the most popular, heavily promoted dolls are stereotypically sexualized, and marketed to girls as young as seven.

Look for toys are open-ended, that can be used in many ways, and encourage children to invent their own games and pretend worlds. Blocks can become a dollhouse, a zoo, or a ramp for toy cars. A single block can be a phone, or a peanut butter sandwich, in a pretend game. Open-ended toys will be used longer and enjoyed more because there are more things to do with them.

"I had my five-year-old granddaughter, and her friend, for most of the day. I suggested they might want to set up an ice cream store, like our local one that they love to go to. With just a tiny bit of prompting from me, they made ice cream cones out of paper. I helped them make a sign where they listed the flavors—they loved putting down their favorites, and they wrote everything themselves, with me telling them how to spell the words. Then they used blocks for cell phones, and they were calling the store to ask when it was open. One would stand in the kitchen asking on her cell phone about were they open yet and what flavors did they have, and the other one answering from the living room. They made a lot of calls. Everything they see grown-ups do! They had an old, canceled credit card of mine and they thought of making receipts themselves, so they would sell each other ice cream and then give a receipt. They did this for hours, I got them to sit down and eat lunch only by making it part of the game."

See the Resources at the end of this chapter for websites and books that help you choose. The classic toys you remember playing with yourself,

and that your children enjoyed, might be great for your grandchildren. There are also plenty of new toys that are not connected to media, and encourage open-ended creative play.

Diane Levin's book *So Sexy So Soon: The New Sexualized Childhood and What Parents Can Do to Protect Their Kids* has good ideas for parents and grandparents who want to avoid toys and videos that promote sexual images to young children.

Nancy Carlsson-Paige writes about the changes in media consumption, toys, advertising, and play in her book, *Taking Back Childhood: Helping Your Kids Thrive In A Fast Pace Media-Saturated Violence-Filled World*. This book, too, has good suggestions for parents and grandparents on protecting children.

Everyone has heard of the videos for babies that claim to make them smarter, and amuse them at the same time. Are these valuable? No. All the evidence is that they don't help babies learn, and actually do harm. Babies need hands-on play with actual, concrete objects, and relationships with real, responsive people, to develop their intelligence and their skills, not images on a screen. Time spent watching a screen is time wasted, time not used for the active play that does develop babies' minds. To learn more about the research on this topic, see the websites in the Resources at the end of this chapter.

When shopping:

• Look for toys that encourage open-ended play, instead of single purpose toys.

- Look for toys not tied to movies or television shows.

- Check the Consumer Product Safety Commission for recalls or warnings.

- Avoid toys that contain harmful chemicals including phthalates, lead, and other toxics. There are organizations that test toys and post their findings online; consult the current lists before shopping.

- Look for toys that are consistent with your values. Many

highly advertised toys are full of violent and sexual imagery but you can find plenty of appropriate toys you feel good about giving, too.

It can be fun to get the grandchildren things that were favorites with their own parents. Many wonderful elaborate building toys, or a train set, can lead to fun times for parents and children together.

Don't forget those boxes in the back hall or the attic, the things you packed up when your own kids were too old for them. Grandchildren might love the actual toys their parents played with. They might just like to see them, to unpack that box with you, and hear about their parents as children.

Other ways to give.

Betsy found a way to use her sewing skills and give her twin granddaughters something they love, although her first idea of how to do it was a failure. She is an accomplished quilter, and first planned to make beautiful, heirloom quilts for the girls for their thirteenth birthday. She had thought carefully about their favorite colors, and about patterns that would be individual, yet compatible, in their shared bedroom. When this idea was discussed, and her drawings and fabric swatches laid out on the kitchen table, the girls weren't interested at all.

"These would have been my masterpiece quilts, something

they could have all their lives. I was going make Ohio Star pattern, and use everything I'd learned in the Master Quilter class I took. I saw after a while that they really didn't connect with this, they didn't want heirloom quilts. What they wanted was their own rooms. Which is just not possible in that house. So, it was disappointing. I went back to the drawing board, and I came up with an idea. I talked to them, and they loved it. We got them loft beds. It's like a bunk bed, with a top bunk only, and space underneath for a desk, or whatever. And once I got into it, I had ideas about moving their bookshelves to make walls around the space underneath, and rearranging everything so they couldn't see each other as much. And I made curtains around the lofts, to make the space feel separate. One of the girls picked out chiffon, lined with a gold metallic fabric, and she has this diaphanous ethereal look that seems transparent but it's not, and then she put up a string of tiny lights in there. The other girl chose completely opposite fabric and colors. So they have a little privacy, visual privacy at least. I did transform their room, but in the way they like."

Another sewer had a five-year-old grandson who couldn't care less about room décor.

"My daughter likes fixing up her house, too, and she sews, too, so we're excited, and there we are, her and me talking to him about, Grandma's going to make you new curtains, and fix up your room. It was like we were speaking Latin, he couldn't even hear us, it was so not something he could ever be interested in. But, I got him to a fabric store with a big section of juvenile fabrics. Then he was beside himself. It was between motorcycles, space ships, and fire trucks. He went back and forth, trying to choose what he wanted, and finally settled on space ships. I made him curtains, and his mom told me later that his friends were coming in his room to see, because no one else has space ship curtains. Later on, I made him a motorcycle pillowcase."

Money.

Should a gift of money have strings or conditions? If it's for your grandchild's education, or something else specific, make that clear. A grandmother who watched her best friend find this out the hard way says:

> "Our best friends, another couple, gave their kids money for the grandkids' education. Just like we want to do. We've known these people forever; our kids grew up together and are still friends. We were as surprised as they were when the parents didn't save it for college. No, they went to the Space Center in Houston, a great family trip, and they said later that it was 'educational.' Everybody's mad now, and the money's gone. So we learned a bitter lesson from that, and we've told our children, and our grandson, he's seventeen now, that we can help him get a college education. We've said how much we can contribute, for each of four years, and we'll write checks then. Probably checks directly to the college."

Writing checks directly to the college might not always be necessary, but when money is changing hands, it is important to have clear communication of some kind.

Talk, and perhaps send a follow up email or letter to make sure everyone remembers what was said in the same way. What started out as a loving and generous idea can lead to hurt feelings on all sides if there's not a clear understanding.

If you are thinking about helping with college costs, take the time to learn about the tax implications of various ways of giving money to your grandchild or adult child, and the effect on financial aid and scholarships.

If you are giving a teen or adult grandchild a gift of money to use as they wish, then let it go and don't criticize. Once you give it, it's theirs. If it's truly a gift, it might go for a tattoo, or a motorcycle, or maybe time off from work to ski, or to write a novel. You might have envisioned a nice outfit to wear to job interviews, or down payment on a condo.

What if they use it to open that vegan restaurant? If you aren't going to feel OK about this, give in other ways, making it clear exactly what you mean.

Think about:

- Are you financially able to make this gift without risking your own well-being?

- How much money are you planning to give?

- What is the money for?

- If the gift is for something specific, what is the right age or stage of life for the grandchild to be when they get it?

- Are there any conditions?

- If you want to help with college, what do you mean exactly? To contribute what you can afford when the time comes? Or, are you committing now to a certain definite amount for each year of college? Is this only if the child remains a full time student in a degree program?

- If you have more than one grandchild, you may want to give to them equally, so think that through before you impulsively make offers.

Giving experiences instead of things.

There are other ways to give, too, ways that will be more memorable and special, and will promote the childrens' growth, and not add to clutter in the house. Consider sometimes giving experiences instead of things.

Try this:

- Special outings to a ball game, museum, or maybe a day

trip to an amusement park, beach, or state park. Or offer to take your grandchild and a friend kayaking or horseback riding.

• For teens, two tickets to a concert so they can invite a friend.

• Start a birthday tradition of lunch at her favorite restaurant and a bookstore trip where she gets to choose any three books she wants.

• Consider a family membership in an Aquarium or Children's Museum.

• For an older child who really wants this, give a musical instrument and lessons.

• For an adolescent grandchild, ask. Tell them what you are thinking, and talk over whether there is something they want to do, or somewhere they want to go, that could be your gift. You might hear about a plan or dream that means a lot to the child, which you would not have thought of.

• It might make sense to put some money in a college fund rather than buying more things now.

One set of grandchildren has more than another.

Many grandparents would like to equalize this disparity. It's probably best not to do it by giving more elaborate presents on birthdays and holidays, because that will be noticed and resented by the more affluent children. They won't think of the things they already have – they may not have noticed the differences – they'll just compare what you got them and what you got their cousins.

Instead, consider paying for clothes, sports equipment, lessons, or camps, or covering dental bills.

"I get my son's little girls to swimming lessons. I pay for

it, and I take them. I make sure they have those kinds of things."

In another family, the grandparents thought that stability, and a good preschool, was the best gift they could give.

"My daughter is a single mom and there have been years when there was no money around, everything was hard. We paid for Montessori school for two years. So the kids could stay in the same school, and no one had to worry about that."

The gifts of generosity and empathy.

Grandparents can give the gift of generosity, too, sharing with children the satisfaction of giving, which can continue all their lives. In addition to buying them presents, you might want to involve them in your charitable giving, or help them donate things they don't use anymore in a thoughtful way.

A grandmother who worked for many years in various human services organizations says:

"Every year after Christmas, I go over and we figure out what they don't want anymore, things they've outgrown, or never play with. We check to make sure things are in good condition, and box them up. I talk to the kids about where they're going, maybe to a social worker I know who can get them to a specific family, or to a daycare center, or a shelter. The kids are really into it, they feel good about it. And their parents love it, it gets the clutter out of the house."

I talked with a grandparent couple who have a family charitable foundation. Each of them is also on the board of several other nonprofit organizations. They have started to talk to their grandchildren about giving, and bringing the children in on the decisions.

"We have a family foundation, and we talk to the kids about it, each one beginning at ten years old. We bring them into a quarterly meeting and invite them to help us think about what to give to. And each year on their birthday we make a donation in their name, which they help us pick. It's been so beautiful to watch them grow in this, to really start to care. They're proud of the birthday donations. The oldest child is really involved, really thoughtful about it. He's eighteen, and he is starting to work on researching the options, background, thinking with us about our long term strategy. Someday, he'll have a leadership role in the foundation."

Travel with grandchildren.

There are several organizations offering group trips and tours especially for grandparents and grandchildren, or you may prefer making your own plans. Realistic choices about what your grandchildren can handle, what they'll enjoy, what you'll enjoy, and how long to be away from home can make all the difference.

The children's age is the biggest factor. A younger child who is used to overnights with you might do fine on a short trip to a familiar place, especially with other familiar people. An overnight to a family cottage on the lake, or a family reunion with cousins they like to play with can work for some elementary school children. Preteens can enjoy some trips, others aren't ready at all. Adolescents are a good bet for more adventurous and unfamiliar travel. Some children are ready much earlier than others.

> "We took him to New York City for a week when he was eleven. We saw everything, it was wonderful. He still talks about it."

Claudia told me about wonderful trips with her granddaughters.

> "With teens, it is great to get away, do something new with them. Their parents really appreciate it too. We took our teenage granddaughters to the bottom of the Grand Canyon. Then the next year, to Iguazu Falls in Brazil. It was amazing, life changing, for them."

Bonnie and her husband included a grandchild in their volunteer work.

> "My husband and I have been Habitat for Humanity volunteers for years. We're not carrying sheetrock anymore, but there's lots we can do, and it's really satisfying. Last year, my granddaughter wanted to go too. She was eighteen. We told her in advance, this is serious and it's not about you. It's hard and it's not always comfortable. She stepped up and we were so proud of her. And it's the best thing we ever did for her."

Another grandmother said,

> "I took each of my granddaughters with me to Yearly Meeting of the Religious Society of Friends (Quakers). There was a good teen program, very structured, with their own workshops, people their own age. They stayed up real late, I only saw them at meals sometimes."

Janice and her husband, Pete, had a windfall, money they hadn't expected. They wanted to use it for a special trip, to Paris and London, famous fantastic places they had never expected to see. They'd never done anything like this before, and they saw it as a once in a lifetime chance for themselves.

They decided to bring their two grandsons, eleven and fourteen years old. They worried about whether Tyler, the younger one, could be away from his parents for two weeks. Both boys had spent overnights at the grandparents' house, and Tyler was aching to go. He hauled a suitcase out of the basement and started to pack while his parents and grandparents were talking over dessert about whether taking him along was a good idea. In the weeks before they left, he studied maps, and he talked about it all the time, to everybody he knew. He helped his grandfather reserve their seats on the plane using the airline's website.

The trip was a wonderful adventure, but not exactly what they expected. Tyler loved every minute of it, he wanted to see everything, touch everything, buy every postcard, go to the top of every tall building. He did regress some, asking them to put him to bed at night including reading a story. He held their hands whenever they left the hotel. His enthusiasm made him a wonderful companion. He rode on the London Eye, a huge Ferris wheel, and on double decker buses. In Paris, he enjoyed croissants for breakfast, and sailed a toy boat at the Jardin du Luxembourg. He was delighted with the fancy Parisian artisanal chocolates and didn't want to eat his until he had a photo of it. He took pictures everywhere with his own camera. He was stunned and fascinated to hear children his age speaking French. He wondered whether the British really spoke English, since he couldn't always understand them.

It was the fourteen-year-old, Ryan, who was a problem. "It's no fun traveling with a xenophobic slug," Pete told me afterwards. Ryan was overwhelmed by the strangeness. He was too proud to say so, or to ask for help ordering meals. He just shrugged when asked what he'd like to see. He shuffled silently behind them through art museums, parks, playgrounds, and early morning open-air food markets, with his earphones on, listening to music he'd brought with him. He wanted to eat only at McDonald's.

Tyler's enjoyment, and their own thrill at seeing more of the world than they ever expected to meant they could roll their eyes and laugh about Ryan when they were alone.

But apparently it wasn't a complete failure even for him. After they'd been home a few weeks, Janice and Pete were surprised to hear from Ryan's parents that he talked happily about the trip as if he'd been an enthusiastic and pleasant member of the group. At school, he wrote about the Catacombs in Paris and showed his snapshots around.

For Barbara, travel with a teenager was surprising in a different way.

> "We already had the trip planned. We didn't have tickets yet but we had planned the vacation time from work and we were committed to going, months ahead. Bob, the man I love and live with, and I were going to work for a month in an orphanage in Cambodia, and then travel some in the region. Bob is a Buddhist, and it meant a lot to him to see these places. Then, my grandson Andrew started to have a really hard time. He was fifteen, he was angry, depressed, he hadn't done anything really self-destructive yet. It seemed like he was going to. It was scary, real scary. He cursed at his best friend's parents, he didn't come home all night, just

sauntered in at dawn after his parents had been driving around looking for him, frantic. He was smoking cigarettes. His parents were terrified because their older son had had a real drug problem, and they had just gotten him through it. We were all terrified. So we decided to bring him with us to Cambodia. It was a desperate plan, really. My son, his father, said take him somewhere far away, get him out of here. And it was incredible. Andrew was a completely different kid from day one. He took care of the babies and toddlers, he got really attached to one of them right away, and spent time with him every day. His whole face was all opened up, he wanted to talk to us. He and Bob really got along. Bob never had any kids, so he didn't know how to treat my grandson like a child, he talked to him like an equal. They're both the same height, both quiet. They played chess, and took walks together. Andrew started meditating every morning, although no one told him to, it's just something Bob does. We brought home a completely different grandson than the one we left with."

So, how can you plan a successful trip with grandchildren? You can't plan everything and you can't guarantee success. There are always going to be surprises, and you'll have a better time if you don't count on things working out exactly the way you expected. Be ready for disappointments and glitches, and prepared to cope with them. But the surprises can be lovely ones, too. One joy of traveling with grandchildren is that they, and you, can see unexpected sides of each other. Being with only you, and not the rest of the family, gives your grandchildren a chance to step out of their family roles. Their parents, who are angry that the kids usually leave their clothes and possessions strewn around everywhere, aren't on the trip, expecting them to do it in the hotel room.

Older grandchildren have a chance to try out more grown-up behaviors. They may see that the situation is new to you too, and appoint themselves map reader, subway route expert, itinerary planner, or translator. A grandmother in her late seventies took her granddaughters to Florida, and was very touched to see how solicitous they were about her comfort. They took her arm going down stairs because they know she has a bad knee, and for dinner they both urged her to choose restaurants she would like. At home, they left all that sort of thing to their parents. At home, they came to meals with their iPods and headphones. At home, the older one expected to be able to use the family car any time, but was shocked when anyone suggested she do her own laundry. On this trip, they remembered sunscreen, and they offered to make lunch.

There are some things you can do to make a good trip more likely. Once you've done them, be prepared to enjoy yourself even if things don't go the way you plan, and to appreciate new aspects of your grandchildren that no one in their hometown has seen before.

Planning your trip.

• Do your grandchildren actually want to go? Talk to them realistically about what food will be available, and how long they'll spend sitting in a train, airplane, or car.

• What are your days there actually going to be like? Are you willing and able to spend most or all of the time doing child-friendly things?

• Make decisions in advance, with the parents, about whether older teens are allowed to go anywhere by themselves. If yes, what's the curfew, and what's off limits?

• If your grandchild has a driver's license, check on any restrictions it carries in the state you are going to. He or she might be a big help with the driving.

• It's far better for the trip to be too short, rather than too long.

• Being able to communicate with their parents by e-mail or Skype could stave off your grandchildren's homesickness; consider what electronic devices you want to bring along.

• Once you're there, consider giving older teens a break

from you. Do separate things some afternoons, if safe and appropriate. Or see a museum separately and meet in the cafeteria for lunch.

• Consider bringing a blank notebook and creating a scrapbook of the trip. You, or they, can write about what you did that day, and leave space for your own snapshots. Save a menu, or receipts, or admission tickets, to remind you, and encourage kids to write a few sentences from their point of view.

• Be prepared for preteens to act younger and more dependent. Check with the parents about bedtime rituals, comfort foods, and reassuring consistency about rules and expectations. A child might be sadly and tearfully homesick at bedtime, and cheerfully adventurous all day.

• Use books, maps, and weather reports, to help your grand child plan ahead. It's a good chance for them to learn to be organized as they think about what to pack, and learn something about their destination in advance.

The long-distance grandmother.

There are lots of ways to stay connected between visits. Use letters, pictures, calls, e-mail and small gifts. Learn how to use Skype, and other video calling technologies which let you see the person you are talking to on a phone call.

Email is no substitute for being together in person, but it can keep you in touch, after the children are old enough to use it. Learn to send and receive text messages too.

When you do visit, take pictures, and mail copies with a letter to the children after you get home. Some grandparents send very small gifts regularly.

"I don't bring presents when I visit. I'll send something small other times, to let the children know I am thinking of them. Sometimes a toy, or a book, or a puzzle or riddle or joke. My grandson loves raspberries, which are very expensive in the stores. So I got in cahoots with my daughter, and I sent a gift card, to be used just for that. He asks her, 'Can we get some today, with Grandma's berry card?' One time I sent him a funny pen that can write in a lot of colors."

If you don't see them often, be prepared for changes. They might like to do the same things they did last time, or they might have outgrown a formerly favorite activity.

Traveling to visit is, of course, a classic for grandparents.

"I am sad that they live so far away. But, I just get on the airplane and go."

Travel together can be wonderful for families that don't live near each other.

As the children get older, one or more of them might want to come by themselves to visit you. This might be just for fun, or it might give their parents a chance to travel, do something special for themselves, or to have some time alone together.

Planning for a grandchild to visit alone.

Talk with the parents so you can be consistent about rules, bedtime, and food. Unless the grandchildren are adolescents, they might be a little more rattled than they anticipated at being away from home, and consistency helps.

If the visit will be for more than two or three days, consider trying to find a local child for them to play with. Or, have siblings or cousins who play together visit at the same time.

Does a university in your town have a summer program for high schoolers, or allow them to take courses? There are many programs focused on specific interests from making music, to cellular biology, or writing. One engineering school offers several high school programs in the summer, including one just for girls, taught by women. This could be wonderful visit, and also a chance for your teen grandchild to broaden her experience of the world.

Teenagers.

There is a powerful stereotype of adolescents. They are famous for distancing from adults and being difficult, hostile, unreasonable, and taking scary risks. These things do happen, and they may happen at an earlier age, now, because of marketing to children that convinces pre-adolescents they should consider themselves teenagers.

Adolescents are also deeply thoughtful, idealistic, and eager to try new things.

There is a stereotype of grandparents too: they are emotionally frail, easily upset, conservative on social issues, and can't cope with either personal or social change. These things are true, too, sometimes. Grandparents are also often calmer and, because of their long experience of life, more able to put the extreme fashions, peculiar behavior, and even the hostility of adolescents in context. Grandparents are also energetic, wise, and able to see what's really important.

One mother of two teenagers told me she had dreaded letting her own mother know that her granddaughter had shaved one side of her head and dyed the remaining hair electric blue. The mom thought it was best to prepare the grandmother in advance for the shock. She herself was quite upset by this and found herself cringing and looking away when she saw her daughter, especially the shaved side of her head. When she described it to her own mother, the grandmother laughed and made a little wave as if brushing away flies. She said,

"Oh, she can do that, she's a good girl. Hair grows."

There will probably be some hard times as your grandchildren make their way through adolescence. Often, the best thing you can do is support the parents, and help the whole family remember what is really serious (like depression, or risky behavior) and what is not (like hair). This might be easier for you than it is for the parents.

If you don't find it so easy, try to act like you do. If your family be

lieves that you will be devastated by family problems, or undesirable behavior, you'll never be told about them. And don't take your grandchild's
rejection or moodiness too seriously. It's probably not about you.

> "They are interesting as teens. They need so much and they
> are so angry."

Show up and listen to your teenage grandchildren, even if you don't
understand everything they are doing. Every issue or potential disagreement doesn't have to be discussed. There will be times you need to set a
limit, like objecting to misogynist music lyrics or remarks, but even then
ask them what they think. Rather than delivering a condemning lecture,
encourage them to analyze and clarify.

Your longer life experience can help you stay poised and thoughtful.
In the novel, *Domestic Pleasures*, by Beth Gutcheon, the wise mother
easily sees past her teenage son's unkempt disheveled appearance,
slang, and odd sleeping habits to the kind, responsible person he truly
is. Grandparents can be good at this, too. Although the stereotype of
grandparents is that they will be conventional, and easily shocked, in
reality many grandparents have seen all this before.

Grandparents can be a refuge when teens need to separate from their
parents but still need somebody.

Hope chests.

Edna enjoyed her three granddaughters the most when they were
adolescents. She was good at helping to launch them into adulthood.
When each girl began to dream of independence, and find her mother
unbearably constraining, Edna started a Hope Chest with her. It didn't
have anything to do with getting married. As Katie, the oldest, cheerfully explained it, "I'm hoping to have my own apartment someday
soon." She and Edna hit all the yard sales together. They weren't in a
hurry – Katie was just thirteen – so they had time to search out kitchen
gadgets in good condition, and find linen napkins without stains. Katie
decided she didn't need matching dishes. She liked old-fashioned floral
designs. By the time she left for college she had ten dinner plates,
none matching. This was fun for them, and also a small but significant

message to Katie that her grandmother supported her fondest hope, which at that point was to get away from her mother and be on her own. Years later when Katie unpacked her Hope Chest in her first apartment there were some laughs – "Why did I think I would want *this*?" There were also ten beautiful dinner plates, and a lot of happy memories of yard sales and planning with her grandmother.

Show them the world.

One mother I talked with remembers her own grandparents and how they were the ones who took her seriously as an adolescent. They let her know that they thought she wouldn't always be living with her parents, and she wouldn't be going to high school forever either. They asked about her plans.

> "They said to me, you need a five year plan. Where do you want to be in five years? No one else said that. It really helped me, I started to think about it, like I had a future I could have some control over. They had plenty of time to listen to me. My grandfather would get out his pipe, and they would settle back in their chairs."

For many families, grandparent time is mostly fun. Sometimes a grandparent can do something that is really helpful, or is rewarding for you when it wouldn't be for the parents. A busy mother told me about her daughter's visits to college, with the grandparents.

> "It was a bad time for me, my daughter's senior year in high school. The other two kids were much older, launched, on their own. My marriage was coming apart. I had just started art school, which I guess I should have waited another year for, until she was out of the house but I felt like I'd waited my whole life already to do what I wanted. Face it, I was very depressed. So when my dad asked real politely if I'd like them to take my daughter to visit colleges, I said sure. They probably did a better job than I would have. They have tons of energy, even though they're both seventy.

Education means everything to them, they've both been teachers, my mom was a high school guidance counselor. They had checklists, a clipboard, info about each college all printed out, a list of questions. They took her everywhere she had any interest in … Grinnell, Hampshire, University of Texas in Austin, some school in Seattle I can't remember the name of. They gave new meaning to the word 'relentless.' I don't know what my daughter thought of it, we never discussed it. After that trip, she did know where she wanted to go, and she got in there, and she's there now and likes it."

Your time with your grandchildren can be a great joy, a source of satisfaction, and also fun and funny. They will enjoy memories of happy times, how you nurtured their skills and interests, and will cherish the deep knowledge that they are loved and valued. Everything you do with them models your ideas about how to have an enjoyable and meaningful life. You have so much to give them.

Resources

Nonfiction

The World According to Toddlers, by Shannon Payette Seip and Adrienne Hedger

Dr. Spock's Baby and Child Care, 9th Edition, updated and Revised by Dr. Robert Needlman

Baby Play and Learn: 160 Games and Learning Activities for the First Three Years, by Penny Warner

The Long Distance Grandmother: How To Stay Close To Distant Grandchildren, by Selma Wassermann

Consuming Kids: The Hostile Takeover of Childhood, by Susan Linn

Born to Buy: The Commercialized Child and the New Consumer Culture, by Juliet Schor

Taking Back Childhood: Helping Your Kids Thrive In A Fast Pace Media-Saturated Violence-Filled World, by Nancy Carlsson-Paige

Unplug the Christmas Machine: A Complete Guide to Putting Love and Joy Back into the Season, by Jo Robinson and Jean Coppock Staeheli

Fiction

In This Sign, by Joanne Greenberg

Goodbye Without Leaving, by Laurie Colwin

Domestic Pleasures, by Beth Gutcheon

Websites

Campaign for Commercial Free Childhood website, for ideas about toys, products for young children, and tips for parents and grandparents.

TRUCE: Teachers Resisting Unhealthy Children's Entertainment website has excellent specific recommendations about toys promote healthy creative play, and also what to avoid.

The American Academy of Pediatrics website has a section on media and lots of other useful information.

Part Three:

All Kinds of Families

10

Stepfamilies

Finding your way with grandchildren by marriage.

Being a stepgrandmother can feel like a new, modern family relationship created by higher divorce rates. But it's not really new. Marriages, or partnerships that produced children, have always ended, whether through death or divorce, and new partners have entered families. So there have always been stepgrandparents. One difference now is that we live longer. In previous generations, life spans were quite a bit shorter, many more people died young, and their spouses frequently remarried, bringing children to the new family unit. Sometimes, a widow or widower even brought their stepchildren, the children of their deceased spouse's earlier marriage, so households could contain children not biologically related to either adult.

There are two ways a stepgrandchild can come into your life. Either you partner with someone whose grandchildren become your stepgrandchildren, or your adult child has stepchildren, who are then your stepgrandchildren.

Your partner may bring you stepgrandchildren, whether you meet him first as a grandfather, or much earlier in life. Time makes a big difference. You might know his children for years, build warm relationships with them, maybe even help raise them, before they become parents. It is very different if you are woman later in life, who marries a man who already has grandchildren. You may be just getting to know your new husband's adult children, and may feel hesitant about how to relate to the grandchildren.

Or, perhaps it is your child's new partner, not your own, who brings you stepgrandchildren. Your adult child becomes a stepparent, and you get to know your new daughter-in-law or son-in-law along with his or her child.

> "Of course I want those two boys to be comfortable in my house, but part of it also is welcoming my new daughter-in-law."

If you've known the grandchildren since they were born, you may be treated as the grandmother by everyone, and never question it yourself.

What little children are thinking.

Preschoolers don't understand abstract ideas like genetic connections. They understand concrete things that they can see and touch, and they think about the world mostly in relation to themselves. At this age, they don't really comprehend that their parents were ever children, and the idea that a grandparent is their parent's parent seems ridiculous. The way they see it, a grandparent is someone who has a certain kind of relationship to themselves.

> "When we started to explain it to the kids, the relationships among the adults, the four-year-old burst out laughing. My three-year-old granddaughter, my stepgranddaughter literally, was really interested though. She listened to the whole explanation, especially because she had two new baby cousins, one on each side of the family. We thought she got it. Then she said, 'I'm the cousin of every kid!' Turns out that now she thinks her friends at daycare and her baby brother are her cousins too. The idea that some grown-ups are the parents of other grown-ups was beyond them. We were

kind of surprised because they are both so bright but there it is. They're little. So whether I am genetically related, whether I am a stepgrandmother, is meaningless to them."

As children get older, they begin to understand abstract ideas. Then the literal, black-and-white thinking of a five-to ten-year-old child takes over. They become logical, and exact. Many love games with rules, or playing school, with themselves in charge. One of them could announce unexpectedly that you are not really their grandmother. They don't mean to reject you, and they aren't saying their feelings about you have changed. They are talking about their new understanding of facts.

They may also be looking for responses from important adults, asking indirectly what it all means. They are starting to wonder about relationships.

Really my grandchildren.

Sometimes adults have this question too. Some people feel that genes are all-important and other relationships are not as valid. For others, marriage and other legal ties create family relationships. In this view, a woman becomes a stepgrandmother through legally marrying the grandfather. For other people, the time spent together, and affection create family, more than genetic or legal connections do.

> "They are all my grandchildren, all completely. Some I have a genetic connection to, some I don't. It doesn't matter. To me relationships are about caring, time, love. I mean, think about it, if you go back far enough we all have the same genes somewhere, anyway."

You may hear "not really a grandmother" from someone, especially if the biological grandmother is involved. You may feel that way yourself.

> "Of course I treat them the same, but they're not really my grandchildren. We are not related."

Or you may be needed, wanted, and invited in right away, and this grandchild could become a great joy.

You may be the only grandparent the children have.

Although Norma hasn't known her husband's family long, she did not follow the advice she got from everybody to move slowly. That was probably good sense on her part. This family had a big empty space labeled "Grandparents" and Norma was the only one capable of filling it.

Norma and Ken married when they were both in their fifties. It was a second marriage for each of them. She first met his daughter Erin and son-in-law Jeremy as adults. The two couples lived thousands of miles apart, and Ken was in the habit of visiting once a year, so Norma didn't get to know Erin or Jeremy very well. But when Erin's baby was born, Norma dove right in, sending presents, calling, assuming the new parents would need help, and heading right for the kitchen when she visited with Erin's father. She admired the baby, she cooked, she cleaned up, she cooked some more, and when she got home, she sent another present, a high chair she had heard Erin talking about.

Erin and Jeremy were sadly aware of a lack of grandparents. Jeremy's parents lived in Beijing, teaching at an International School serving the children of Europeans and North Americans. They had four other grandchildren already and were not especially excited about a faraway baby. Jeremy didn't expect that to change. Erin's parents had divorced when she was eight. Her mother had remarried, and lived in a remote part of Costa Rica, where she didn't have reliable phone service or Internet. Her visits to the United States, every year or two, were exciting, loving, and fun, but everyone knew Erin's mother wasn't going to be an active grandmother. Erin also knew that her father wasn't comfortable with children. She understood that he was very shy, and noisy or unpredictable events made him nervous. He ignored holidays and birthdays, or he had until he married Norma and she took over those things. He would fly across the country to visit Erin, then spend hours reading the newspaper or focused on one of his hobbies, which included trains, and the maps of big city mass transit systems.

Erin and Jeremy didn't expect much from him.

Norma calls, just to hear about the baby. Norma asks for pictures. She sends presents of baby clothes, and toys, and she urges them to " … tell him his grandma loves him."

Simply by taking on this role so cheerfully and energetically, Norma is accepted in it by everyone involved. Erin and Jeremy consider Norma to be their child's only functioning grandparent, and they want their son to have that relationship. They invited her to his first birthday party, and she traveled across the country with a suitcase full of presents and her husband in tow. They expect her to be at his graduations and other special occasions too. He's started to talk, and he's learning to say Grandma Norma.

Yours, mine, and ours.

In other families, it's not so clear. Adults may have more mixed feelings, and aren't always in such agreement. The passage of time has an effect, too. You may feel differently about a child who has been part of your family since infancy than you do about an older child you meet for the first time. The child feels very differently too. And those feelings can change, as both adults and children get to know each other. If they develop a history of happy experiences together, and act "like family" which means staying in touch, helping when help is needed, being at important events and holidays together, having some good times together, then they'll be closer. If they don't, then they may never really feel that they are a family, even after years.

Too young.

If your partner is older than you are, or had children early in his life, you may feel much too young for the role of grandmother. You may still be raising children of your own and have no time or energy for new little ones.

Connie doesn't consider herself a grandmother at all. She married for the first time at thirty-six. She had no children. Her new husband was forty-nine, with a married and pregnant daughter, and a toddler grandson. Connie desperately wanted a child and they started trying right away. They succeeded in a few months, but Connie was a stepgrandmother before she was a mother. Her stepdaughter gave birth to twins just after Connie's wedding.

> "It feels weird, I can't be a grandmother at thirty-eight, and my husband and I have a baby ten months old. I'm a new mom! But I do try to help out. When my husband's oldest daughter had the twins, I brought them dinner every week for the first two months. I'm more like a friend, or an aunt."

Mildred's husband had become a father when he was nineteen, before he met Mildred. He then became a grandfather in his forties, when he and Mildred were quite busy raising their four children. She's not ready.

> "I don't feel like a grandmother, I haven't earned it. It's too soon, too, all my energy goes to my own kids, I just do the symbolic things, I send presents, cards. They come to the house for family parties, holidays and all. I don't babysit over there. I'm swamped already! Those kids deserve more, they should have involved grandparents, and luckily the other grandparents are that way."

This could be your only grandchild.

For some women who have never had children, a "grandchild by marriage" can be a wonderful, unexpected blessing.

> "I so much wanted a child, but I never had one. I married late and then went into early menopause. I devoted myself to his children, I spent every weekend, and all my vacations with them, I went to all their games. I loved them, I considered them my children by marriage. But I was never really the parent, always a little bit on the outside. I never made the decisions. My husband is a good father, a devoted father. That's something that I respect and love about him. It also meant he wanted to do it all. He saw other men hand the parenting over to their new wives and he wasn't going to do that. So, when I wanted more of a role as a parent, I couldn't get it. I felt like an appendage, and I tried so hard to do everything a mother would do. I cooked, I had family gatherings with his kids and my relatives, my nieces, parties, a lot of cooking, and I tried to take care of the house, the homemaking, make a pleasant welcoming home for the kids. I organized the holidays. I bought presents. But I was never a full parent. There was a lot of sadness in it for me. Every graduation or holiday just meant, I lose again.

> "Now, with the grandbabies, a lot has happened. Over those

years, gradually, my oldest stepdaughter, and I became close. I was there for her. She got to know me. She grew up, too. This paved the way, yes. The real shift in who I am in the family came with the first grandchild.

"Now, with this baby, my stepdaughter sent me a book about grandmothers as soon as she got pregnant, included me in everything. She saw what it meant to me. Now there is a full place for me. I'm the one they call to take care of her sometimes if they need help, they send me pictures, she calls me Nana. It's such a joy, such a delight. And the second one, my grandson, just as dear.

"And I can really be a help now, instead of just background stuff. My husband and I take our granddaughter to the ballet, because she's taking lessons and she just loves that. It's delightful. But I am the one who thought of it, I talked to the parents, I got the tickets. And when my stepdaughter had surgery, she was exhausted of course and I could be the one to call her, I could offer to take the children for a Saturday, and to bring over dinner. My husband and I are equal partners as grandparents."

Daniel married a woman with a young daughter and he is very glad to be part of a family, after he had given up on having one. He's an only child, and he was past forty years old, and still single. He knows his own mother had stopped hoping for any descendants or a bigger family.

"I didn't find the right woman until I was forty-two. My mom had given up on grandchildren a long time ago. I'm a bike mechanic, I have my own shop. Melissa used to come in all the time, with her bike and then she bought a two-wheeler for her daughter from us, and we got friendly, and then I asked her out. Our first date was children's concert in the library. The singer was actually quite good. It was a really nice time. Sitting there with them, I was thinking, it seemed like it was too late for me to have a family, but maybe not. Best thing that ever happened to my mom. She loves when we visit, and telling her friends, having grand-children pictures to show, like her friends have."

If you both have grandchildren.

If you marry or remarry later in life and you and your new husband both have grandchildren from previous relationships, you face another set of dynamics and questions. You are secure in feeling like a grand-mother but it can still be confusing. Do you have to love them all the same? What should they call you?

> "For me, I needed to know they were going to always be my grandchildren. My husband and I met in our late for-ties, when we both had teenagers. Over the years, they all grew up, and my kids had kids first, and I just loved it, loved being with them, doing things for them. When his daughter had a baby on the way, I considered this another equal grandchild, just like the ones my daughters had, I was ready to commit to this baby. But I needed to know if my stepdaughter saw me that way. Or, would it not really count, like if my husband dies first, or god forbid we split up, that would be the end of it and I'd never see her again?"

For Carlie, things are complex.

> "I married a widower. I am taking the place of someone who died very young. One night I was walking the baby, my stepgrandbaby, and singing to him, I started to cry. Is this fair that I am getting to do this and his real grandmother isn't? So I can imagine how my husband's first wife's family must feel ... or maybe even my husband.

> "I have grandchildren myself, I did when we met. So I kind of knew the kinds of things grandparents can do. At the little girl's first birthday party, they invited me, and I brought copies of several of my favorite children's books, Charlotte's Web, and Eloise, and Misty of Chincoteague. And I inscribed them, saying I had loved these books and

I would read them to her. And my husband's daughter, the new mom, she cried over it, she loved it. Another time, I bought a beautiful dress for one of the little girls, very nice, from a very lovely local children's store, for a special occasion. A grandmother can give that. My husband is happy that I do all this. I wondered at first. He says he sees them more because of me. I guess I know how to do it."

Your children's stepchildren.

When your stepgrandchildren come to you through your child's new partner, in some ways, it's similar to your partner's grandchildren. These are children you are related to through marriage. In both situations you are making a connection to an adult, the stepgrandchild's parent, before or at the same time as you try to figure out your role as a stepgrandmother.

But it's different because you connect to these children through a new son-in-law or daughter in-law, another important new person in your life. Everyone involved is adjusting to big changes and new relationships.

Evelyn is seventy-six years old, and has raised four children and helped raise eight grandchildren. She has the wisdom to know that relationships don't happen instantly.

> "When our son remarried, his new wife had two boys, three years old and ten. Of course, we welcome them; we immediately put their pictures up on the wall with our other six grandchildren. We treat them the same. But truly we don't have the same relationship with them. At the beginning I was so anxious to do the right thing that early on when they came into the house one time I hugged the older one, and he felt so stiff in my arms I knew it wasn't right. He doesn't know me very well so why should he want me to hug him? Now I know that I need to treat them equally in presents and all that, and be open to things developing, but not push it. We might have a deep connection someday and we might not."

She also thinks about the bigger picture, the stepfamily and her hopes for her son's marriage.

"I care about the little boys, sure. Just as much, it's my son's new wife, I really want to make her comfortable. We have a big family and I know it could be kind of overwhelming, and it must be hard to be the second wife, coming into a family where the first wife was part of all our lives for over a decade. So partly I make a point of welcoming her kids so she will feel welcome. There are lots of divorces in second marriages and I don't want to do anything to drive a wedge between her and my son."

Grandparents can have a hard, anxious time watching their adult child form a stepfamily. You are meeting these children as they face huge adjustments and perhaps losses. They may have lost a parent through death or be grieving over a divorce or abandonment. They are probably anxious about changes in their own lives. Of course, you worry first about your own adult child and your grandchildren. Will your child's new partner treat your grandchildren well? Will anyone get lost in the turmoil of creating a new, blended family? Older stepchildren can look very big, especially if your grandchildren are the youngest ones.

Try to remember that someone who looks to you like a huge hulking hostile teenager may be a frightened twelve-year-old trying to figure out what this new stepfamily will mean for him, and whether he has lost his own parent's love and attention forever.

Daniel spent years getting to know his fiancée's daughter, and had a warm relationship with her. She was happy to see him, and accustomed to fun times that included him. Still, when she was told that her mother and Daniel would be marrying and Daniel moving in with them, the child said nervously, "He'll go by our rules, right?"

Vera liked her new son-in-law, but was anxious about her daughter's new stepfamily.

"I was so worried for my daughter and especially for my granddaughter who was only two. There were these three bigger kids. Hadley is so little, she could get lost in the crowd. And I was worried my daughter was taking on so much."

You wonder what to do. How will these children feel joining your family's holidays and traditions and customs? If they're older than preschoolers, they have traditions of their own, and another parent they miss.

Judy Osborne, author of *Wisdom for Separated Parents: Rearranging Around Children to Keep Kinship Strong*, advises grandparents,

> "Back off on the holiday traditions. It's not going to be the way you always did it. Your child has to compromise with a new partner."

You may also see your child struggling to stepparent, which is never easy, and perhaps making mistakes. A grandfather found himself highly critical of the way his own son, Kevin, handled stepparenting.

> "Kevin is ridiculous. That boy is thirteen, he's a kid. Kevin expects way too much. He's way too hard on that kid. I've talked to the mother. I've given her money so the kid can take guitar lessons, and for a few other things he wants to do."

Grandmothers worry about how and when to get involved, especially if they have married a grandfather and are just getting to know the children's parents.

> "I didn't want to push myself on them."

Women who already have grandchildren are often very confused at first. Whether or not you love them all the same, should you treat them the same?

> "I didn't know what to do. We were taking our two grand-daughters, six and eight, to the circus like we do every year. Honestly I didn't want to bring anyone else along, especially a rude teenager I barely know. My husband was no help, he was still stunned by the divorce. I finally went and talked to my rabbi. Luckily she's a good listener because all I needed was someone who wasn't upset, wasn't involved, didn't have an agenda in this situation, to listen to me. I just told her about it and found myself saying, 'Am I going to tell a fourteen-year-old child, who is hurting and scared,

adjusting to a new home, obviously unhappy, am I going to tell him that other kids are going to the circus and he's not going?' No. I am not that person. I am not going to do that. So I invited him along with the girls. I didn't think he'd come, but he did. I didn't think he'd like it, but he was mesmerized by the acrobats. And he stuffed himself with popcorn and cotton candy. I think he had a good time.

"Did it help anything? I don't know. Nobody thanked me, he never said thanks, the parents said nothing. Everything is just as tense as ever. But at least I know where I am. When there's a holiday or a birthday, I look for some clues what he'd like and I get him something kind of equivalent to what I get the girls. When we go anywhere with the girls we invite him. I greet him warmly, I have a picture of him on the wall in my house. Maybe we'll have a close relationship someday, feel like family, maybe not. For now I feel that I'm doing the best I can do."

Learning to be a stepgrandmother: making connections, respecting boundaries.

Sometimes the creation of a new stepfamily goes smoothly, but when it is closely preceded by a divorce or death, everyone is upset, rattled, and in pain. They often want other people to quickly ratify their decisions. Sometimes they want to recreate a nuclear family, or what looks like one, as fast as they can. The recently divorced often want their new partner or spouse accepted instantly as part of the family – including pressing their children to accept that person as a parent.

If both adults in a new stepfamily are already parents, they often have a house full of scared, unhappy, or angry children who do not feel at all like siblings or even friends, but who have to accommodate to each other's schedules and interests, and maybe even share a room.

If your adult child marries a widow or widower, children are mourning a terrible loss, the death of a parent. They may feel their surviving parent has started to date too soon. No matter how long or short the interval, any time can be too soon. Even if everything is handled slowly and sensitively, and the new stepparent is warm and appropriate, children may feel it's disloyal to accept or like the new stepparent. It can take years – decades – for children to make a relationship with a stepparent that feels separate to them, and not a slap in the face to their divorced or deceased parent. Even adult children, who are genuinely glad that their father or mother has found happiness and is remarrying, can find themselves angry, sad, or insulted with the resulting changes. One young father, who had welcomed his own father's late-middle-age remarrying, said sadly,

> "I'm glad my dad found somebody and is happy, but it's hard to see her renovate my mother's house, get rid of things."

Everyone has thoughts and feelings about what makes a family relationship. Is it genetics? Love and caring? Legal connections? You'll be sorting this out while also hearing from others, both people you are close to and people who aren't involved but will tell you what they think.

Big milestone events bring up all the difficult issues and feelings. People who have gotten along peacefully and been calm and friendly can suddenly be in an angry struggle about details of planning a wedding or who goes first to see a new baby. This happens because these special moments are seen as revealing the true roles, priorities, or precedents for how it's always going to be. Who is really loved, who is the real parent, who gets to make the decisions?

Try not to get caught up in these symbols.

> "When the second grandbaby was christened, my husband's in-laws – his first wife's family – wanted a picture. I stayed back, I'm not in the picture. That's fine."

You don't have to be in every picture to be in your grandchild's life. Stepfamilies mature over time. Move slowly and welcome developing relationships and affections. The surly frightened teen who wonders what it means for him that your daughter has married his dad, may in fifteen years be teaching his toddler to call you Grandma, and sending you the link to the website where he posts family photos.

Try this:

• Don't assume anything. Many stepgrandmothers don't call themselves grandmother until they see what the parents want. Especially if the children's biological grandmother is involved, this can be just right. But the parents may eagerly welcome your connection with their children, and they may be hoping and watching for signs of warmth and caring from you.

• Look for a place in the grandchildren's lives that is light, affectionate and fun. Until you are sure what everyone is comfortable with, avoid more symbolic and ceremonial roles unless specifically invited.

• Children need to hear you speak with respect about their parents.

• Create a welcoming atmosphere in your home, with some toys or other activities. Put breakables away when toddlers visit, and consider talking to the parents in advance about what food the children like.

• Remember that big milestone events bring up all the difficult issues and feelings from the past.

• Be patient. Take some time to think about how this all feels to the children involved. Or to the adult children.

Resources

Nonfiction

Wisdom for Separated Parents: Rearranging Around Children to Keep Kinship Strong, by Judy Osborne

Stepfamilies, Love, Marriage, and Parenting in the First Decade, by Dr. James Bray and John Kelly

My Father Married Your Mother: Writers Talk about Stepparents, Stepchildren and Everyone In Between, edited by Anne Burt

The Way We Never Were, by Stephanie Coontz

Fiction

This is My Daughter, by Roxana Robinson

Other People's Children, by Joanna Trollope

The Ogre Downstairs, by Diana Wynn Jones

Prodigal Summer, by Barbara Kingsolver

11

The Adopted Grandchild

Some things about adoption have changed
since you were raising your children; other
things are universal.

What has changed.

Adoption has changed in your lifetime. Throughout much of the 20th
century, secrecy about adoption was the norm. This attitude, and assigning babies to adoptive parents by race, appearance, religion, and other
factors were standard practice, and of course this policy made it possible to keep the fact of adoption secret, even from the child. Since the
1970s, unsealing records, open adoption, and transracial and international adoption all have become increasingly widespread and accepted.
Now, families created across lines of nationality, ethnicity, and race are
much more common. Interracial and international adoption have made
adoption visible. Adoption professionals no longer tell parents to keep
the adoption secret; instead they work with parents on finding the best
way to talk about adoption in affirming and sensitive ways, rather than
how to conceal it. There are still secrets in some cases, or just lost information, and adopted children may need to find this information. But
the overall picture is much different than it was a generation ago.

Adoption can be domestic, including through the foster care system, or international. In an open adoption the birth and adoptive parents exchange identifying information and often make a plan for some continued contact. The adoptive and birth parents may stay in touch, sometimes meet and visit. The adoptive parents may regularly send photos and letters about the child to the birth mother. The child may be able to get additional information about her background and other birth relatives more easily in an open adoption. In this kind of adoption, you may meet your grandchild's birth parents and birth grandparents.

Kinship adoptions connect people who are already related. An aunt and uncle adopt a child they have known since birth when the birth parents can't raise the child. A stepparent adopts a child she is already living with and caring for.

A grandmother whose two grandsons were both adopted says,

> "It's just wonderful. My daughter adopted from Vietnam as single. I went with her on the first trip, my husband on the second trip and brought the baby home. My grandson knows the whole story. He likes to look at the map and see Vietnam. They have the name of the person that took care of him in the orphanage. He can contact that person later when he's older. Then our daughter met Rosemary, who has a birth child, and when they married, they co-adopted each other's child. So we have two beautiful grandsons."

Who can adopt? Laws and policy have changed. Single women and single men adopt, and in many places gay and lesbian couples can adopt. In some states, both partners in a lesbian couple can have equal parental rights when one gives birth to their child and the other mother adopts in what is known as a second parent adoption.

This is very different from the way adoption was done, and thought about, when we were raising children. These changes offer many benefits and options that previously did not exist. If your adult child is a single person, or part of a same-sex couple, there are more opportunities to become a parent. Your grandchild can grow up knowing much more about his origins, and his parents are spared the burden of keeping secrets. A child may be able to stay in touch with birth parents or other birth relatives who are important to him after he is adopted, which can make it easier for him to attach and be comfortable in his new family.

Before the adoption.

Grandparents, or grandparents-to-be, can have a wide range of reactions to hearing their adult child's plans to adopt.

You may be reluctant and sad, wishing for a grandchild who carries your genes. You may be very fearful about how difficult the process will be for your adult son or daughter. You may be focused on your own child's welfare rather than on a potential grandchild. Many people, especially if they have no experience with adoption and have seen media accounts of everything going wrong, are worried that the child won't be healthy, or do well in school, or that the process will involve financial fraud or require dangerous travel.

Keep in mind that the drama and difficulties are what get attention. The many families who adopt and then live normal lives don't make news, or generate anecdotes worth repeating, so you don't hear about them.

Other people may want to tell you upsetting stories they've heard, just like the anecdotes of pregnancy or birth difficulties that pregnant women are subjected to. You don't need to listen; you can politely introduce another topic of conversation.

Or, if your adult child and his or her partner have struggled with infertility, you may be hoping they will adopt, while they are still trying to let go of the dream that has been woven into their romance from the beginning, of a child who is part of each of them. You may be eager for a grandchild and urge your adult child to stop the invasive, painful and risky medical procedures, and adopt. One woman who wished fervently for a grandchild said,

> "I feel like my grandbaby is out there somewhere, waiting for us. I am so ready to give up on biology, everybody can see it's gone on too long and it's not going to work."

Flora wanted grandchildren. Her family carries a severe genetic disease and she desperately wanted to avoid having the next generation suffer the heartache of this disease, as she had. She could not understand why her adult son and his wife were even thinking about a pregnancy. She said,

> "To me adoption is a wonderful beautiful thing. A baby not genetically related to us is just so much what this family needs. Our genes have to stop right here. Adoption I feel it would be a gift from God."

If your adult child is single, or didn't seem to have any plans for a family, you may have given up on grandchildren. Hearing of your child's plans to adopt can be wonderful, opening the door to grandchildren and to seeing your child have the joys of parenting.

For many people, both parents and grandparents, starting or expanding their family is the goal and they are comfortable with adoption from the beginning.

"I just want to be a mom," said one young woman I met through my midwifery practice; she was a good friend of some of my patients. She patted her abdomen and added cheerfully, "I don't care if it comes from in here, or on an airplane. I just want to be a mom." A little more than a year later, she came to see me with her new son, born in Guatemala. He was sleeping on her chest in his baby carrier. "Do I look like a mom?" she asked, laughing and laughing with joy. I got happy tears in my eyes watching her.

I told her yes, yes, yes, a mom for sure.

Many grandparents feel something like this, too. Genes don't matter to them.

> "People have asked me what my feelings are about him. They say, 'he's not your blood.' But from the moment I held him, he was my grandson. I adore him."

Doubts and reservations and fears.

Many grandparents who at first thought an adopted grandchild would never feel like theirs find their fears assuaged as they eventually get to know their grandchild, and as they see their own child loving and caring for him.

If you do have doubts and fears when you first hear about the adoption plans, it's a good idea to think carefully about how to handle them rather than immediately sharing them with your adult child.

It is usually a mistake to verbalize these fears to your adult children. Your misgivings will probably change, but if you say them aloud they'll never be forgotten.

After a few months, or after that first visit, this child is a beloved grandchild.

Often the grandparents can't really remember having felt any other way.

The problem is that you may not remember what you said, but other people certainly will, including your adult children. If you are all very lucky, they may be able to laugh it off, as this father could:

> "My mom didn't think he'd be like her other grandchildren,
> but she's wrapped around his little finger now."

More likely, your reservations would be painful for your adult child to hear.

I talked about this with the mother of three adopted children. These children are a ten-year-old and two teenagers now, and the mother still remembers her mother-in-law's fearful and negative comments about adoption and her efforts to convince them not to adopt. Years have passed, but these are still vivid and painful memories.

> "It was awful to hear. We never doubted our plans to adopt,
> but it was ghastly to keep hearing that."

You don't want to be remembered as the person who didn't want this child, so don't say it to your children.

Instead, talk things over with your husband or partner, a trusted friend, or someone else who can sympathize. Choose someone you can really trust to keep the conversation private. It can be very helpful to talk with some other adoptive parents or grandparents and hear their stories.

Adoption process.

The adoption process may be a challenging experience: exhausting, grueling and expensive, and especially difficult if it follows years of trying to conceive.

Or, your adult child might be very happy with the valuable support and education from adoption agency social workers, and find a community of other adoptive parents who become treasured friends. Your child may feel good about moving forward in a process that does lead to becoming a parent, even if it takes a long time.

Or *all* of the above.

It's going to involve what seem like vast quantities of paper, and usually – but not always – long waits. The adoptive parents-to-be can feel out of control of the most important thing in their lives.

> "First time they laid eyes on Mark, he was an adorable little child, not quite two years old. But he was left in his crib, not picked up and loved, and they heard foster parents yell at him. They said, 'We want him right now, right now.' And they pushed and they did get him very quickly, and he's thriving now."

Adoptive parents-to-be appreciate a cheerful, patient attitude from waiting grandparents during all this.

Not feeling like the real parent.

Adoptive parents may think that everything that is difficult, awkward, or is not going well is because their child is adopted. If they're first time parents, they don't realize that parents who give birth also feel ambivalent or overwhelmed, and may not love their baby instantly. They may not know that everybody finds parenting hard.

Lisa talks about the first night with her new baby. She tells the story openly now, hoping it will be helpful to other adoptive parents. The infant cried, dozed for a few minutes, and went back to crying. In the middle of an endless night of walking, rocking, and carrying him around, helpless to comfort him, she thought, "I can't do this." Lots of parents have thought that. Lisa was fearful that she actually couldn't parent her child and she really thought that in the morning she would have to call the social worker and send the baby back. She tells what did happen the next morning, too. Around three in the morning, her baby fell asleep and so did she. When the baby woke at dawn, her husband hustled the infant out of the room and fed him in another part of the house. Father and son watched the sun come up together, and then they took a walk around the neighborhood. When Lisa finally woke up after eight hours of sleep, she felt great, and she never looked back.

Most new parents feel awkward and incompetent. What Lisa didn't know then is that some mothers give birth and then wonder if it was a terrible mistake. Just about everybody, at some point, has painful doubts about their ability to be a good parent and most parents at times feel overwhelmed, frustrated, or inept. But if their child is adopted they can attribute those feelings to the adoption, wondering if a child born to them would be easier to understand (probably not). They may think that had they given birth to this baby they would naturally know how to stop her crying (they wouldn't) or they'd be instantly adept at getting her into a snowsuit and then buckled safely into her car seat (not easy for anyone).

Adoptive parents sometimes feel they have to justify having the children, and show they are worthy. They may be hypervigilant, and anxious. They may not feel entitled to have the child, especially if they aren't perfect … and no one is.

Some adoptive parents don't experience this at all, of course, but as a grandmother it may be useful for you to know it's common and natural if you see it happening with your adult child.

The first days and weeks may be harder than expected.

Other people may naively ask questions that minimize adoption, making it sound second rate. This isn't done out of malice, yet it can be upsetting especially in the early weeks or months when new parents are told myths or clichés such as the mistaken idea that a pregnancy is sure to follow an adoption.

The new parents may feel sad and angry and powerless, too, if they know or suspect their child was neglected or treated badly before they were able to adopt him. They wish desperately that they had had him from the moment of birth so they could protect him. You may feel this yourself as you hold this child, and get to know him.

I can't complain.

The new parents may also feel that they should not have any mixed or negative reactions. After waiting so long, and making so much effort to become parents, how can they say they're exhausted, or that it's not fun? Birth parents are expected to complain a lot; there are many books on the market now on how difficult and tiring raising children is. Adoptive parents often think that's not allowed for them. Other people may even make remarks like, "Just be glad you finally got him."

It's challenging because love might not be instant, but the lost sleep, effort, and strain are.

So, for many reasons, those long-awaited first days can be harder than imagined.

This is my child.

It can be upsetting when, in the early weeks or months after adoption, the news of the new child is greeted with questions from friends or coworkers about the "real" parents, or the new parents are asked if they have "any children of your own."

All new parents need to claim the child as theirs. Every parent looks at their child, looking for similarities, physical resemblances, shared traits and talents. Biological parents see physical resemblance even when it's not there, or at least no one else can see it. A round-faced sleeping newborn is said to have "his father's eyes," and a fractious toddler is fondly excused for being "just like" a temperamental, emotional parent. Adoptive parents look for signs of connection and similarity, too, and in much the same ways.

Names are very important to any new parent, and parents often spend lots of time looking for the right one, trying out various names. Months can be spent discussing and considering them. It's a way of picturing the child as a real person, and a way of claiming him, making him part of the lineage, and the family. For an adoptive parent it may be important to name their child in a way that emphasizes membership in the family. They may also need to keep the name the child already has been given, perhaps as a middle name. If the child is internationally adopted, many parents want to make sure the child has a name from her culture of origin. If you are still getting used to the idea of the adoption, think ahead so you will be prepared – and happy – to hear this grandchild called by a name important to you, perhaps your own spouse's or parent's name.

Although it's rarely mentioned, grandparents can go through the same stage, of not feeling entitled to the child and looking for ways to feel she's theirs, or feel they are entitled to have her.

> "I needed to claim her, I didn't feel like her grandmother because she didn't look like me, like anybody in the family. I loved her completely, I would have done anything for her, but it didn't seem like she was mine, I sort of thought we'd have to give her back. I wasn't sure I had a right to her, this delightful, perfect baby granddaughter. I used to take care of her every Monday but I felt like a babysitter. Of course I couldn't say this to anybody. One day when I had her, my arms were getting tired carrying her, and I put her in the baby carrier on my back. I went to check in the mirror to make sure she was in there securely. I saw us together and suddenly it looked right. I said to her, 'You are right where you belong, right where you would be if you were back in Korea, carried on your grandma's back, only now it's me.' She just looked so natural; we looked natural together that way. So that was the turning point. Right after that, I brought a picture of her into my office. She is the joy of my heart."

Grandmaternal feelings develop when you think of yourself as a grandmother and become attached, and begin to love your grandchild. For many women, it's the same process no matter how the child enters the family. Sometimes it's instantaneous and sometimes it's not. For some women, grandmaternal feelings develop differently with adoption.

For Claudia, the attachment to her fourth grandchild was a bit slower because the child was adopted.

> "I remember it was a little harder to connect and yet when you see your kids loving this baby as much as their others … It took me a little time, because we didn't go through the birth, I was with my daughter for the births of the other babies. But now I love them the same, you get to the same place. It's seeing your own child be a parent to them."

Another grandmother wrote to me about how much it meant to see her own daughter happy,

> "To see her after these years of waiting and doing everything to have a baby, finally with her arm casually tucking little Tyler against her hip while she moves around the kitchen…"

One emotional phone call was all it took for Lorna to bond with the newest member of her family. Her son and daughter-in-law held the baby they were adopting in the hospital on the first day of her life.

> "My son called me on the cell phone, and he said, 'Oh, Mama, she's so tiny and she's beautiful and she's going to be ours.' I was just bawling, sitting in the grocery store parking lot in my car. Just bawling. I loved her without even seeing her."

For many grandmothers, the day the adoption becomes legal makes a difference. Melanie, whose story we read in Chapter 3, was eager to welcome her first grandchild, but felt tentative until the child was legally adopted. He was placed with her daughter and son-in-law as a foster child, and the social worker said it was almost certain that they would be able to adopt him. The parents bonded with him right away, organized their lives around him, and referred to him as their son. At that point, Melanie, who hadn't seen him yet, didn't feel quite like a grandmother. She sent presents, she supported her daughter. She still waited anxiously for the court date. Her daughter called from the steps of the courthouse right after the adoption was final, and Melanie, in her kitchen, burst into happy tears. She immediately scheduled a trip to visit her new grandchild, told all her friends, and put up pictures of him in her house.

Some adoption agencies, where it's possible, create a ritual with birth parents and other relatives formally handing the child to the adoptive parents, and entrusting them with his care. This can be a lovely and comforting moment for everyone.

Some families may mark the adoption with emotionally significant gifts, and many create a lifebook for their child, which is similar to a scrapbook but with an age appropriate story of the child's life and adoption.

Think ahead about how you could participate, if invited, in any of these lovely rituals. You might offer a meaningful gift. It doesn't have to be expensive or elaborate. A children's book that your own children enjoyed, lovingly inscribed, or a hand knitted hat, could be perfect. If you have saved baby clothes that your own children wore, this could be a nice time to present them. Or you might write a letter for the child to read when she's older, describing her arrival from your point of view, or a snapshot of yourself and your household on the day she arrived. Chapter 14 on Family History, has some ideas, and Chapter 5 on Celebrations has other ideas, for welcoming this child.

How little children think.

Small children may be surprised to find out that an adult was adopted. They may think "adopted" means a characteristic of a child, like themselves. They may be quite confused the first time they meet an adult who tells them he was adopted. When younger, the transracially adopted child may not even realize that to other people, the adoption is visible. When just a little older, the same child may be uncomfortably aware of not looking like his parents, and feel very conspicuous. This can happen at varying rates and in different ways even to siblings in the same family.

Preschoolers may also surprise you because they can repeat what parents have carefully told them about adoption, yet they don't really understand it at all. They may think that everybody in their family is adopted or that everybody of their own gender is. A little boy may conclude that he and Daddy are adopted because he knows there is something they have in common but he doesn't really comprehend what exactly it is yet. Or, they often think all little children are adopted, that's just how it works. A little boy was heard asking his friend, "Where were you adopted from?" It never occurred to him that his friend wasn't adopted, like he was. All this is part of normal childhood cognitive development.

Even though children don't understand everything, it's still useful to talk naturally about it all, and explain. They'll understand more as they grow, just as they do about everything, and they'll know that adoption is something they can talk and ask about.

Many preschoolers who acquire a sibling see the infant as a usurping intruder and suggest the baby be sent back. The parents laugh over their young child asking after a week or so when the baby is going "back to the hospital," or suggesting that today would be a good time to take him back. Siblings of adopted children may have exactly the same feelings. A three-year-old who had a new baby brother asked his parents several times, "When are you taking him back to Columbia?"

Preschoolers are quite self-centered, and most love to hear about themselves when they were babies, things they did or said when they were younger, and the details of their adoption. They see the adoption as their own story and don't empathize yet with feelings of their parents – either birth parents or adoptive parents.

As they mature, that changes. When they gain a more realistic idea of adoption, they often start wishing and pretending that they were born to their parents who are raising them. As they get to school age, they will develop a more complex view that may include some sadness, some speculating about the birth parents, and questions about why they were placed for adoption.

You are probably familiar with the idea of telling adopted children that they were "chosen." The aim was to make them feel loved and wanted. This was common practice years ago and even if you never adopted, you probably heard this explanation given. Now it's not considered the best way to talk about it. Children take things literally, and they are likely to picture a room full of babies with adoptive parents wandering around looking for the one they want. Instead of the desired effect, it can make them feel anxious. Why were they chosen? If they stop being good or special, in whatever way it was, will they be sent back, or be a disappointment? Also, this explanation is not really true. Parents choose to adopt, but they don't pick their child out in the way this statement implies. So it's better not to say this to your grandchild, even with the best intentions.

In school.

The child may encounter intensive questioning from other children by the time he is in school, whether he looks like his adoptive parents or not, but especially if he does not. Even well-intentioned teachers and other school staff may question him tactlessly about the adoption, or may interpret everything he does or says as caused by the adoption. Some may be sure that adopted children are always "troubled" or "have problems." This can lead to ignoring ways the school or other agency needs to improve its services by blaming any difficulties the child has on the adoption, rather than on what's going on in the classroom.

Some schools still have family tree projects, or ask children to bring in baby pictures, which will probably embarrass your grandchild if he doesn't have such pictures, or has to explain his origins to everyone. Your grandchild's parents may be caught off guard when something like this happens, and rush to respond amid all their other parenting responsibilities. Or, they may be proactive, talking to each teacher before the school year starts. See Chapter 14 on Family History, for ways grandparents can help support the child with a positive, confident view of the family.

Adopting an older child.

When a child past infancy is adopted into your family, there's more to getting ready. The child has lost familiar settings and people, and will need time and understanding to adjust. A grandmother eager to welcome and nurture this child, excited to finally step into the role of grandmother, can find it hard to be patient, to wait until everyone has settled in and the child is ready to meet new people. Or, she may also need some time to adjust herself, to change the pictures in her mind of fantasy baby grandchildren, and to include this actual older child, who has a personality, and a history.

Adults may think that adoption by a stepparent or foster parent will be a wonderful solution for an older child, who already lives in the family. The child may feel the same way, but he may not. Or he may struggle with intense mixed feelings. He may not want to be adopted, even by a much loved stepparent, out of loyalty to the birth parent. This is not a rejection of your adult child's parenting or of you as a grandparent. In fact, when important adults accept and empathize with the child's feelings, they create a stronger and more comfortable bond. Look for ways to celebrate the new connection the child has to the adult who is raising her, while accepting her mixed feelings and her need to also stay connected to the other people who have been important in her life.

Mother's Day, Father's Day, birthdays and Adoption Day.

The family may celebrate the day the child first came home with them, or the day the adoption became legal. Some parents call this Adoption Day, or Family Day, or Gotcha Day. Some parents have a party, others have a solemn ceremony of gratitude, some a family outing with favorite activities for all. Children may appreciate acknowledgement of this part of their lives at one point, and change their minds later. A young child can be delighted with a party focused on her, all the talk about how beloved she is, even favorite foods and presents—what could be better! Such a celebration can be a joyous day for you, too, and something you look forward to every year. You might tell her every year about the time you first saw her picture, or held her, and how happy you were. If you don't live nearby, you might call or send a card, to let her know what a joyous and important day this is for you.

Yet later on that child might want to stop observing this anniversary because it makes her feel different, or draws the attention of peers to her being adopted. Or the observance may become calmer and simpler, but be deeply meaningful and comforting as the child matures. If there are both adopted and nonadopted siblings in a family, parents have to figure out what will feel best, and feel fair, to all their children.

Either the parents, or an older adopted child, may find Mother's Day, Father's Day, and birthdays complex and full of mixed emotions.

Especially if there was a long wait and struggle to have a family, these special days may carry an extra layer of happiness and gratitude for the parents. You may find that you feel this way, too.

> "It seems like he's always been ours, and my kids just had to go farther to get him and bring him home. He's just a wonder, a precious gift. On his birthday every year I make a donation in his honor to an organization that benefits children, and I am full of gratitude all day."

Everyone may also think sadly of the biological parents, wondering where they are and if they are all right. A grandparent can feel this way, too, on birthdays or any time. A grandmother wrote,

> "I felt so sad for her biological family. When I was alone, I would find tears running down my face thinking of them, wishing so much I could somehow, somehow, let them know she is happy and well. Find them and bring a letter,

appear to them in a dream, anything, something. Especially the grandmothers, could I somehow reach out to them and tell them, she's safe, she's loved, we will tell her about you."

For the child, her birthday may revive questions about why she was placed for adoption, and about the birth parents. A child may simply revel in friends, party venues, and presents one year, and be moody, teary, or angry another year, as she copes with her identity as an adoptee.

In an open adoption, this may be a time to send the birth parents pictures and a letter about how the child is doing, or the birth parents may visit on this day. These communications can be comforting for everyone involved.

It can be a challenge for grandparents to accept that the adopted child has sustained a real loss. It's important to accept and understand if your grandchild feels sorrow at the loss of his birth parents and other biological relatives, and at the loss of the full story about the beginning of his life. It might seem to the grandparents that he's come to live with loving, capable parents, and he has you, so why would he feel sad? In fact, he needs your support in order to make sense of his feelings and origins.

None of these feelings mean rejection of you, your adult children, or the life he has with you. As a grandmother, you can plan presents, develop birthday traditions that are lots of fun, and help kids make a Mother's Day or Father's Day card for their parents, all while staying open and sensitive to your grandchild's range of feelings.

Everything isn't about adoption.

The mother of an adopted daughter said,

> "We talk about it, she has a picture of her birth mom in her room, we celebrate the day we got her. I wonder if we've done enough, or right. But right now her whole life is about gymnastics and dance, her close friends are all in that. If she had to describe herself, it would be 'gymnast,' or 'ballerina.' It wouldn't be anything about adoption."

Lisa, mother of two adopted children, worried when her second child walked late, very late. The child was still crawling when everybody else her age was walking. Even though pediatricians could find nothing wrong, it was frightening and led to endless loops of worry about what the cause could be and what other developmental problems might show up next. Thinking this way made Lisa wonder anxiously about what had happened to her daughter before the adoption, what she didn't know. No one could answer those questions. Lisa says now,

> "Actually the only helpful thing that ever happened was something my mom said. She just said very casually that I walked really late too. It just reminded me that everything isn't about adoption."

The grandmother's calm, and her long-term point of view, helped Lisa stay calm and optimistic. Within a few months, her daughter was toddling, and then walking, then running.

There is no simple answer to the meaning of adoption in a child's life, and no single, correct way for families to feel, to think about it, or to handle it. As a grandparent, you want to be sensitive and supportive of your grandchild, and also of your adult child and child-in-law.

It's a mistake to act as if the adoption doesn't matter, and shouldn't be talked about, as if it never happened. A deep and loving bond with the child doesn't mean forgetting his origins. If important adults never talk about it, the child can't either.

It's also possible to make children anxious if we act like being adopted is the most important thing about them, by talking about it constantly.

No one gets this balance perfectly, and you don't have to either. The child's needs and feelings develop over time. As you get to know your grandchild, and see the meaning various parts of his life have for him, your love, your commitment to him, and your willingness to hear him will be a valuable and enjoyable resource. You will figure out how to re-adjust as the child grows, and sees things differently than he did earlier. You can respond sensitively when adoption is on his mind, or shaping his reactions, and when it's not.

If the family includes siblings who are both adopted, they may not react the same way as they get older. One might focus on the adoption, while to another it is much less important.

A mother of two daughters sent me this story in an email,

"We adopted our two daughters, and they are completely opposite in personality, including in the way they think about the adoption. The older is more of a planner, very articulate. She has her future planned out, and she has always been interested in her origins. The younger is more happy go lucky, and always following her sister. We once had this conversation at dinner, when Amber was eight and Samantha was four:

Amber, [our elder daughter] When I'm grown up, I'm going to find my birth mother.

Us, the parents: Sure, good idea, we'll help you.

Samantha, our younger daughter: Me too, me too. I'm going to do that, too. I'm going to find Amber's birth mother, too."

Other people's questions.

You may get lots of comments and questions from friends and acquaintances. While many will be happy congratulations, others may make you uncomfortable. Some of these are the same things your adult children are being asked, and some will be directed specifically to you by people who are curious or anxious but don't want to confront the parents. Adoptive parents and grandparents are often asked about the "real parents" or about "what is wrong" with the child or even whether the "real parents were on crack." Friends, relatives or people you scarcely know may tell you that adopted children "have problems" or "never adjust." One grandmother, when she was happily telling everyone she knew about her newly arrived grandson, got a critical lecture from one friend condemning international adoption, while another asked repeatedly whether the birth parents were in jail. Negative stereotypes kept these friends from sharing her joy.

Many grandparents and parents are very surprised when strangers or acquaintances demand to be told "How much did he cost?" or ask if the child is healthy.

"My other daughter has a biological kid. No one would

dream of asking such personal things, no one asks if the pregnancy was a birth control failure, or if her husband is really the father. But there don't seem to be any limits on what people think they can ask about adoption. If you don't fit the mold, don't conform to expectations, then you have no privacy, there is no politeness."

If the child is of a different race, then the adoption is visible, leading to questions and comments from strangers. Chapter 12, Multiracial Families, has suggestions from parents and grandparents who have thought through how to handle this.

Some parents and grandparents answer questions more thoroughly when the children aren't present, using the questions as a chance to educate people about adoption. When the children are hearing the conversation, the way you handle it is primarily for them. Your tone is important; try to keep it calm and cheerful. You can express your pride and delight in the children, show that you are proud of them, and also model for them that they don't have to tell their life stories to people they don't know.

A mother of two daughters has often gotten the question, "Are they real sisters?" She simply says,

"Sure they are. Watch them fight."

An adoptive grandmother suggests,

"Just say yes. Then if they persist, ask them, why do you need to know?"

The grandmother of two adopted grandchildren, now in their teens, says,

"It's hardest for me with people I know but am not real close to, who ask for way more information than I want to give them, way more than they would tell me about themselves. I can't just start to talk about something else or walk away like I do with a stranger. So, after bumbling a few times, now I say, 'This is his story, and his parents want to let him decide when he gets older how he wants to share it. I don't know how he's going to feel, let's leave it till then.'"

Another grandmother says,

"You can see it coming after a while, people who are staring and then approach, asking something like, 'Are you a foster mother?' I answer with a question about something else, like isn't this a great bookstore? Or I'll ask, I'm sorry, have we met? They say no ... and I can just nod and smile and say something pleasant, and leave."

A house full of teenagers, and a new grandbaby, gave a grandmother a chance to educate. She had time to think about what she wanted to do, and she found a way to set limits on questions that felt intrusive, but to do it in a kind and informative way.

"We had two teenagers at home, and our nephew in college was living with us that summer. So the house was full, with them and all their friends. And our new grandbaby, who is adopted from China, was with us several times a week. One young woman, a friend of our daughter who was around a lot, she was about nineteen I guess, kept watching the baby and staring at her. Every now and then she would ask something, like, 'did her parents have to go to China to get her?' Or, another time, 'was she in an orphanage? What does she eat?' So after this went on for a while, I took this young woman aside and said, Is she the first Chinese person you've met? It seems like you have a lot of questions, let's talk about all of them. I waited until the baby was down for her nap, and sat down with this young woman, and we talked it all over. She seemed curious but also kind of anxious about it all. I told her a lot about adoption and international adoption and cleared up some misconceptions she had, which are common. Then, I told her, let me make a suggestion. You didn't know, but people ask her parents those things all the time and as she gets older, it's going to make her embarrassed, so it's better not to ask in front of the kids. There are a lot of good books on this stuff."

The grandparents' understanding and support can be important to both the parents and the child. Responding sensitively to your grandchild's experience of being adopted can deepen your connection to her. At other times, your relationship will be like that of any grandmother and grandchild, focused on enjoying each other and things you do together.

Try this:

> • During the seemingly endless waiting times don't keep asking your adult child if they've heard anything, or how long it's going to be. Stay upbeat. They'll tell you when they know.

> • Don't repeat the myth that if they adopt, they will conceive.

> • Remember that adoption is part of your grandchild's identity and experience of the world. What that means may vary over time, and for different children.

> • Just as with the arrival of any new child, remember to pay attention to the siblings and let them know they are also important and special.

> • Your grandchild needs acceptance of all her feelings and questions about her origins, her birth parents, and being adopted.

> • Never ask about your adopted grandchild's "real" parents. They are right there in front of you. Don't refer to the child as your "adopted grandchild." You don't say my "genetic grandchild," and saying "adopted grandchild" implies you have a different –and perhaps lesser –relation. Gently correct other people if they use this language.

> • Birthdays may bring up many emotions for your

grandchild, including sadness, and questions about birth parents, along with the usual enjoyment of birthday celebrations. You can learn to enjoy parties and plan presents, while staying sensitive to these feelings.

Resources

Nonfiction

The Family of Adoption, by Joyce Maguire Pavao

Adopting the Older Child, by Claudia Jewett Jarrett

China Ghosts: My Daughter's Journey to America, My Passage to Fatherhood, by Jeff Gammage

Are Those Kids Yours? by Cheri Register

Weaving a Family: Untangling Race and Adoption, by Barbara Katz Rothman

Fiction

Digging to America, by Anne Tyler

Then She Found Me, by Elinor Lipman

Brother and Sister, by Joanna Trollope

Theory of Relativity, by Jacquelyn Mitchard

Film

Juno

12

Multiracial Families

Grandparents can help grandchildren develop
a positive self image that includes all of their
racial heritage.

What has changed in your lifetime.

Although there have always been some multiracial families, much has changed in your lifetime.

In the 1950s, half of the states still had laws prohibiting interracial marriage. These laws remained in effect in seventeen states when the 1967 Supreme Court decision aptly named *Loving v. Virginia* struck down the last laws prohibiting people of different races from marrying. Since then, the number and percentage of interracial marriages has increased. As our country becomes more diverse, and barriers to interracial unions fall, more mixed-race babies are born. The 2000 Census reported that nearly seven million Americans consider themselves multiracial, and the 2010 Census reported nine million.

Interracial domestic adoption and international adoption also create multiracial families, and these too have increased in recent decades. Although a few transracial adoptions were made in the middle of the 20th century, they became far more common after 1970, and include both domestic and international adoption. In the last quarter of the 20th century, Americans adopted more than a quarter of a million children born outside the United States, many of a different race than the parents. Added to that are households that bring a stepchild and stepparent of different races together.

For a grandmother, these changes have happened during her lifetime. She may have always been comfortable with the idea or she may have struggled to adjust.

Multiracial families are formed and structured in many ways. They include parents of different races and their mixed-race children, single parents with mixed-race children, and families who have adopted children of a different race than the parents. Children may be the same race as one of their parents, but not the same as the other one, or not the same as a step parent. Children may be biracial, and have an appearance that is ambiguous to other people, or they may be seen by other people as belonging to just one race while they identify themselves as biracial.

Good to know.

It's useful to grandparents to understand their grandchildren's experience of race, especially if it's different from the grandparents' own. It can make your adult children's parenting easier to understand and support, too.

This is an enormous and complex topic, including a huge variety of life events, and reactions to them. We won't attempt to cover nearly all of them, but simply to describe some common experiences that may happen in your family, and some descriptions of how other grandparents have thought about, reacted to, and handled these.

What information and ideas are useful for your family depends on many factors, including where the grandchildren live, family composition, and the parents' beliefs and plans. Being part of the only multiracial family in her community is not like living someplace where her family blends in. It matters whether a child's race matches one or both of the parents. It matters whether the child and the family mainly encounter outright hostility, or mild curiosity, or if they live in a generally supportive neighborhood, with other people like themselves. It matters whether or not the child sees other people who look like her in her extended family, her neighborhood, and her school.

The one drop rule.

If you are not already familiar with this idea, it's good to know about. The one drop rule is a custom, a belief, and at times has been the law. It means the idea that anyone with any African ancestors is defined as African American, even if the person had far more white ancestors, looked white, or looked more white than African American. Originally rooted in slavery, this idea came to be custom and belief among both whites and African Americans. The one drop rule has become more controversial recently, as biracial people and their parents claim the right to a choice of how to identify, or to a biracial identity, instead.

"Colorblind" doesn't work for children.

One thing that won't work is to ignore race, and tell ourselves and our grandchildren that it doesn't matter. Race makes a big difference in how people are treated, and children will find this out right away. They need help from the trusted adults in coping with this.

Young children.

What race means to young children will depend on many factors, including what they know or have been told already, what they have seen in the behavior of important adults, and their developmental stage. At one point they may notice physical differences without assigning much meaning to them, at another point – often earlier than adults expect or hope – they become very aware of racial stereotypes and derogatory ideas about race and appearance. They often pay attention first to skin color, as they notice all kinds of details about the world, but that doesn't mean they understand or are interested in the concept of race.

How little children think.

The ideas of your toddler and preschool grandchildren may be quite surprising, until you remember they don't think the way grownups do. After about age two, they can use symbols, they can play pretend games, using toys as props and taking roles in the pretending (although they still can't always tell what's realistic, or distinguish what they wish was true from what is actually so). They start to be able to see things from another person's point of view, although they aren't very good at it, and still mainly see the world as revolving around themselves.

At this age, they still don't think the way you do. Many adults are surprised to realize that very young children may believe they are going to grow up to look just like, and be the same race, as their parents. It's logical from a toddler's point of view. Preschoolers don't realize that gender is permanent, either. They often believe that gender can spontaneously change as they grow up, too.

They may also express a wish to resemble one of their parents. Parents can be upset and worried when a mixed race child or a child of color expresses a wish to have blond hair or white skin like one parent. This certainly can happen because they have heard their own race or appearance talked about negatively. Or, it can be just because they identify with their parents, and want to be like them in all ways. At this age, they try to involve themselves in whatever you are doing. They copy their parents' ways of speaking, and yours, too. It can be very cute and amusing to hear a parent's favorite phrases spoken by a three-year-old. In the same way, they want to look like their parents, too.

Small children think differently than adults about categories. They might appear to understand race, perhaps they have been read children's books addressing the issue, or their parents might have tried to explain. They still don't understand how it applies to them. It's useful to know that small children think that something can be in only one category at a time.

As an example, a little boy I know had been given a toy lion by his grandparents, which he carried around with him and showed to everyone. He'd often be asked by friendly adults, "What's the lion's name?"

"Lion," he replied. He couldn't think of the lion as being named more than one thing. It was a lion. He got a little annoyed that adults kept asking the same silly question.

In the same way, young children may surprise you by not realizing that racial categories describe their own family. An adult can read an appropriate children's book, talk about how certain differences in skin color and other physical characteristics are due to race, explain that all people are beautiful and valuable. The child seems to understand, and parents and grandparents feel they've done a good job, and they have. That doesn't mean that very young children understand that these ideas apply to them, or people important to them. To a toddler, Mommy is Mommy. She can't also be in another category. She can't be Mexican, or Korean, too, even though a stranger, or someone in a book, is.

Children this age also mix up reality, pretend, and wishes.

A family with two small children took a while to make sense of their older daughter's claims. She's four, and has a Korean father and an Irish-American mother. She also has a one-year-old little brother, who she sees as a serious rival, as older siblings often do.

She started telling everyone that she was half Korean and half white, but her little brother wasn't. No, she said firmly, he's Brazilian. She agrees that he has the same parents as she does, but she's still sure he's Brazilian. It's not always easy to figure out what preschoolers are thinking. This child's parents eventually came to understand it this way.

> "She goes to Korean preschool, with other kids half Korean like her, and also Korean kids, they learn to write Korean, and do crafts, and it's really fun. Her best friend is Korean, and also goes to this preschool with her. So what we think now is that the Korean part seems more interesting and high status to her, and more like her best friend. We realized she's always saying her little brother can't do what she can do, doesn't know what she knows. So she wants to exclude him from being Korean, and she wants the preschool to always be for her and her friends, and he'll never get to go there. Where she got the Brazilian we don't know, except that we go to a Brazilian bakery in the neighborhood and they have a baby and when her brother was newborn, she was jealous like most kids, and she suggested we give our baby to them.
>
> "She obviously doesn't realize that she looks white to most people, and he looks much more Asian."

No matter what they are thinking, young children can start learning positive ideas about all kinds of people. There are wonderful multiracial children's books and a variety of books for parents on countering racial stereotypes and raising children with positive ideas of themselves, and of people who are not like them. Some are listed in the Resource section at the end of this chapter, and your local librarian is a good source for more. *Does Anybody Look Like Me? A Parent's Guide to Raising Multiracial Children,* by Donna Jackson Nakazawa, has lots of good ideas for talking to children.

Children will gradually understand more and more, and they'll also understand that race, and skin color are OK to talk about.

Starting school.

Whether it's daycare, nursery school, or kindergarten, this is the time when children move out of the more protected and controlled world of their family, and are exposed to more people. A child may feel conspicuous and be the victim of teasing or harassment. Even if that doesn't happen, she may hear racist remarks from adults. Children may be questioned by other children, asked, "What are you?" if their race is not apparent, or be pressured to explain their family, if not everyone in the family looks like the same race.

As children get a little older, and go to elementary school, they think and talk more logically. Their lives begin to involve more people outside the family, they become part of groups of children, and they have friends who are very important to them. They get better at negotiating about their play with their friends, although they still need adult help to learn social skills.

Children don't want to be different.

Children like to connect and be accepted. They don't want to be the different ones. Because of this, your grandchildren's parents may think carefully about where to live, looking for a town or neighborhood where their child will see other people like himself. They may join a social organization of families like theirs. They may look hard for schools and try to find one with supportive staff and a diverse group of students, so their child does not stand out.

"My granddaughter is adopted from India, she's dark and looks quite unlike the rest of the family. When she was in kindergarten, I was there for her birthday party. Her parents had invited lots of families, and there were many little children from India, with their white parents. I knew they had stayed in touch with the other adoptive families they met. At the party I saw so vividly how wonderful it is that my granddaughter regularly sees other families that look just like hers. I hope they can stay in her life as she grows up."

This can mean extra driving, or other inconvenience, even moving, but it can give your grandchild an important peer group and a comfortable secure environment.

"We switched to a synagogue where there are lots of other adopted Chinese girls. They have grown up together, gotten bat mitzvahed together."

Classes in dance, music or other arts are a great way for children to learn about and participate in a culture that is part of their heritage, and may be a place to connect with other children and adults of their race.

Other people's questions.

As the child goes outside her own home, relationships with other people and the reactions of other people are going to be more and more important in her life.

Everyone needs to make sense of the world and categorize what they see. In this country most people think of a family as two opposite sex, same race parents and their biological children. A family that deviates from that, or appears to, confuses them. Race is important in our culture, so most people use it as an important way to classify and identify what they see, too. Some are uncomfortable if they don't know what race someone is, so they ask, or try to figure it out.

Both parents and grandparents will probably find that other people's discomfort and curiosity lead to a lot of questions, either the occasional friendly conversation starter, or sometimes very persistent intrusive questions from strangers and from people you barely know.

Most of these people don't mean any harm. Yet the questions can make children feel uncomfortably conspicuous, or that there is something wrong with their family, or something wrong with them. If it only happened once or twice, it might not matter but many families find that the kinds of questions discussed below are frequent. Hearing remarks about how they look different from their parents can be deeply embarrassing to children and can make them feel that they are not really connected to their parents or that their family is strange.

Your grandchild needs to know that there is nothing wrong, odd, or embarrassing about himself or his origins. He also needs to know that he doesn't owe the world an explanation and needn't answer personal questions. His origins and his family are his own to share or not as he decides. He does not have to explain himself to strangers.

However, you also don't want to give him the impression that being part of a multiracial family is embarrassing, or that race shouldn't be talked about.

It can be hard to figure out what to do. You may not always get it right, and there's no one simple answer about what "right" is. It will change over time. You and the parents may decide to use these incidents as an opportunity to educate, or you may just want to protect your privacy. It's different when the children can understand than when they are babies. Siblings are different. This issue may just not bother one sibling much, while another is angry and humiliated, and glumly withdraws when strangers keep asking her where she's from or how her parents got her.

It's much easier if you know what to expect. You can plan on how you want to respond, rather than being overwhelmed, surprised and angry, and thinking later of what you wish you had said.

> "I thought it wouldn't happen to me because I live in Cambridge Massachusetts, the world capital of diversity and multiculturalism. It did, though. Every time we left the house, strangers would approach us and question us, even touch her hair. After a while I decided I didn't want to be upset all the time, and defensive, so I thought about it and made some plans of how I would deal with the various questions I usually got, which are very repetitive, and now I feel more in control."

A mother who adopted three children of a different race than hers suggests,

"I don't want to have a conflict in front of the kids, but I want to make it clear they don't have to answer to people. So I will offer to call the person. I have even given people my card saying, 'Let's talk on the phone, but I can't get into it now.' No one has ever called."

Whose kid is that?

While your grandchild is a baby, always held and carried, or in a stroller with an attentive adult, everyone sees that baby as belonging to that adult. Belong in what way? For a white grandmother with any non-white child, people who don't know you will typically assume the child is adopted and they may start a conversation by asking where he's from.

If the child actually is adopted, some families are happy to talk about it. Occasionally it turns into a connection with another adoptive family with children of the same background, who are asking because they think you might be part of the same community of families.

Other grandmothers just say the name of the town where the child lives and then move on, or firmly change the subject.

"Bellingham. Where are you from?"

Of course, the assumption that the child is adopted is often wrong.

"I just tell them, 'You seem to be assuming that she is adopted. Actually, my daughter gave birth to her.'"

For an African-American grandmother, or another grandmother of color, with a white or white-appearing grandchild, strangers and acquaintances often assume the child is not part of her family, and ask if she is babysitting or running a day care.

"This is my granddaughter. I just say that, and walk away."

Anna says,

"I took my granddaughter, at age ten months, to the baby

music time at the library. The woman next to me took one look at her and demanded, 'What is she?' I was stunned, I fumbled, I said 'She's a baby, how old is yours?' This woman just repeated it louder and louder, 'What is she?' I got up and moved to another place in the circle. It was upsetting. I never went back."

Donna has grandchildren who look like her, and others who do not. She decided it's a chance to educate. She looks for chances to explain.

"I'm sure that I have said thoughtless things, too, in situations I'm not familiar with, or when something comes up that I have never thought about. I give everyone the benefit of the doubt, and try to raise awareness. If it's a friend, or someone I know slightly, I'll just talk really openly about how these questions make me feel, without blaming. I think some people feel like it's a normal social overture. When I remind them that they don't ask white people where they're from, most people get it. And I talk about how it's embarrassing for the kids. I've had some good conversations. I have to be a good listener, too."

Once a child is mobile, and more apt to be playing at some distance from you or her parents, the relationship is often missed completely by people who don't know you. At the playground, the library, lessons and sports, a doctor or dentist office, the parent and child are simply not seen as a family by people who don't know them. Of course the same happens to the grandmother with her grandchild. Adults will look around for the child's parent or caregiver while you are standing right there.

Florence Ladd and Marion Kilson's research about mothers raising biracial children is published in their book *Is That Your Child?* Some of the mothers they interviewed had the experience of not being recognized as their child's mother. Families I spoke with had the same experience.

To deal with this, some parents make a point of acting obviously like the parents, and giving easily recognized cues. They will hold their child's hand, or start a conversation with, "This is my daughter..."

Meeting new people, or arriving at a school, or a medical appointment, they learn to introduce themselves first, to avoid misunderstandings.

> "I've learned to start with, 'Hi, I'm Betsy and this is my daughter Elizabeth, we're here for her to see the hygienist' instead of saying, 'We have an appointment at three'. It's just easier."

The white father of a Korean daughter says that his daughter realized very early that they weren't seen as a family.

> "When we would be out in public she would make sure to call me dad frequently, she wanted people to know we were her parents. Later after she hit puberty, she didn't want people to think she was my girlfriend so she would always call me dad."

This same thing might well happen to you when out with your grandchild. The grandmother of an internationally adopted child found herself doing this without realizing it. She wrote to me in an email,

> "I have just realized since I talked with you about this, that I am not acting like I did with my own kids. I pick up my grandson after school, and when he seems friendly with another child there, I will go up to the parent, and introduce myself, I am Jakob's grandmother. When I was raising my own kids, it just sort of happened while we were all there together waiting at the school."

Because many families are both adoptive and multiracial, there is more on this topic in Chapter 11, on The Adopted Grandchild.

Oh, she looks just like you.

Some biracial children have an ambiguous appearance: other people can't classify them by race. These children, who have parents of different races, may be seen differently depending on which parent they are with. She may look white to others, if she is with only her white parent.

She may be seen as the same as her other parent's race when with only that parent. She will notice the treatment she gets.

People may talk to your grandchild differently, depending on what ethnic or racial group they assume she is part of. Appearance matters, but even just her name can elicit different treatment. People who don't know your family may be confused and look twice, or ask for an explanation if your grandchild's last name gives a perceived message that doesn't match her appearance, such as an Asian or African American child with a name that sounds Jewish or French.

A mother who had changed her name when she married told me,

> "People said very different things to me sometimes when I was Jean MacNamara than when I was Jean Cohen."

Parents of multiracial children also get a lot of comments on how good-looking their children are, sometimes including elaborate discussion of their features and statements that racially mixed people are the most beautiful. This is probably well meant, and it can be a bit confusing to figure out why it feels bad. It's a compliment, after all, and it's certainly not intended to be hostile. Many parents and grandparents don't like these comments because it's another way of saying their family is different, and it's usually said by adults who realize they've been staring at the child, and are a bit embarrassed. One grandmother handles it this way,

> "I just say, all kids are beautiful, aren't they?"

Full siblings may look very different.

One sibling can look much more like one parent, and be clearly seen as of that race. His full sibling can have a more ambiguous appearance, and therefore have a very different experience.

The parents in a multiracial family, with one white parent and one African American parent, told me how different things were for their two daughters. The older child looked clearly African American, and she always thought of herself as African American. Their younger daughter has lighter skin and a much more ambiguous appearance. She gets attention and questions, from strangers and from people she knows. She's very aware that how she does her hair and other details of how she presents herself can determine whether she is seen as African American, Puerto Rican, or whether people are uncertain—and some of them therefore ask. Friends her own age, and even some adults, have told her what race she "really" is, and strangers ask her questions like, "So, your father's Black, huh?" or "What are you?"

Parenting her has been more complicated. Her father, who is African American, says,

> "It's harder for her, it's taken up much more energy for her to decide who she is, and how to deal with other people. At times she has felt she doesn't fit in anywhere. She doesn't want to pass for white, but other people sometimes think she does."

Siblings may be different in other ways too.

If there is more than one child in the family, and they are of the same race or mixture of races, parents and grandparents hope the children can support each other, and help each other feel normal by sharing the same experience of the world. This often works wonderfully. It's great to look around the dinner table, or family photos, and see other people who look like you. But, like all the other issues in child raising, children are separate individuals, with widely divergent personalities from the beginning. They can be allies, and can really understand each other's experiences. They won't always react the same way, or feel the same.

Adolescents.

As your grandchildren get older, they are navigating the world without their families. They need to define themselves, in their own minds, and they will rethink what they've been told by parents, grandparents, and other influences. They need to figure out who they are, and want to be, on many dimensions.

Multiracial teens often experience intense pressure from peers to choose one race. Or, they may be repeatedly told even by adults, that they have to choose one. They may be told they "want to be white" if they do not decisively and exclusively identify with the non-white part of their heritage.

They are very often subject to intense questioning, from strangers and acquaintances who ask, "What are you?" Or even people who know them may tell them they "can't be" or "don't look like" the race they identify with.

> "My daughter is Vietnamese. She works in retail, and people often ask her ethnicity and then when she says Vietnamese, some argue with her saying, no you are Hawaiian, or no you look Chinese."

It's normal for teens to be self-conscious and it can be humiliating for them to be questioned and made to feel different.

Yet, you may be amazed at the way they get used to it, and that they can nonchalantly answer questions that you, as a grandparent, find very intrusive. When out with them in a public place you may find yourself stunned and upset at the kind of things that are said to them, and impressed at your teen grandchild's ability to cope.

As they work on this, many of them will probably be told by other people that they are not really part of the group they think they are part of. If they are biracial, or transracially adopted, they may consider themselves African-American, Guatemalan, Chinese, or Indian, yet find they have to prove to other people in this group that they belong. How they talk, whether they speak the relevant language, who they are friends with or date, what they know of the history and culture, can all be badges of belonging or things they have to do to be accepted. Food, ways of speaking or dressing, hair, and various cultural markers may become important as signs of authentically belonging to a group. Adolescents may try very hard to conform to the expectations, to prove they are "really" who they feel they are. They may decide to have friends, or date, only peers of one race.

Or they may insist on a biracial identity and refuse to be classified as one race.

If they choose a biracial identity, they will probably spend a lot of time explaining, insisting and countering other people's views. Institutional forms with boxes to check describing demographic information including race can become a big issue because they rarely offer the option of "multiracial."

One adolescent girl says,

> "I'm Black and I'm proud to be Black, but I'm really mul-
> tiracial. And if I just say I'm Black it's saying my mother
> doesn't exist. I won't do that."

Your grandchildren may reject the efforts of supportive adults to offer
an affirming racial identity and connection. The father of an adopted
Chinese daughter described this.

> "Now she does not identify with China or want people to
> say she's Chinese. She says, "I'm American." Her friend is
> half Chinese, raised by a Chinese mother and white father.
> The Chinese mother always invites our daughter to her
> house for Chinese food. She wants no part of it."

All this can take a lot of your grandchild's energy. It's a struggle that
can leave her hurting, angry, and insecure. But over time, this emotional
work, and examination of the meaning of identity, can also contribute
to an adolescent growing into a confident young person, who is more
secure, as can many kinds of struggle or stress that are successfully dealt
with. Some grandparents are amazed and proud of grandchildren whose
thoughtful awareness of both self and other people is much greater than
the grandparents' was at that age.

Siblings can make very different choices about how they think of
themselves and how they respond to peers, strangers, and important
adults in their lives, either because of how they look, or what school or
social group they are in … or for no reason you can see.

For some adolescents, racial identity is very important. For others,
it's not their biggest challenge in adolescence. They may focus on other
things. How they deal with this, and what it means to them, can vary
from one child to another. Like other aspects of parenting and grandparenting, you think you've learned a lot and know what to do and what
to say, after raising one child, and the next child is different. You are
back to wondering what to do, and what their behavior means.

If parents and grandparents have tried to support a positive biracial
identity that honors all of the child's heritage, they will probably be quite

dismayed to see their efforts swamped by other influences, interests, or peer group concerns.

We tried to teach them to appreciate all of their heritage, but …

One reason that some adolescents might reject a multiracial identity that the adults have tried to foster is that adolescents are figuring out what interests, talents, and ideas they want to be known for, and what kind of adult life they want. Adolescents are simpler thinkers than adults, and they have a lot to sort out. They may not be able to handle a complex multifaceted identity in their own minds, especially in addition to coping with pressure from others. It can seem easier to take a simpler stance, especially as they are busy defining other aspects of who they are.

These white adoptive parents told me about their sixteen-year-old son,

> "We wanted to honor his Guatemalan birthright. We have the art on display in our house, we learned about the culture, we learned to cook some dishes. We talked about it. We told him many times that we can go there, visit. I'm glad we did that. For now, he's not interested; he just says he's Jewish, which we also raised him as. That's it for him now. Maybe later he'll be interested in the Guatemalan part. Sometimes I think it's too complicated for him right now – he's sixteen and the world is rough for teens. Maybe he wants a simple answer, with people he's known all his life – our congregation is very warm, and welcoming. Later maybe he'll identify with both. We hope so, but we realize we've done what we can and it's his choice now."

When they leave for college, things can change again. They have a chance to remake themselves, claim a new identity, and they often find a very different social milieu.

A young woman, half Vietnamese and half white, wrote during her freshman year in college,

> "Growing up I never really thought about it. My town is mostly Caucasian and since I look very white I never felt

like I stuck out or anything. Also, living in the same town my whole life, everyone knew my racial background so there was never anything to explain and I never felt that people didn't know about this other half of me that wasn't apparent from looking at me.

"Then when I got to college, things were different. Getting involved with HAPA (Half-Asian People's Association) made me think more about racial identity and how rather than trying to be Asian or be Caucasian, it's possible to just be mixed or HAPA and that can be a category in and of its own. In this way, my conception of racial identity was greatly changed, and I'm still trying to wrap my head around it."

Grandmother's feelings and reactions.

When a white grandmother becomes part of a multiracial family, race becomes part of her daily life too.

"I'm white and I have two sets of grandchildren, one white and one family that is racially mixed and the children look Black. And it's been an education, how differently they are treated. The darker ones really are watched in stores, treated with suspicion. It's heartbreaking to me, and I do realize that African Americans deal with this all the time."

Some grandparents carefully plan to teach their grandchildren about family history and the culture they are from. You can teach them about the other cultures and races in their background, too. Grandparents can also have a role in teaching children to respect and value all people. In Chapter 14, Family History and Childhood Memories, are some ideas on how to do this, including teaching your grandchildren about your own and other people's ethnic background and history, talking about admirable people in your own lineage or group, as well as those different from you. You can have good times sharing the art and culture of the world with grandchildren, and at the same time give a message of inclusion and respect for everyone.

Angela, an African American grandmother in a mixed family, advises,

> "It's important that children learn that white people have varying cultures too and are not just the standard that makes other cultures 'exotic.'"

Parents and grandparents sometimes disagree.

It can be hard to understand your adult child's parenting choices. For some perspective, see Chapter 6, Parenting ... New and Improved? for a discussion of the many ways, in addition to racial issues, that your children are parenting under very different circumstances than you did.

An African American mother, married to a white man, with two biracial children says,

> "My kids look white. And we live in a very diverse, very accepting community and race isn't a big focus for me. I relate to all people. And our family isn't unusual here. This year, I am just starting a practice as a fee-only financial planner, and in addition to all the parenting stuff which is enough to keep most anyone busy, most of my focus is work, the clients, keeping up with new legislation. My parents and my aunts say to me, How are your kids going to know they're Black? I know they think the way I live isn't going to give my kids that, I know they're very critical of my parenting. So my aunts and my parents have the kids for visits in the summer, and try to immerse them in their version of Black culture. I know my aunts don't think I'm Black enough."

A white grandmother of biracial children felt strongly that her grandchildren would benefit from talk about race. She knew the parents didn't want her to do that.

> "Their parents never talk about race. If it were up to me, I would. I would be teaching the children about all the people they are descended from, all sides, I'd be teaching them some history, and the heroic people and accomplishments

in that history, and also talking about what stereotypes they are going to encounter. I know my daughter-in-law doesn't want that, neither of the parents do. They would flip, they would both be really upset with me, it's not my place, so I never say anything. I just show the kids I love them, and I think they are wonderful, and smart, and beautiful."

Parents of biracial children who are both African American and white know that the children will generally be seen as African American by other people. Some of these parents decide to raise their children as African Americans for this reason. To them, it seems best for their children to concentrate on a strong African American identity, since that's how the world will treat them.

Other parents see it differently. They think it's better for children to have a positive biracial identity that honors everything in their heritage and both sides of their family. They raise their children to think of themselves as biracial, and hope their child will identify as biracial.

Some grandparents worry that the parents' strategy is the wrong one. Many grandparents feel that a child who identifies as biracial is a child lost to their community. Actually, throughout human communities, the older generation often is worried about whether their children and grandchildren, as they go out into the world, will stay connected, identified, and be part of their group, their race or religion. To your grandchild, though, the multiracial identity doesn't mean leaving or rejecting the race of their grandparents. To them, it means acknowledging and including *all* of their family and heritage.

These can be difficult, painful topics in a family. Knowledgeable, aware people of good will can disagree.

Other issues can complicate the situation and make it hard to talk, or sort out, feelings and what it all means. People in each generation are shaped by what they have lived through. The next generation is living in a different world.

A mother in a multiracial family told me about the hardest parenting issue she and her husband faced. It was not what any of the grandparents, on either side, thought was important.

"My daughter is mixed, and we live in a mixed neighborhood, and she fits in. There's all kinds of families here, and people from all over the world. What we deal with that's difficult, is there is a huge range of income, and she is friends, good friends, with some kids who have a lot more money than we do. They go skiing in Europe over spring break. We could never do that. Even if we had that much money, we wouldn't spend it that way. And my daughter said to me, 'It makes me feel poor. And I know we're not.' This is the challenge of raising her here. Because it's only going to get worse. We need to teach her about our family's beliefs and why we live the way we do, and to feel good about that, and not envy these other people all the time. But we also don't want to criticize her friends, or their parents."

Grandchildren may not handle this the way you want them to.

The grandchildren's ways of coping can create very difficult situations for you, too. As the children get older, there will be times when they just want to fit in. It can be even more difficult than a child saying she's biracial, rather than simply identifying with your race, although that it itself is tough for some grandparents.

As preteens and teens, they may even hide part of their racial identity or keep secrets about one of their parents, especially if that parent does not live with them. The result of all this can be that as a preteen or an adolescent, she may for a time identify with only one part of her racial heritage and this can mean – or feel like – rejection of your side of the family. Teens and preteens do things like this all the time, trying out new ways to see themselves and rejecting things they've been taught, including ideas or ways of living that are important to the adults in their family. But most are not so emotional for grandparents.

A grandmother who is of African American and Columbian ancestry, with an adopted son and a biological son, tried to support all her grandchildren as they grew up. She wonders:

"My only grandchild that shares my genes looks white. Will she stay part of our community or will she want to only be part of the white world when she's grown?"

Adolescents also change fast. At one point, a grandchild may be immersed in one interest, or way of seeing himself. You listen, you understand, you support his choices. A few months – or weeks – later, everything's changed.

You might be surprised.

Grandparents are naturally anxious about their grandchild's welfare and safety. We have focused on potential problems and difficulties in this chapter, and these are real. You may also be pleasantly surprised. You may find the family comfortably living in a diverse neighborhood, where the children have friends like themselves and also friends of very different backgrounds and races. Some grandparents have been amazed at how much their grandchildren know about the world and how comfortable they are with a variety of people. Some families and older children have benefited greatly from organizations or consciously planned social groups that connect people and families like their own. Some have found diverse schools with very aware and supportive teachers and principals who are thoughtful about creating a comfortable environment for all families.

> "When I raised my children here in this town, everybody we saw looked just like us. Now, I pick up my granddaughters from school, and there is no one main group, it's just kids from every race, every culture, all over the world. They run around the playground together and nobody looks different, nobody stands out. I feel really good about this."

Another grandmother found ways to contribute beautiful images to her grandchild's environment.

> "There are lots of lovely kids' books with people of different races, and we have those. But nobody who looks just like my granddaughter, who is half Bengali and half white. I am a decorative painter, so I bought an unpainted wooden dresser for her room, and painted it with a mural of children playing, children who look like her. I did one other thing, too. I have some photos of the whole extended family, one of the few times we were all together. I enlarged

two of the best ones, and framed them, so whenever she is in my house she sees all of her relatives, both sides, together in these beautiful photos. I stay in touch with the other grandparents, too, by cards and email. My granddaughter is growing up very self-confident and a very secure young lady in her identity and I think I have contributed a little bit to that."

Grandparents have a very important role in multiracial families.

"My granddaughter is mixed, a mixture of three races. It's different for her than for anyone else in the family, probably from other people she knows. I want to really be there for her as she grows up, I want to be someone who can understand what she's going through."

Grandparents can form a buffer between the nuclear family, and the outer world. They provide an affirming and understanding presence beyond the parents. They can help grandchildren develop a positive self-image that includes all of their racial heritage. They can support parents in teaching grandchildren how to cope in a healthy way with a world that sometimes sees them as inferior or exotically different. They can set a good example by seeking friendly respectful relations with the other grandparents and other family members of another race. A grandmother may take on the responsibility of teaching grandchildren about her side of the family's culture, traditions and history, and encouraging the child to learn about the other side, too. You can have good times sharing the art and culture of the world with grandchildren, and at the same time give a message of inclusion and respect for everyone.

As you demonstrate your respect and support for all members of your grandchild's family, you are also teaching and modeling a respectful, unprejudiced attitude towards other people in general, a wonderful gift to your grandchild.

Try this:

- For toddlers and preschoolers, read them some of the

many beautiful children's books about families of all races, and about the people on both sides of their family.

• Consider donating a multiracial children's book to your local or school library. Or donate a useful book for adults to your local library.

• If you sew, it might be fun to make a doll that looks just like your grandchild.

• Welcome the other side of your grandchild's family into your home. Learn about their race and culture.

• Show grandchildren that it's OK to talk about race, and that you are comfortable hearing their thoughts and questions.

• Don't allow other family members or friends to express racism in front of you.

• Develop a plan to respond to public scrutiny, and questions from strangers, family members, and friends that make your grandchild feel different from you and from their parents. Children should not have to educate other people, especially adults. Try to do that yourself as much as possible.

• Grandparents can also have a role in teaching children to respect other people, those who are like them and those who aren't. In Chapter 14, Family History and Childhood Memories, are more ideas on how to do this.

Resources

Fiction

The Bean Tree, by Barbara Kingsolver

Nonfiction

Does Anybody Look Like Me? A Parent's Guide to Raising Multiracial Children, by Donna Jackson Nakazawa

Mixed: Portraits of Multiracial Kids, by Kip Fulbeck

Movies, videos and podcasts and events

Mixed Chicks Chat, podcasts of interviews and discussions on the experiences of racially mixed people, by Fanshen Cox DiGiovanni

Off and Running, A documentary movie, by Nicole Opper

www.mixedrootsstories.org, a website about the multiracial experience

13

Gay or Lesbian Parents

Your grandchild has two moms or two dads.

What has changed in your lifetime.

Most of us grew up in an era of silence and shame about homosexuality. We have seen important social change in our lifetimes, including greater freedom and acceptance, and increased legal rights. Change is uneven; some parts of the country are very different than others, both in laws and in social norms and behavior. Younger Americans tend to be much more accepting of gays and lesbians than older people are, although there are many exceptions in both age groups.

Gay men and lesbians can now live openly with their partners, and in some states can have the legal protections of marriage or civil unions. In some places, there are wedding announcements of same-sex partners in local papers, and same-sex couples can be comfortable and safe in their neighborhoods and schools. In other regions, gays and lesbians fear for their safety, and their children can face harassment, discrimination, and violence.

Many of these couples are raising families. Some of these children were conceived in heterosexual marriages; others were born or adopted into gay- or lesbian-headed families. Major professional organizations such as the American Academy of Pediatrics now formally support these families as healthy and normal, a far cry from just twenty years ago.

Unfamiliar territory.

For some women, having a son or daughter come out as gay or lesbian is sad because they believe this means no grandchildren. If the adult child then does have a family, the grandchildren will be a welcome surprise to a grandmother who didn't expect to have them.

As these grandchildren are born or adopted, or if a grandchild's parent comes out, grandparents find themselves in unfamiliar territory. This family constellation is not what you grew up expecting. Even when completely supportive of their gay and lesbian children as parents, most grandmothers have some learning to do.

Big changes.

Diane is the grandmother of a one-year-old girl. She described a series of events she's had to get used to, each one surprising at the time but ultimately enriching.

> "It's like whiplash with my son. You get used to something and then suddenly it's the opposite.

> "First, you don't expect your son to be gay. When Jeffrey told me he was, I had to adjust to it. It was a shock at first. Very hard … I wanted to know what I had done to make him this way. But, I love my son. He's a wonderful, good man and I went through an adjustment but I completely accepted it. There's been a lot of sadness, not at him, not at being gay per se, at what it means. No family, I thought at the time, no grandchildren. No wedding, no looking forward to my son bringing his family for the holidays. And of course I was fearful, that he would be snubbed by people, shut out of things, hurt.

"Then, after dating a few different people, he settled down with Patrick. And after 9/11, that really affected me, watching on TV those buildings come down. It made me see what's important in life. I felt, I am so glad Jeffrey has someone. I went from just accepting, to being very glad my son loves and is loved.

"OK, so then we're fine, they do come for the holidays, we're all doing fine.

"And then the law changes in our state, now they can get married. So now, it's back, everything I put aside is suddenly happening, the cake, the rabbi, the invitations, the music, the expense, even the arguing over who to invite, every classic wedding thing happened. And when I saw my son standing up there making those vows, I cried with joy just like any other mom. Things are so much better than I feared when he first told me he was gay. He and Patrick are happy, they're married, they have a nice apartment, things are good.

"Then, within the year, Jeffrey calls and says 'Mom, we're having a baby.' I almost burst out laughing, it's a good thing he called instead of telling me in person because I stifled it, I made it sound like a cough, I'm kind of coughing and choking on the phone there. Because I'm thinking, Jeffie, society can change, the courts can change, some things don't change, and two men can't have a baby. It turns out Patrick has a cousin, a single woman in her thirties and she really, really wanted to be a mother. She lives about half an hour away, and Jeff is the biological father, they did artificial insemination I guess, I don't really need to know about that part, not my business.

"When they put that little baby girl in my arms, everything came full circle. She looks like me, she's my granddaughter, the joy is just incredible, even more because I had given up on ever having this.

"How's it going to go? How are they all going to get along? I decided, every family has that question of how the parents are going to get along, every grandmother is affected by that, so I don't worry about it, and I just try to be as kind and helpful to my granddaughter's mother as I can, and she is a really good mother.

"I consider myself a very fortunate woman."

Your gay or lesbian child may – or may not – share with you the months or years of planning and the details of the process as they conceive or adopt. You may learn a great deal about donor insemination, and second parent adoption, and the international and domestic adoption options for gay men and lesbians, either as couples or as singles. You may help your grandchildren cope with the surprise of one parent's coming out, or with their parents' possible subsequent divorce.

Who is going to take care of the baby?

Even as legal rights expand, and even if your grandchild's family lives in a safe and more accepting region, gay and lesbian parents commonly face skepticism about their parenting, even from well-intentioned people. Grandparents experience this too, and they also think about how they can counter it, and support their adult child's parenting.

When Martha told her closest friend that her son and his partner were adopting an infant, the other woman said incredulously, "Who's going to take care of the baby?" Martha answered, "They are."

She admits she wondered at first herself.

"When I visited the first time I thought I would be doing a lot. I didn't expect to get much sleep. Forget that. I had to fight to get them to let me take care of Darren at all. They had studied all these books. They told me about swaddling, which they read about. When Doug showed me, I said to them that's just what I did with my babies."

Martha's son Doug encounters the assumption that men can't take care of babies all the time. He says,

"We are a novelty. No one would make a movie called Three Women and a Baby, but with us they are amazed that we can do it at all. People are so surprised that the baby looks great and is obviously so well cared for, so we get a lot of attention. It's impossible to get out of the bank in less than 45 minutes because everybody wants to hold him."

Some gay fathers have found this expectation that men can't take care of babies or young children to be less amusing and more of a burden. Diane's son Jeffrey says,

"It's OK on the weekend, but if I'm at the park with her like on a Wednesday morning, the mothers there with their kids look at me kind of suspiciously. Baby swim class, even worse."

Diane listened to Jeffrey and Patrick, her granddaughter's fathers talk about this, and she began to be careful what she said.

"I tried to show with my comments that I had confidence in them, that they were good parents."

Who is the real mom?

It's not just fathers and babies. Gay and lesbian parents are frequently challenged in what should be ordinary, routine interactions, and have to explain themselves to strangers. Grandmothers may hear about this from their adult children, or they may be involved when they're with the family.

"My granddaughter was eighteen months old. She'd had diarrhea for about twenty-four hours and I was getting worried, so I wasn't surprised when my daughter called me around dinnertime and said they were taking her to the hospital. I said, I'll meet you there, OK? And she agreed. So, they took us in pretty quickly, and we were at the desk where they get your insurance information. My daughter-in-law is holding the baby, and my daughter is reading off

223

her insurance card, and the clerk says 'So who's the real mom?' And they say, 'We both are.' And she says in an irritated way, 'But who's the mom mom?' And they say again 'We are both her mothers.' Finally she just rolls her eyes and puts them in an exam room. They were upset by this, my daughter and daughter-in-law, naturally, and I said something that was kind of stupid. I said something like, 'It's so much better than it used to be, they've come a long way.' I think I hurt the girls' feelings, like I wasn't on their side. We haven't talked about it. I feel awful about that now. My daughter-in-law doesn't have any legal rights because she didn't give birth to Zoe, and it must be awful for her to be treated like she's not really the mother to her own child."

If one parent is biologically related to the child, and the other parent is not, such as a lesbian couple in which one partner gives birth to the child, the non-biologically related parent may encounter constant challenges. Schools, summer camps and pediatrician's offices may not accept her as a parent. Even if she has adopted the child and is a legal parent, she may not be treated as one. Grandparents can help by treating both parents equally, and by noticing the ways the child resembles and learns from the non-biological parent.

Anna says,

"Show me a grandmother who doesn't enjoy finding resemblances to the rest of the family! I just think my daughter and her partner should've said something right away. Finally my daughter said it was hurting Sally's feelings to talk about how their child looks so much like my husband, and he gets his athletic ability from my side of the family too, and I guess I can understand that since Sally isn't his biological mother. I wouldn't have hurt Sally for anything, and she's a wonderful mom to him. They should've told me at the beginning. Now I still have those conversations, but I have them with my sister because it's enjoyable for us and I don't do it in front of the girls. I see now she felt it lessened her parenthood."

You're different.

Even well-intentioned people, including friends, professionals and casual acquaintances, may focus only on what makes this family different, ignoring all the ways that gay and lesbian parents are similar to other parents.

Even good things in your grandchildren's lives may be interpreted by others as always related to sexual orientation and nothing else.

Elizabeth's grandson has two lesbian mothers. When Elizabeth talked to her friends about how her grandson and her husband enjoyed their time together, some of her friends always responded that it must be just because the child lived with two mothers, and didn't have a man in his household. This was the only thing they could see. Grandchildren had been a deeply enjoyable shared interest for this group of women friends; they had shared photos, cute stories, worries, and celebrations. It wasn't fun for Elizabeth anymore, because she felt pushed out and different. Her husband had a way of swooping toddlers up into the air over his head that made them laugh hilariously. He taught kids to make frog and duck noises, and tell knock knock jokes. When they got older, he showed them how to rewire a lamp and took them cross-country skiing. Elizabeth's friends saw only his gender because they thought something was missing from the child's life, and his mothers weren't enough.

At first, Louise was just grateful that her grandson's doctor was affirming.

> "They found a pediatrician who is very supportive of them. I was so happy about that. Still, every time they take Robbie Ray in, the doctor says, 'All that matters is he has two good parents.' Like she always, always, always has to comment on the fact that their family is different. She's really trying to be good but she can never just relate to them like she would other parents. It's never about, is he ever going to sleep through the night, is he a healthy weight, is there any way to get him to eat vegetables, and is that a rash on his neck. It's always, his parents are two gay men, two fathers and no mother, and he might have a rash on his neck."

Grandparents who admit any doubts or worries about their grandchild (and everybody has doubts or worries sometimes) may find the reactions of others focused solely on the parents' sexual orientation, rather than on the many issues and influences that all children face.

What are little children thinking?

Preschoolers accept their family structure, as they do everything in their daily life. They will ask at some point why they don't have a mom, or a dad, when they realize that some other kids do. That doesn't mean they think something is wrong. It's part of their curious questioning of everything; it's how they learn to understand the world.

Preschoolers can't keep secrets, so they won't hide the facts they do understand about their family, the way an older child who is afraid of being different, or afraid of bullying, may do.

Preschoolers may think that any two men or women they see together, or who live together, are a couple. The first child I knew who thought this was the three-year-old daughter of a straight couple. These parents explained to all their kids that some people love and want to live with a person of the same sex, just like Mommy and Daddy love each other and live together.

Their older children understood; they had a friend with two moms. But the three-year-old concluded that the two carpenters working on their deck were gay, and the two women she always saw working together at the bakery, and their nephew and his college roommate.

In another family there were two young cousins. The older one had two moms, and the little girl, just three years old, had a mom and dad. When the older cousin and his mothers were visiting from out of town, both grandchildren were spending the day with their grandmother. The little girl asked about her cousin's other mother.

The grandmother explained to both children that he had two moms, and she had a mom and dad.

"There are different kinds of families," she said, "Parents always take care of their children. You both have two parents who take care of you."

The older cousin, age six, nodded, yeah, he knew that. But the little girl was quite competitive with her cousin and wanted to do everything he did, only better. She saw this as a chance to get ahead of him. So she immediately announced that she had the same thing as he did, but more.

"Yes, yes," she insisted happily, "I have that, too. At my house, I have two mommies *and* two daddies." She told her parents this, when they came to pick her up that afternoon, and she talked about it everywhere she went for several days. Two mommies and two daddies!

Trying to explain or reason with her just gave her another chance to talk gleefully about how she had surpassed her cousin, so the parents and grandparents laughed and gave up. It went down in family history as a cute anecdote, and she confused her daycare teachers quite a bit.

Even before they fully understand, talking about same-sex couples makes children realize that it can be talked about, and that the important adults in their lives are comfortable with the idea.

The environment matters more as they get older.

As children get older, much depends on where they live and go to school. They move out into the world and people outside the family affect them more. It's harder if their parents are in the closet, the children don't know anyone else with gay or lesbian parents, and they hear hostile, prejudiced remarks regularly. It's difficult for them to move to a new school or town where they wonder how they'll be treated, and who they can safely be open with.

Teasing and harassment can be a big problem. It's very common for children with gay or lesbian parents to be teased and insulted mercilessly by other children, and even for teachers and other adults to ignore or condone it.

The child may be told by neighbors, acquaintances, or even someone in the family that their parents are going to hell, or are sinners, or they may be told other hostile, frightening messages.

Other children may tell your grandchildren they are gay because their parents are, forcing them to focus on sexuality long before they have thought about their own sexual orientation and before they want to, and to think about their parent's sexuality – which children never want to do.

They may go to great lengths to hide their parents. They may end up having to defend and explain their parents to other children, and even to curious or antagonistic adults.

Just act "normal."

As the children get older and understand that their family is seen as less legitimate or adequate, they may feel that they have to act "normal" all the time, or better than normal. They may feel they can never let themselves have any problems or difficulties, because if they do it will immediately be blamed on their parents' sexual orientation. A child of straight married parents can have school troubles or emotional problems, be a failure at sports, or do dangerous things as a teenager, and no one ever says that his parents shouldn't have gotten married. A child with two dads or two moms often finds every misstep blamed on her family structure.

Fear.

If only one parent has legal custody, older children who understand this may worry that if that parent dies, they would be separated from their other parent and put into the foster care system. Media accounts of violence against gays and lesbians may make them very frightened for their own parents. Depending on where they live, these fears may be more or less realistic. Children don't know how to gauge that. A news story about something that happened far away can feel very relevant and threatening to them. Political speeches and campaigns that vilify gay and lesbian adults can be disturbing for them too.

How the parents respond will depend on many factors, including the child's age. Parents may try to protect young children from disturbing news stories. When they're older, or if they will surely hear the bad news, it may work better to talk with them before they hear something frightening or hurtful.

Hearing about violence against gays, or listening to verbal attacks, is going to be upsetting for you, too. Take your cue from the parents and plan an honest yet reassuring approach to talking about this with children. Try not to blurt out your fears in front of children.

Your grandchild's parents may decide to move to a more diverse and accepting neighborhood, or even to another part of the country. It's much better if they are in a neighborhood with many kinds of families including some just like theirs.

They may devote time to working with an advocacy organization, or with other families trying to make schools more fair and inclusive. They may join a social organization of other families like theirs. It helps if the family lives in the same place for a long time, where they have friendships and secure connections with neighbors and teachers.

Schools.

Schools, afterschool programs, summer camps, and the like, can be a nurturing and educational part of a child's life. They can also be the places where children encounter prejudice. The family 22may face real problems that you don't expect and didn't have to deal with when raising your own children. Your grandchild's parents may work with the school to improve things, perhaps with a group of other parents.

Sometimes, schools don't acknowledge both parents at all. Some have classroom activities like family trees with a set format for a biological mother and father only. Often consent forms for school activities have space for a mother, a father, and no one else, which actually excludes many families, such as single parents, and stepfamilies, as well as gay and lesbian parents. Some teachers or principals are very uncomfortable and don't know what to say, so they may actively discourage children with gay or lesbian parents from talking about their families. Surprisingly, even in a school that doesn't allow language denigrating a racial, ethnic, or religious group, homophobic language is sometimes tolerated. Teachers sometimes even join in. Principals may make excuses for staff, citing their background as justification for their prejudices, rather than protecting children.

Some schools have suggested that only one parent participate in the school. In this kind of environment, parents may decide to stay invisible, or "in the closet" in order to let their child decide when to share information about his family.

Equal rights up for debate.

Marriage equality – the right of gays and lesbians to marry – may be discussed in front of the child. Schools may even promote, debate, and give equal weight to "both sides" of the issue. The child is then forced to listen to denigrating remarks about her parents, or speculation by adults in authority that his family is inadequate or immoral.

This can happen outside of school, too.

> "My grandson's mothers are a lesbian couple. When he was about four, I was in a pizza restaurant with him, and at the next table, a group of people started discussing gay marriage, in loud voices, arguing about it. I was just horrified, I didn't want him to hear what some of them were saying, that his parents are terrible, and they shouldn't have children. I hustled him out of there as soon as fast as I could. The thing is with a four-year-old, you don't know if he was listening, or understood. So I didn't say anything to him, like I would have if I was sure he understood it. I still worry about how I should have handled it, should I have talked to him about it?"

How the children handle this.

If the family lives in a community that is not accepting of gays and lesbians, the children will quickly notice stigma attached to their parents. They may avoid inviting friends home, and they may not talk about their parents at school. If your grandchildren are embarrassed, or fear persecution, they might ask their parents not to be involved with the school, or other activities at all, or for only one parent to show up. One teen negotiated with his two moms that they could both come to his band concert. Actually, he wanted them to, but they could never sit together, or even act like they knew each other. "Take two cars," he said, "and sit with your other friends."

An eleven-year-old girl with two dads asked one of them to come to school activities, and the other to soccer and gymnastics. One of her fathers told me about this, saying,

> "We're living in the same town we always have. Everybody at school knows us. We both volunteered in her classroom in grade school. She doesn't seem to realize it's not a secret."

Some children don't try to keep their family hidden, especially if they have accepting long-term friends and trust their teachers, and feel safe. Much can depend on where they live. Children can quickly size up new situations. One family with two lesbian mothers noticed a big change when they moved to a more diverse area, with a wide variety of families including some like theirs.

"Suddenly, our kids were bringing their friends home."

Siblings may react differently, for many reasons. One may have a confident, assertive personality, and not bother to keep secrets, while another is embarrassed, frightened, and dreads being conspicuous. They can change as they get older, get new friends, or transfer to a new school and lose a group of long-term friends.

Older children are less likely to tell their parents about negative experiences at school. They are more likely to try to handle it or endure on their own. They may want to protect their parents, or they may be afraid that the parents' intervention (such as talking to school teachers or principal) will end up making things worse. Sometimes children think their parents won't understand, especially if parents have told them in the past to just ignore prejudice, which doesn't always work.

Grandparents are often worried for the grandchild's family, and may even disagree with how the parents handle things. It's important not to take a "What did you expect when you had him?" approach. Be on your adult child's side.

When I talked with a lesbian mother concerned about her son's education, I felt sad for the grandparents. I'm sure they didn't intend to make their grandson's parents afraid to talk to them about such an important issue.

This mother said,

> "Now that he's older we're getting really worried about what he'll encounter when he goes to school. We're looking at private schools, trying to figure out if we can afford it and if we can find one that would be supportive of our family. We can't talk to either of our parents about it because they just say, 'That's why you shouldn't have had a kid.'"

Being prepared for problems that may or may not happen.

Your grandchild might encounter all, some, or none, of these troubles.

It's better for grandparents to be prepared and have some idea of the problems the family may face so you can offer knowledgeable support.

If your grandchild's parents were in a straight marriage at first.

If your adult child has his or her children in a heterosexual marriage, and then divorces, and comes out as gay or lesbian, the family faces homophobia at the same time as coping with divorce. This can be overwhelming for children – or anyone. Children will usually be distraught over a divorce at first, even if it leads to a better life for the adults. If you are the parent of the straight partner, then some people around you may speak very negatively of the parent who came out as gay or lesbian. This is awful for children. They love and identify with their parents, even when they are angry or sad about a divorce. It's best for grandchildren if you can protect them from these negative comments. If that's not possible, let them know that you respect both their parents.

You will probably be upset yourself. You will be worried about your grown child and about the grandchildren's welfare, emotional state, finances and custody arrangements. The parents of an adult who divorces can lose a beloved daughter-in-law or son-in-law, and this can be a further source of sadness for you.

This is a situation where calm grandparents, who can use the wisdom acquired in long years of living, can be an anchor for children. Make your home the place where children's feelings can safely be expressed, and where both parents are accepted and respected.

Where did that baby come from?

Most grandparents love to talk about their grandchildren. Telling the cute anecdote, keeping a picture at work, celebrating the arrival of a new grandchild: these are some of the universal pleasures of grandparents.

When grandparents of children in gay and lesbian headed families do this, people are often curious about how these children were conceived or adopted. Many grandparents find that just mentioning their grandchild who has two moms or two dads can unleash a barrage of questions.

A Boston grandmother says,

"People who hardly know me ask me things they don't have the nerve to ask my daughter, like how did she get pregnant? Did she know who the father is? How did they get the donor and how much did it cost? I find it all pretty annoying and insensitive. My son, who is straight and married, has two children and when I mention them nobody would dream of asking such personal questions."

Marilyn sees it differently. She's written many letters to the editor, and op-ed pieces for her local paper. She does continuing education trainings for social workers and school principals on supporting gay and lesbian parents. She feels fine about talking about how the children were conceived and born, and has no problem explaining the details of donor insemination, and second parent adoption.

"People are curious, and it's my chance to educate them. If I don't explain, it may seem like there's something to be ashamed of, and there isn't."

Hadley, whose daughter is a lesbian with a baby on the way, says,

"The conception? I explain. I am very, very open, I tell them it's artificial insemination, they went to a sperm bank, and I explain what that is. People ask a lot of questions, they get artificial insemination and in vitro confused. Other people are doing the same thing who aren't gay or lesbian. It's just another way to have a baby."

Each family is different in the amount of privacy or openness that feels right to them. Some explain anything people want to know. Others learn to set limits in a polite and firm way.

Either way, grandmothers sometimes get the brunt of public curiosity about how same-sex couples become parents. You may want to be prepared for this, and decide in advance how you would like to handle it. If you are open to talking about it, you may get further and more personal questions including, Whose is he? How did she get pregnant? Where did they get the sperm? Will he ever know his father? How much did it cost? Which one is the real mom? Many grandmothers told me they were surprised and caught off guard at how persistent these questions were. Being prepared can help you respond in ways that you, your adult child, and your grandchild are comfortable with.

If the children are present, think first of what they are hearing. You want the children to feel comfortable about their family and their origins, so don't act upset when people ask questions, even though you might be quite annoyed. A grandmother who has dealt with this for years has a strategy that works well for her.

> "I say in a pleasant cheerful manner, I can't get into this now. Let's talk later."

One grandmother has learned a lot, and has suggestions,

> "I figured out after a while that the thing to do is decide how much I am willing to tell people, and then if it comes up, with someone I am talking to, I tell them everything I want to tell them right away, all at once. It's better not to encourage a series of questions, because that can go beyond what you want to share. If it's a total stranger or someone I just see in the park, I say something like, that's a private family matter."

If someone asks "Who's the real mom?" you may want to say something like "They both are. My daughter's partner gave birth to him, and they are both his mothers." It's good for children to hear you affirm the legitimacy of both parents.

Whatever you decide, you will probably need to reevaluate when the children are old enough to understand the conversation. Children usually don't want their conception discussed in public, so the frankness that might have been just right for your family at one point may need to be reconsidered. If you've been very open with everyone, explaining all the details of the conception, pregnancy and birth, or the adoption, think about how that sounds to a ten-year-old who is standing right there.

Coping with all this can be a lot of work for your grandchildren. But if they get support, and have trustworthy friends, these challenges can help them to grow up to be open-minded and complex thinkers with an ability to cope with difficulty that surprises you and makes you proud of them.

Grandparents coming out at work and in the neighborhood.

Babies and children make it impossible to stay in the closet. You will have to figure out what to say, and when.

> "When my son was single, it never came up. People I am close to knew he was gay, but at work or with people I didn't know very well, people I have just very brief chats with, I would mention that I had a son, or that he came for Thanksgiving, and sexual orientation just never came up. Now that he has a family it's different. I can't say the simplest thing about my grandson without getting into him having two dads. So now I am 'out of the closet' myself. And it's not always easy."

Grandparents go through some of the same stages that their gay and lesbian children faced – making a decision to be open, telling friends and coworkers a truth that may bring a negative reaction, and learning to cope with the homophobia.

Anna felt fine about having a lesbian daughter, and thought of her daughter's partner as her daughter-in-law. But she became frightened when she tried to mention the couple casually in the same way she talked about her straight son, to her neighbors, or people at the hospital where she volunteers. She was haunted by fears of violent attacks on her daughter and daughter-in-law, like the frightening things she read in the newspapers, even though the people she knew were unlikely to do such a thing and her daughter and daughter-in-law lived hundreds of miles away.

She decided not to let this fear stop her. She tries to talk about both her children in the same way. She says,

> "I think everyone is getting used to it anyway, to lesbian

and gay people. So often, it's someone they know, or kids of someone they know."

Joan decided it was all or nothing. She teaches math at a community college in a conservative state. The beginning of the semester is a time to reconnect with colleagues, after the summer when most of them haven't seen each other. It's a friendly group, people who have been working together for years, so they usually take time to catch up on each other's lives. People talk about vacations, or report on major home decorating projects, and ask about each other's families.

Joan thought in advance about what to say. When family news came up, she said,

> "My daughter is going to visit next month, with her girl-friend and their baby. They are a lesbian couple. The baby is three months old now, and this is my first time to see my grandchild."

There were awkward silences. A few people looked stunned and backed away. Joan is glad she did it, but she lost friends and now has to work with some people who are extremely uncomfortable with her, and who she knows harbor antagonism and prejudice toward her daughter.

Betty was afraid to tell people she had a gay son, and only her sister and one close friend knew. She says,

> "I can't deny my grandson."

She decided a picture is worth a thousand words.

Her new grandson's adoption was finalized on a Monday. Tuesday morning she had a picture – a very big picture – of the two young dads, and one-year-old Michael up in her cubicle. She beamed out the picture by e-mail to everyone she knew, too, with a subject line "my new grandson" and no other text. Michael doesn't look like his parents – he's African American, and they're white – but in the picture he certainly looks like he's theirs. Betty's friends and coworkers got the message. That Friday afternoon at a surprise "grandbaby shower" they gave her toys and children's books. She says,

"It turns out there weren't any mines in the minefield."

When Louise was expecting her first grandchild she devised a controlled way to deliver the news. She advises,

> "Don't give anybody a chance to say something you aren't going to like. Tell them how to react first, then give them the news, then get out of the room before they have a chance to say anything stupid."

Her conversations go something like this:

> "I have wonderful news. I'm so excited about this. My son, Bobby, and his partner, Raymond, are going to adopt a child. They have a great social worker who says they'll probably get a baby or toddler by the end of the summer. Well, I've got to go, I've got a meeting in two minutes, but I wanted to let you know."

Another grandmother says,

> "People get confused and can't follow what I mean because they are expecting a mom and dad family. So now if I want to say something about my grandsons, I just start right off with, 'It's a two mom family, they are a lesbian couple.'"

Even if your grandchild's family lives in a safe inclusive place, you may have worries and fears for them.

> "Where they live, in Park Slope, there's a large lesbian community, incredible, and they are not unusual as an interracial couple, the schools are like a mini UN. Families of all kinds. They don't stand out because of what they look like. I know it's a great place for them. The only thing is my anxiety level. I can't help worrying about the state of the world for them in the future."

How to talk about it and what to say.

"We had to figure out the language. My daughter is a new mother. Her partner gave birth to their baby. I wanted to put it in the church newsletter, where we have that kind of news. I didn't know how to put it, because my daughter didn't give birth, and they haven't been able for her to adopt, either. Her and her friends use words like co-mother and 'the other mother.' My church and my friends won't know what that means. My husband and I finally decided to just make it like any birth announcement, she has a new baby. We'll explain the details when we talk to people."

Your extended family.

Some grandmothers have challenges in their own extended family. For some, it's the grandmother's own parents, the child's great-grandparents.

"The tension would be that my mother does not know. That the two moms are lesbians. We just haven't told her. I know her. She is a right wing fundamentalist Christian of the most right wing, most fundamentalist, type. I don't what she would say ... I don't know what she would say to the boys. I don't want them to hear something awful from her about their mothers. She sees them only with me, she's in assisted living and we go there together to visit her. We have explained it to the boys this way, your great grandma thinks everything in the world is a sin, TV is a sin, wine and beer are a sin, and movies, and she would think this is a sin too. All things upset her, and that's not our problem, but we aren't going to contribute to it. She is eighty-four years old and not going to change is she?"

For another grandmother, her sister was the difficulty.

"My sister does not accept my daughter's partner. Like she will send Christmas gifts to our daughter and her son only, not to their whole family. That's really painful. I intercept them and get them to Goodwill."

Others have found it easier than they expected.

"When I told my parents, who are in their eighties, - the kids' great-grandparents – with much trepidation and worry, my parents said, 'We know. We wondered when you were going to figure this out.'"

Things may go better than you expect.

Many parents are very fearful when their adult children come out to them, fearful of just the kinds of prejudice discussed above. They worry that their adult children's lives will be very hard, and they worry even more when a grandchild is added to the family.

Your grandchildren's family may encounter an unpredictable mix of prejudice and support. You will probably encounter prejudice. You may be surprised at the positive changes in our culture, too. A gay father told me,

"People don't hate gays as much as they think they do. They vote for all these repressive laws, but when they meet us, they like us. "

A town, or a school, can be transformed very quickly. Siblings in the same family who attend the same school a few years apart can find that things have improved, and they could have quite different experiences. Parents who think they will need to advocate endlessly for equal treatment when their child starts school may be delighted to find instead that their school already includes aware, helpful principals, training for teachers, and an anti-bullying program.

Your grandchildren may find a caring community of families like theirs. Or they may have a group of peers who share an intense interest in music, or computer games, or travel, or vegan food and aren't concerned about each other's parents, outside of commiserating together about how embarrassing and clueless they *all* are.

Depending on where they live, the family may not encounter the problems that they expect in their neighborhood or town either.

A grandmother who had been quite worried told me her story.

> "I was always anxious about my daughter and her partner, but even more when they were going to have a baby. You just never know how people are going to react. The girls had moved out to a far suburb, not known for progressive views. They moved there because it was a good location for both their jobs, and they liked the small town. I would visit; I'm about three hours' drive away, and it seemed nice, friendly. There was a block party every summer, and their neighbors fed their cat when they were on vacation. No one asked them anything personal. And once my daughter was visibly pregnant, life just went on. Nobody said anything, except to ask when are you due, how are you feeling, just pleasantries. When my grandson was born, I went down to bring them home from the hospital, and stay with them for a few days to help out. We drove up to the house and there were balloons tied to the porch, and a big banner saying Welcome Baby. And for the next three weeks neighbors brought us dinner every night. There was never anything said or asked. The girls never came out, they were just part of the neighborhood. They're still there, everybody knows their family, they're in the PTA, and soccer, and school volunteers."

Another grandmother realized she was more fearful than she needed to be.

> "I didn't tell anyone for a long time. Didn't tell my friends, very afraid that they would hold it against my daughter and they would not like her. That never happened. Other people had gay children, too, but I didn't know that."

A lesbian mom talks in amazement about a neighbor who changed. Their children were in the same school, and they had seen each other at parks, and swim lessons and school events. This man came up to the two moms one summer evening as all their kids were busy playing in the sprinkler at a local park. He told them,

> "I want you to know I've always been homophobic, I was brought up very traditional, but I've watched you raise your family and I really believe you deserve to be married."

Grandparents can help.

Grandparents can make a big difference in how children experience having gay or lesbian parents, for better or worse.

Grandparents can be an important safe and reassuring part of the child's life, another house besides their own home where their family is completely loved and accepted. There are many ways grandparents can create a safe comfortable atmosphere, by doing small things to show that they see the family as normal and good.

Dottie made baby quilts for all her grandchildren and all her grand-nieces and nephews. She used her favorite craft to wrap her baby grand-daughter in a loving message,

> "When I made her baby quilt, I made a border and I machine quilted her name and Mommy and Meema, all around it."

With a toddler or preschooler, as you read stories, tell stories, sing, or play pretend games don't make everything mommy and daddy. If you sing with your grandchild, create new words that make the the song reflect her family. Make up some pretend characters like your grandchild and his parents. You can have fun embellishing these imaginary people and their stories. A pretend character, or a dollhouse, could have two moms, or two dads. A pretend game could have people in it like your grandchild's real family. Shop for toys and books that reflect your grandchild's life.

Dottie had a lot of fun with this.

> "I was in the toy store because I had my eye on these ador-able little stuffed animals, bears and dinosaurs and lions.

And it hit me all of a sudden I could get him a family of them, a family like his. They had little outfits on and I just picked out two big dinosaurs because lots of little boys really like them, dressed as females and then one of the little baby ones. I put a little card in the box, saying one is a Mommy Dino, one is a Meema Dino, and one is a baby Nickie Dino. They loved it, in fact they had all three dinosaurs arranged up on a shelf in full view, and after a while I had to say, no, let him play with them."

As the children get older, you can continue to find ways to reflect their world. If they make or draw something with you, help them give it to, or label it for, both parents. Or help them draw a picture of themselves with both parents. As they start to write, help them write both parents' names. Talk about both parents naturally, as full caretakers, don't refer to just your own adult child.

It's also important to clearly include both parents equally in all the activities that define a family. Have photos of your grandchildren with both the parents in your home, and on holiday cards. Include both parents in special occasions like weddings, graduations, funerals, and family reunions. Welcome the other grandparents into your home, as you would any in-laws.

I talked with the parents of a gay son who, with his partner, is raising three children. They advise,

> "Don't treat them any differently than your other grandchildren, but know they are going to need some kinds of support you would not need to give grandchildren with straight parents."

Another grandmother says,

> "I don't know that we do anything different. But I think we may do a little more, because the mothers are lesbians."

It's important not to allow other family members or friends to express homophobia in front of your grandchild. If you just ignore these comments, the child can feel that you condone it. Making excuses for prejudiced family members by saying they aren't going to change leaves children defenseless. Yes, there may be someone in your life who isn't going to change his mind, although it's hard to be sure of that, because many people do grow and rise above the bigotry they've been taught. Whether their thoughts change or not, you can expect them to control their behavior, including what they say.

Even just keeping silent on the issue can make children feel worse. Daniella, the grown daughter of a lesbian mother, told me:

> "My grandmother really loved us. We had a good time with her. But when we went over there she never asked about Lillian, my mom's partner. She would avoid any mention, wouldn't admit she existed, would talk like it was just me and my sister and my mom. There was just this complete silence, and I always was left feeling there was something wrong. My grandmother could have done so much more to help us feel safe."

As you demonstrate your respect and support for your grandchild's family, you are also teaching and modeling a respectful, unprejudiced attitude towards other people in general, a wonderful gift to your grandchild.

Try this:

   • With toddlers and preschoolers, make your pretend play, songs, toys, games, books and stories reflect the two mom or two dad or single parent family.

   • Include both parents in all the activities that define a family, including photos, holidays, and special occasions.

   • Ask about and talk about the child's other parent in a warm positive way. Welcome your child's partner into your home. Introduce him or her to family, friends, and neighbors.

   • Respect both biological and nonbiological connections.

Show that you respect both parents equally, by noticing their caretaking and what they give the child.

• Don't allow other family members to express homophobia in front of the children.

• Children should not have to educate other people, especially adults. Try to do that yourself as much as possible.

• If the child's parents were originally in a heterosexual marriage, and divorced when one came out, then speak of both divorced parents in a respectful way. The child needs support for continuing to love both parents, just as all children do when their parents divorce or separate.

• Your grandchild may want to keep same-sex parents secret, to avoid being teased and stigmatized. Be supportive of the grandchild's feelings and needs, and also of your adult child.

• Your adult children encounter many people who think they should not be parents. Show that you have confidence in their parenting.

• Be mentally prepared for the possibility that your grandchild will encounter threats, harassment, or even physical violence, in schools, camps, or even from people you know.

• Consider donating a book featuring families with gay or lesbian parents to your local library.

• Find out how you can support legislation or influence your local school department or faith community to be inclusive and fair to your grandchildren's family.

Resources

Nonfiction

Homo Domesticus, Notes From A Same-Sex Marriage, by David Valdes Greenwood

The Family Heart: A Memoir of When Our Son Came Out, by Robb Forman Dew

Families Like Mine, by Abigail Garner

Fiction

Until the Real Thing Comes Along, by Elizabeth Berg

Websites

COLAGE

Familyeqalitycouncil.org

Part Four:

From Generation to Generation

14

Family History, Childhood Memories

Storytelling, scrapbooks, genealogy, newsletters and recipes. Sharing your culture with grandchildren

Grandparents are in a unique position to give grandchildren the gift of their family history, their cultural, religious, and family traditions, since they are usually the people who know family history the best, and often have the most connection to other relatives. They often have the deepest, or the only, connection to the family's ethnic background. They frequently have more time than parents. And because they have more life experience, grandparents know that stories or mementos that are of no interest at one stage of life may be fascinating later.

A grandmother can also record a grandchild's life in scrapbooks, mementos, letters, notes, and recipes. She can create a keepsake that will be treasured in later years. It can be simple, casual, and done in spare moments, or it can become an elaborate and fun project, perhaps one the grandchild shares in.

Family History.

If it interests you, and is fun, you could learn more about your ancestors. The Internet makes it very easy to start. Marie got started on genealogy research when she decided to make a family history scrapbook for each of her three grandchildren.

> "I got interested for myself. I found my father's birth and death dates, and his parents, in about my first ten minutes on the Internet. I saw that my grandmother had eight siblings, which I had never known. She died when I was about twelve or thirteen, and I wonder why I never met these people. I got curious, and I just followed the threads from there."

Another approach is to look into what life was like for your ancestors, rather than just details about individual people. It might be interesting to learn about immigrating to this country in the era when your family came. How did homesteaders live? What did Jim Crow laws mean in day-to-day life, both for African Americans and for white people? What was life like in your parents' hometown when they were children?
Barbara said,

> "I never really knew my paternal grandmother very well. I knew she homesteaded in South Dakota as a young woman. I'm older now than she was when she died, and my aunt sent me a book, "Land in Her Own Name," histories of women homesteaders. It was amazing to read, and I feel I know my grandmother better now. I'm definitely passing this story on to my children and grandchildren."

There are specialized museums, too, as well as books. If your relatives were immigrants who lived in New York's Lower East Side in the 19ᵗʰ or early 20ᵗʰ century, you could visit The Tenement Museum in New York City. This unusual museum will show you, and your older grandchildren, in vivid detail, the immigrants' first American homes, which initially didn't have the utilities and ventilation we now consider standard. There are many other institutions, specific to various ethnicities and places, from the tiny Danish Immigrant Museum in Iowa, to the museums in Washington D.C. highlighting the history and heritage of African Americans, and the new National Museum of American Jewish History in Philadelphia.

If you want to do something much simpler, you can easily draw out a family tree on a piece of paper. Just record what you do know; don't be deterred by all the missing information. Most people don't know their own parents' birth year offhand. Few people know about all the offspring or siblings their ancestors had.

A simple hand drawn diagram can be valuable to your grandchild and fun to do. Include dates people were born and died and any other details about them you know, and that's plenty. Or, there is computer software available that's extremely easy to use. You just type in people's names and birth and death dates, and the program gives you a nicely drawn family tree.

Some grandchildren may never be interested in all this, while others may be quite curious at some point in their lives, and want to hear about the people they descended from, or whose traditions they are inheriting. You may be asked to tell the stories, and perhaps be pressed for more detail than you know. Yolanda and I talked about her granddaughter's sudden curiosity.

> "They never took an interest, any of them, in the old stories or my parents or the other relatives. Never want to speak Spanish. But suddenly when Lucia was a freshman in college she wanted to interview me for a class project. Oral history. Here she is with a tape recorder, and a list of questions and she wants to know every single thing."

You probably know the most about people in your own generation, and your parents' generation, and you probably have the most feelings about them also, both positive and negative.

It's wonderful to give children a sense of their roots, and a feeling that their ancestors were likable and admirable. Hearing that they are descended from capable people who overcame obstacles can give children confidence. But presenting your family in a positive light can be overdone, too. A child should never be left with the feeling that every single person in the family was a great academic success, or an athletic star, or anything that will be too hard to live up to. These stories shouldn't make children feel like failures if they don't have all the identical talents and inclinations. There are many ways to talk about family that are about character, not only about achievement. Everyone can emulate a family tradition of kindness. Any child, regardless of his talents, can try to be like a great-grandfather who was known for his honesty.

Ruth says,

> "To hear my grandmother tell it, our family was all rabbis and professors."

This family story nourished Ruth, because her inclinations were academic. She grew up to be a college math professor, in a time when very few women accomplished this, and she felt that she fit right in. If she had been a child with a different set of talents and interests, or if her grandmother had spoken in a rigid way implying there was only one way to be a valuable person, then that story could have been a burden to her.

A bigger picture.

Family history also offers a natural way to teach about the culture and history of your race or ethnic or religious group. Sharing something of your culture with your children and grandchildren can give more depth in that part of their identity and can counter the simple, distorted and often negative images in the media.

Angela, an African American grandmother, wrote to me,

> "I feel that grandparents should pass along their respective culture, the music, food, literature, art, customs and holiday traditions, to their grandchildren. It typically seems that women are the bearers of culture in most ethnic groups.

> "One thing I did, was I took my then nine year old granddaughter to the African American Museum of History in Detroit last year. This came about because she noticed me at the dining room table reading a book about the legacy of African American women and started asking really poignant questions – it was a book that went all the way from African women being queens and regular folks in Africa, through slavery, then to modern day icons like Oprah and other black women involved in civil rights. In the book, it showed an illustration of slaves in a ship's cabin hold and I

got her and her five year old sister and we laid on the floor side by side; crammed really close; swayed; and thought about leaving home and never returning. My nine-year-old was in awe of this (the five-year-old got scared and went into the den to watch television!). At the museum, it showed the slaves; tied together in the ship with it being dark except for gas lamps and they had prerecorded moaning and screaming. She was fascinated. As we discussed our museum visit, I knew that I had to strike the delicate balance of letting her know that although there were some bad white people that stole slaves (and also bad African chiefs who rounded them up during raids for the white traders), there were also good white people (Quakers and other abolitionists) who sought to hide and protect slaves. Since her DNA embodies both the slave and the slave master, I felt that she needed to understand that both parts of her are "good." I think this is an extremely important role for grandmothers to play."

You can also be a leader in your family in teaching about other races and cultures. Take your grandchildren to exhibits of art and history created by other groups that your family isn't part of, too. Every child can be thrilled by the heroism of Harriet Tubman. Every child can take pleasure in paintings by Rembrandt, murals by great Mexican artists Diego Rivera and Jose Clemente Orozco, and Chinese brush painting landscapes. Every child can enjoy Appalachian fiddle tunes, and Mozart. As you teach your grandchildren self-respect and pride in their own heritage, you can also model respect for others.

What about the sad or embarrassing parts of your family history?

Every family has them.

You may wonder what to say, if anything, about the tragedies and bad behavior. What do you tell children about feuds, violence, drug or alcohol addiction, mental illness, or neglectful parenting? Some important events are part of the story too, even if they're sad or shameful. What is private, and should stay private? As you decide what to talk about and what to leave out, think about the effect of knowing, and of keeping things secret or private. If there's information people need to know to plan their lives, or to be safe, it's clear: you'll need to figure out who to talk to about it. People need to know about significant medical history, or a living relative who has sexually abused a child. Sharing some other kinds of painful information serves no purpose.

You may decide in some situations that an older teen or grown grandchild will need the truth in order to make sense of their own experience growing up in the family. A violent, alcoholic, or mentally ill person's behavior in an earlier generation can explain a lot. So can a painful childhood, or a situation that drastically limited someone's life choices.

Betty told me how she has handled this.

> "My grandfather abandoned my grandmother and their children. Because of that, my father grew up in poverty, and never got an education. He left school very young to work, and that really determined his life. We will talk about that sometime, when the kids are older, but for now I put together a scrapbook for them and I put in it that my grandfather was a carpenter, he emigrated from Russia alone when he was thirteen years old. Which is true."

Or, is there a whole set of relatives whose very existence was denied and hidden? Was a child never acknowledged by the rest of the family or given up for adoption in an era when unmarried pregnancy was considered shameful? Perhaps your grandchildren have living relatives, people they may want to know or who may get in touch with them someday. You may struggle with how to make these people part of the family story. Joyce Maguire Pavao's insightful book, *The Family of Adoption*, has thoughtful chapters on secrecy and connection that make interesting reading for anyone trying to decide such questions.

One grandmother decided after years of worry and uncertainty. She says,

> "I made up my mind that my children and grandchildren had a right to know. These people exist and the reality is they are kin. I didn't want to take secrets to my grave, and I don't think they necessarily stay secrets anyway. I was just haunted by the thought that this would all come out some day and

my daughter would be saying, How could my mother have kept this from me? So, next time my daughter visits I'm going to tell her all about it. She can take it from there."

If you are wondering what to tell, and who to tell, here are some questions to help you decide what to do:

- Will talking about this help anyone?

- Will it hurt anyone?

- Might this story make children feel worse about themselves?

- Could it help someone make good decisions?

- Does it give the next generation a better understanding of why family members are the way they are?

- What do the other people involved want told, or want to know?

- Are you tempted to talk about a sad or painful event mainly because you need the solace and comfort of a sympathetic listener for yourself? If so, would it be best to seek support from a friend, or your spouse or partner, or someone not involved?

- How old are the children, teenagers, and young adults in the family? Is there something you want to talk with them about when they are adults, but not now?

Someone needed to talk.

What about feelings or thoughts you were told during a crisis, or by someone who was distraught and needed to talk? Should you reveal these? Think about what the effect will be. If your son confides in you during his divorce that he never loved his wife, that's probably a private conversation, not family history, and repeating that story helps no one. You want people to feel safe confiding in you. In fact, one role a grandmother can play is to be a safe person to talk to, someone who has seen enough of life not to be easily shocked and to have a long perspective.

Scrapbooks and mementos.

Perhaps researching past history doesn't appeal to you, but you would like to save mementos of your grandchild's life, especially of experiences you have shared.

You can create for your grandchild a beautiful, organized scrapbook, or you can just fill a shoebox or a big envelope with mementos, pictures, and notes. Before you begin, think about the long-term plan for what you make. It can feel easy and natural to combine mementos of all family members, but who's going to have this collection eventually? You may be setting up a conflict among your descendants. In most cases it makes more sense to have separate collections for each grandchild.

Some grandmothers enjoy creating a scrapbook where photos, other mementos, and notes about what happened are preserved and displayed. Start with any sort of blank book or notebook. There are beautiful, bound volumes available for this sort of thing in photography and art supply stores. You may even enjoy bookbinding classes where you can make your own. Or, you may prefer a three-ring notebook so pages can be removed or changed, or more pages added in the middle. A blank scrapbook can also be a wonderful gift to a friend who is a new grandmother. The scrapbook isn't just for later. Your grandchild will probably enjoy looking through it with you as you are making it, and he may even want to choose things to go in or to help you assemble it. He may be fascinated at one time, and indifferent at another.

If that sounds like work rather than fun, there are easier ways. Commercial books are available with pages for each topic organized for you, and questions to answer. You need only fill in the information, and add a few snapshots. Or just get a shoebox, keep it somewhere convenient, so you can toss in photos, and anything else you'd like to save. You don't have to make an album. That box by itself will be a treasure chest someday. A preteen child will probably enjoy looking through the box with you and reminiscing about special events they remember or hearing about things they did when they were little. But it may be even more precious later in life. Imagine your grandchildren at age forty or fifty, looking through the scrapbook or shoebox and finding signs of how you loved them, and pictures, notes, or objects that spark early memories or tell them things they didn't know about their childhood.

Just make sure you label things so they have meaning. It doesn't take long to write the date and the child's name on a school paper. If you took your grandchild to the Nutcracker ballet, or the Black Nativity concert, just write on the ticket stub, "Julia and I went together," and throw it in the box. If there is a favorite restaurant you and your grandchild go to together, save the menu or a napkin with a note like, "Devin always liked to get the double chocolate ice cream."

To help you record the small things as they happen, keep some index cards in a convenient place. That makes it easy to just write a few sentences when your grandchild says something cute, or does something you're proud of, or when you have an especially nice time together. It doesn't take long to write, "Today at the bank, Aniyah held the door for a woman pushing a stroller who came up behind us. I was really proud of her good manners." Or, "We made blueberry muffins, and Danny took some home for his mom." Write down brief notes of things you did together, a park you enjoy, favorite meals, something cute the child said. A few words on a card or scrap of paper are enough. Or, if you enjoy writing longer accounts and stories are wonderful. If you go to a performance, save the program. If you go someplace like a state park, and there is an advertisement or a brochure, save that. Any mail you get from your grandchild should certainly be included.

The computer can be another easy way to record things, and the most compact and portable. Type a few sentences about what happened or something adorable your grandchild did, and the date. You don't have to do this all the time. If you forget about it for months and then come back to it, you'll still have plenty.

Storytelling.

Part of the traditional image of grandparents is storyteller. It's not hard to do. Plan ahead a little, by selecting an interesting event that happened to you or the child's parents, or something further back like how your ancestors came to this country. Think in advance about how you could tell it, with details appropriate for the age of your listeners.

Preschool children can be fascinated by simple stories about a child much like themselves. For inspiration, look at some of the popular books like *The Snowy Day*, or *Bedtime for Frances*.

This is also your chance to be funny, or extremely theatrical, for an easily amused audience. One grandfather started every story about his childhood by saying histrionically, "We had to walk to school every day through the freezing snow, with the blazing sun beating down on our heads, and it was uphill both ways." Grandchildren screamed with laughter every time. With so much entertainment electronic now, a grandparent's ability to come up with something amusing out of their own imagination can be impressive to children. Funny voices, exaggeration – you will never again have such an appreciative and uncritical audience.

Storytelling is very convenient in many situations where there's not much else to do, such as on a long car trip, or waiting in doctor's office or at a bus stop. Many children like to hear a story as they're falling asleep. Erica invented a fictional little boy, Jack, to entertain her four -year-old grandson, Ramon. In her stories, Jack does a lot of the things that Ramon does, but in a more dramatic way. The day before she took Ramon shopping for new shoes, she told the story of how Jack went to a hundred shoe stores, riding on a bus that was faster than a rocket ship. Ramon finds this fascinating, and as he settles down for a nap will sometimes ask, "What has Jack been doing?"

Other possible topics are stories of your own childhood, and stories of what the grandchildren themselves did when they were younger. The grandchild's own parents are a great subject too, once the child is old enough to understand that their parents ever were children.

When talking about their parents, though, resist the temptation to get carried away and describe behaviors that you don't really want your grandchild to imitate. Making a hilarious story of the time the child's father went out on the roof is a lot of fun but can backfire if your grandchild interprets it as permission to do the same.

The child's birth, or the day she was adopted.

Write a letter the day the grandchild arrives, about your thoughts and feelings on that joyous and special day. You could also talk about its meaning to the rest of the family. You could write about where their parents lived, where you lived, a little about what your daily lives were like at the time. Save the front page of the newspaper at the day they were born, or write about what's going on in the world. Some adoptive families celebrate Gotcha Day, or Family Day, the anniversary of the adoption as well as birthdays.

If the mother had a birth experience that was primarily joyous and satisfying, it can be great for children to hear all about it. This tale can teach children of both genders that birth is a normal and happy part of life, and that the difficulty of birth is matched by the strength of women. This can be one part of a calm, positive approach to sex education. If the mother's birth experience was not good, something like "Your parents were so happy to finally see you and hold you" is best. Childbirth can be very painful, but "Your dad and the midwife really helped your mom," gives children a much better feeling than "The pain was awful," or, "It broke my heart to see her going through that."

If the mother does not feel good about her birth, don't tell that story. I have heard many adults talk about how upset and pained they still are by having been told as children that their births were difficult for their mothers. Phrases like, "You almost killed your mother," or "She was crazy to have that natural childbirth," or "They barely made it to the hospital," are never forgotten by children and can make them feel unwelcome and guilty even into adulthood.

Maternal grandparents especially are sometimes worried about the welfare of their daughter at such an intense, overwhelming time. It may be useful to talk over the whole event with a friend or another adult who understands your point of view.

Of course, the parents are the ones to decide how and when to explain birth to their children, but grandparents can help enormously by avoiding any negative or frightening comments. Think about what you say in children's hearing, just as much as what you tell them directly. They are listening all the time.

Birthdays.

Traditional parties with cake and presents are important to children and lots of fun all around. You can also add other special ways of marking these days. On each of their birthdays, you might want to write a letter about the past year of your grandchild's life, especially the growth you have seen in them, and what their interests have been. Save the front page of the newspaper on that day too.

Recipes.

For the grandchild who has enjoyed cooking with you, or loves the meals you make, you could write out favorite recipes on cards or into a little booklet as a gift for when the child grows up and leaves home.

Lucy was modest about her cooking and didn't think she would be passing on any recipes. She loved cooking big meals for her family when they visited, but she never thought any of the grandchildren were interested in how it was done. As soon as they grew up and got their own kitchens, however, they all started calling her, asking how to make pie crust, how long to roast a chicken, and please send the recipe for watermelon rind pickles. She mailed recipes written by hand on index cards, with advice on how to measure, sometimes in handfuls, and what brands she likes, and what can be substituted if an ingredient isn't available. Sometimes she suggests other dishes that go well with the recipe, or whether it's easy to make, or can be made a day ahead. These tattered little cards are treasured by her grown grandchildren.

Another grandmother made a beautiful hand-bound cookbook for a granddaughter's wedding present. She carefully wrote out directions for lasagna, angel food cake, carrot salad, and black bean soup, all the foods she had made that her granddaughter liked the most. She added the directions for roasting a chicken that she had gotten from her own grandmother, and the three bean salad she remembered her own mother making.

School.

School generates so much paper it's easy to save the occasional award, artwork, program from a performance or recital, or typical homework. They don't have to be records of achievement only. Many years from now, your grandchildren may be fascinated to see what kind of math they were doing in fourth grade.

What have they taught you?

Have you learned anything from your grandchildren? Children

usually aren't credited as teachers of their elders, but it's fun to notice and remember when it happens. Many grandmothers I talked with said their grandchildren taught them how to use email. Two women said their grandchildren taught them how to draw. These are good scrapbook or family newsletter items.

Family newsletter.

This can be a fun project for you and a grandchild to do together. Or, it can be your project and various grandchildren can join when they are interested and capable. Not every child will be interested, and their involvement will probably be temporary, probably a few issues at most. An interested child, most likely between seven and twelve years of age, can have a lot of fun creating, or helping you on a newspaper about her family and friends. Current computer software makes it very easy. If you don't know how to put in photos, and put your text into columns, an older child can teach you. A digital photo can be added very easily. Or, if you don't enjoy using the computer, you can do everything with scissors and glue and take it to be Xeroxed. Your grandchild can write up her favorite recipes, and accounts of things she's done or places she's been. A family vacation could be the front-page article. Call up friends, and other relatives and find out what's going on with them. Your child helper can write about his siblings. It's a chance for him to take a kindly interest in them while maintaining control, which can sometimes be very appealing for children. You could write a few paragraphs about family history, too. Most people will enjoy getting something like this in the mail.

You and a child could do this just once, or it can be a more permanent project for you, a way to keep relatives and friends in touch. If you put out your family newsletter a few times a year, grandchildren can get involved as they wish, but you can keep the newsletter going all the time.

Erica started the "Elm Street News," when the youngest of her four children was leaving for college, and her oldest grandchild was a toddler. The News included family friends as well as relatives. She asked everyone to write in about what they were doing. People wrote funny and detailed accounts of themselves. She also published advice columns. Erica's husband, an economist, wrote a column about managing money, entitled "Buy Low, Sell High," and a pediatrician aunt had a chance to give all the health and safety advice she wanted to in her column, which included how to fit a bicycle helmet correctly, and why preteens and teens should get the new vaccine against Human Papilloma Virus. One young child sent in a detailed, full page diagram of a large sand castle she had built on the beach which was widely appreciated. Erica's niece had finished college, and moved to New York to be an artist. She wrote about her exciting new city under the headline "The Big Apple." Other relatives, living in rural Vermont, took the anecdotes in "The Big Apple" very seriously and planned a visit to New York around them. All the new babies, travels, graduations, books and articles published, new kitchens and other home improvements, were described. Later on, some family members sent directions for how to find the YouTube videos they had posted, and Erica started adding her favorite cartoons to illustrate some of the stories. Everyone could read about old friends and former housemates.

> "They make fun of it, mainly the teenagers, but they all read
> it as soon as they get it," Erica says.

One family developed a tradition of sending each other postcards when they were having a good time. They began with vacation postcards from the parents and kids to their grandparents, and expanded to everyone sending to each other from events like day trips to an amusement park, or an afternoon at the beach, or a ball game. There's even one from teenage granddaughters that just says, "Hi Grandma, we are at the mall, I got shoes, love Kristie."

After her three sons grew up and married and each moved far away, Sharon looked for some easy, light ways to keep the family connected. Remembering a round-robin letter on paper sent by her own grandmother and great aunts, she decided to use modern electronic communication to accomplish this. She sends a family news email message out every Friday afternoon to everyone in the family who is old enough for an email account.

The conventional family tree might not fit.

These activities can be fun, keep people connected, and let kids know where they come from. They serve another purpose, too. They can define the child's family as good and normal, even if it is different than the popular model of families … and most families actually are different.

Many children's lives do not conform to the model of two married parents of opposite genders, and their biological children, living together with no one else. Your grandchild might be part of an adoptive, divorced, stepparent, single-parent, or gay or lesbian headed family. She may have godparents, foster parents, or honorary aunts and uncles who are important to her. Today, only a minority of children actually live in families who fit the conventional image of "traditional" family structure. But the fantasy persists that this particular family configuration is both common and superior. If her family does not match this picture, she may feel that she and her parents are wrong, missing something, or inferior.

What grandmother can do.

Sometimes it can naturally fall to grandparents to explain all this, perhaps because you know the older family history the best.

> "My little grandson came to me in confusion last Christmas vacation. He knows all these people but he wanted to know who was related how. His uncle has been married twice and had children from both marriages, I raised one of my nieces when her parents couldn't, and there are two ex-spouses who still are close to us and come to Christmas dinner. So I started to draw a sort of conventional family tree. I had to keep re-doing it because there wasn't space for everything. Eventually I got bigger paper, and I finally got a nice diagram. It was good to get it all down on paper, even kind of raggedly, and show him."

It might be helpful to do this when they are young and curious about everything, so you can tell a confident positive story before they encounter stereotypes. School activities sometimes still include teaching genetics by using students' and their parents' characteristics like eye color as examples. A well-intentioned daycare or nursery school teacher might ask everyone to bring in a picture of themselves as an infant, creating feelings of loss and difference in children who don't have such pictures.

For an adopted child, looking at the family tree that is structured to fit her family, and drawing in what is known about her biological parents, as well as her adoptive parents, might be a good way to think about how she wants to answer others' questions. If a child with two moms or two dads has drawn and written about her family with you for a scrapbook, she'll be prepared with a self-confident affirming story about herself even if schools, and children's books or movies, show only heterosexual families. Divorced and single-parent families can be drawn as healthy and complete, and not as missing something or broken.

How to do it.

There are many ways to create family records that acknowledge the child's reality, including both her biological and her emotional connections.

One way is to draw a Tree With Roots. Children put themselves on the trunk, and then fill in the roots and branches with other family members. They could depict birth or foster parents as the roots, then use the branches for adoptive or stepparents, and grandparents and siblings. A divorced family can add more branches when parents remarry, and emphasize connections rather than separations. Another way is Family Houses: This approach uses drawings of several different family houses, to show links between family members and to show how family members, including parents, have moved from one home to start another with new members.

The book, *Lucy's Family Tree*, by Karen Halvorsen Schreck, gives examples of these ideas in a story about a child who discovers that no one she knows lives in a family that fits the conventional stereotype. These other ways of portraying families can also work for a child who wants to include stepparents, stepgrandparents, godparents or a close friend who is an honorary aunt. For more ideas, see the chapters on Multiracial Families and The Adopted Grandchild.

Marie handled this issue differently at different times.

> "I had a folder with some basic information about my own grandparents and great-grandparents, with a few old letters, that sort of thing. I'm saving it. I figured between my three kids and their kids, someone would be interested someday.

But after my son and his wife got divorced, their kids were really upset. And honestly, I was pretty shook up myself. They were seven and nine years old. That's when I had them for the weekend one time, and we did a few different art projects, including drawing a family tree. I let the kids take the lead, but I gave them some ideas. What we ended up with was, they split the trunk so it was like two trees growing from one root, and they put a parent on each side. They didn't put my son's new wife in at all, I know they don't feel really connected with her at this point. They put their aunt though, my daughter-in-law's sister, over there next to my daughter-in-law, their mother. That aunt has been part of their lives since they were born. I just kept it at my house with other things they've made. I think it was good, it shows that they still have all these people in their lives."

Your life story.

• Don't forget your own life and times. Write down your story, too. This can be easily done in a few pages, and your descendants will appreciate it. You might include:

• Where you were born and grew up, some photographs (label them with the names of the people in them, or they can become meaningless when you are not around to explain).

• Details and anecdotes about your childhood: what you did after school, what your classes were like, how you met your spouse, a little about raising your own children.

• How you left home, and what the world was like then, which will seem very exotic and different to your grandchildren, or their children.

• Your version of any significant political or cultural events in your times.

Choose what is meaningful for your family.

No one is going to do all these things, or even very many of them. This chapter is a resource you can use and adapt for your family and yourself. One grandchild might want to draw a family tree, another might be eager to learn recipes or hear about his great-grandfather's journey to the United States. Another might not care about any of this. Decide what is useful, fun, or interesting to you. You can also be a resource to older children or adult grandchildren who want to know more, and any scrapbooks or family newsletters may be saved and be interesting to the next generation.

Resources

Nonfiction

Lucy's Family Tree, by Karen Halvorsen Schreck

About the Author

Becky Sarah has worked with women, children, and families for decades. After receiving a B. A. in Child Development from the University of Wisconsin, she began her career teaching in parent cooperative free schools, and in day care centers. Later, as a midwife and childbirth educator, she attended births both at home and in the hospital. She received a Master of Public Health from Boston University, served as the Public Health Director for the city of Chelsea, Massachusetts and has worked as a program evaluator, program developer, and parent educator at Boston area hospitals, Planned Parenthood, and the Massachusetts Department of Public Health.

She has two children and three grandchildren and lives with her husband in Cambridge Massachusetts.